THE
DELECTABLE
EGG

THE DELECTABLE EGG

and how to cook it

.... *by* ....

MEL MARSHALL

Trident Press New York

This book is for Aldine,
who very kindly allows me kitchen privileges;
and for Honey,
whose hens provided the raw material.

Introduction

As IS OUR WAY with so many of nature's gifts, we treat the egg too casually.

In the kitchen we approach it with a mental shrug, convinced that all we can do is fry, scramble, boil or poach, then slide the cooked egg on a plate with a slice of ham or bacon. Sometimes we go so far as to put a poached egg on a mound of corned-beef hash, or add a bit of cheese to an egg being scrambled, or drop a few crisp bits of buttered toast into the cup with a soft-cooked egg. But, seasoning? What can be used to season an egg except salt and pepper?

Like a woman who needs a dab of makeup to accent her best features, the egg needs and deserves more attention than it gets. Cooked in one of the four ways to which most cooks limit themselves, served with a dash of salt and pepper, an egg resembles the pretty woman who ignores the aid of lipstick, rouge and powder: basically attractive, but uninterestingly pale. Accent the features and heads turn to admire her.

Restricting yourself to serving eggs cooked four ways is like limiting your wardrobe to dresses of one color; no matter how well that one color becomes you, it soon grows monotonous. For the record, there are not four, but eight basic ways to cook an egg; ten if you

7

allow a few extra motions in the cooking process. Add a few fixings, and the range can be extended almost indefinitely. In this book there are over 500 ways to cook and serve eggs.

In spite of the almost 550 egg recipes here, there are still egg dishes unknown to this or any other cookbook. No one individual could ever hope for the time needed to explore all the back-country byways of every land where local dishes based on eggs have evolved.

Have evolved? Are evolving right now; on a remote ranch in Montana or a secluded hacienda in South America, in a wooded Swedish dell or on a rocky island off the coast of Greece an unsung cook may now be creating a superlatively delicious egg dish, of which the world will forever be unaware.

What this book gives you is an adequate cross section of recipes that have stood the tests of time and taste, many of the great classic egg dishes, some revivals from a forgotten past, some originals from the present—a sampling of what might be called the Eternal, International Egg.

Two rules have been followed in choosing the recipes presented here. One is that the egg must be integral to the dish, not an auxiliary. The second: the recipe must be compatible with today's cooking procedures.

Generally, the obvious and banal have been weeded out, as have the extremely exotic items. The commonplace devices have been repeated until they are worn out; the very elaborate and complicated ones do not fit into today's scheme of culinary operations, or they call for items not now available. Also avoided have been the artificial recipes that mar the pages of women's "service" magazines; too many of them are created for the obvious purpose of promoting a product advertised in the magazine. This book is not intended to turn housewives into package-opening, dinner-thawing-out robots, but to stimulate enjoyment and extend the range of imagination. At the same time, no recipe given here is beyond the facilities of any average kitchen or the skill of any average cook. Many recipes based on unthinkable quantities, or procedures that by today's busy standards are overlong, have been ruled out on these grounds alone.

One such recipe, omitted with regret, appears in the 1808 edition of the *Imperial Cookbook of France*. It reads: "Have 15 poached eggs drain on a platter; also have a dozen ducks almost done on the roasting spit. Carve the ducks close to the bone so their juices drain into a pan, season this juice with salt and coarsely ground pepper. Reheat the juice, but do not let it boil, and use it as a sauce to pour over the eggs just before they are served."

Other recipes have been left out because they are variations on better-known or more basic dishes which are included; a few such variations do appear, but usually because they represent an evolutionary step or have a validity of their own. In some of the variations the differences are less than major, but as the French might remark in an entirely different context, *"Vive la petite différence!"*

Brillat-Savarin wrote: "The discovery of a new dish does more for the happiness of mankind than the discovery of a new star." The dishes are waiting in the pages that follow. It is up to you to discover them.

Contents

THE

DELECTABLE

EGG

1

The Ubiquitous Egg

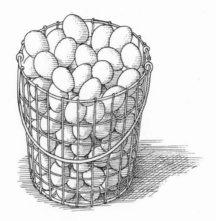

ASKED TO NAME the one universal food, few would hesitate to nominate the egg. Not only is it eaten everywhere; in almost every Christian nation the egg is the Easter symbol of rebirth. In primitive countries an egg is often offered to a stranger as a sign of peace and trust. We say of a man, "He's a good egg," or "He's a bad egg," and no one doubts what is meant.

From penguin eggs at the South Pole to ptarmigan eggs at the North; through hen, duck, plover, turkey and goose eggs in the temperate zones to the ostrich egg of the equator and the gull's egg of lonely sea-washed islands, the egg is everywhere. And everywhere man is, he eats eggs. The primitive man eats them raw, and often values them more if the bird has begun to form inside. The more civilized man wants his eggs fresh, unless he is in China, where centuries of civilization produced the exotic "thousand-year" egg.

Taken by itself, just as it comes from the bird, the egg is an object to admire. It is a self-contained unit of both life and nourishment, still unsynthesized in test tubes, still uncopied for manufacture in a factory. Streamlined in shape and doubly wrapped in a hard outer shell and a surprisingly tough inner membrane, the egg's own packaging not only protects its contents, but serves as a cooking utensil when required.

In its role as a unit of life the egg is nothing short of miraculous, for in liquid form it contains the flesh, bones, skin, feathers and viscera of a living bird. As a unit of nourishment it is no less admirable, for its chemical makeup includes liquids, fats, proteins, iron, calcium, sulfur, magnesium and potassium as well as Vitamins A, B and D, with their attendant thiamin, niacin and riboflavin. It would be possible to live and remain healthy on a diet of eggs alone.

This should not be taken as a recommendation that you go on a diet of eggs alone, or that you go on any diet at all unless prescribed by your doctor. In passing, though, it might be noted that the medical profession itself is anything but united on the subject of eggs in the diet, and especially on the contribution of eggs in the formation of that off-again, on-again villain, cholesterol. Some doctors place the egg in the category of fatty foods; others point out that the egg yolk that contains fat also contains phosphorus-rich lecithin, which breaks fat down into microscopic globules. Adherents of the egg as a non-fatty food say that the interaction of lecithin and fat results in a homogenization which prevents the fat from clotting.

For the record, a raw or boiled egg contains about 6 grams of fat, a fried or scrambled egg about 8 grams. An amount of beef equal in weight to an egg will contain from 18 to 29 grams of fat, depending on the method by which it is cooked. The same amount of chicken contains 7 grams of fat; lamb, from 15 to 29 grams; veal, 6 grams; and liver, 2 grams. Raw oysters equal in weight to an egg have 4 grams of fat; most fish ranges between 4 and 8 grams.

In the kitchen no single ingredient can match the versatility of the egg. It works as thickener and emulsifier, stabilizer and leavener, clarifier and binder. In puddings, sauces and custards it thickens, emulsifies and stabilizes all at the same time; in liquids it clarifies by precipitating sediment; in baking it works in a manner similar to yeast, expanding on exposure to heat and forming millions of air bubbles to lighten the finished dish. When added to minced ingredients, or to dry ones such as flour or sugar, it has the ability to bind their small particles into a whole while still separating them with those same air bubbles, thus keeping the mixture from becoming a soggy mess.

Considered as nourishment, the egg can marry into more combinations with happier results than almost any other food. The egg combines pleasantly with meats, vegetables and fruits in almost unending permutations. Alone, its bland but subtle flavor points up the piquancy of sauces and seasonings; it is equally at home with sugar or salt, as miscible with vinegar as with oil. It is compatible with milk, yet blends happily with stronger waters: broths from the stockpot, liquors and wines.

While it would not be true to say that cooks ignore the egg—it is impossible to ignore such a useful friend in the kitchen—it would be true to remark that most of them treat the egg with a casualness akin to taking an old friend for granted. Busy cooks generally confine the egg's table appearance to breakfast, where it will show up only in one of its unimaginative basic forms: boiled or fried or scrambled. This is understandable, for most of our cookbooks pass lightly over the egg and offer only a smattering of banal suggestions for its service. The average general cookbook will have fewer than a half-dozen recipes dealing with the cooking and serving of eggs.

Even the first cookbook on record, published in 1475, did better by the egg than do most modern volumes, for it contains a score of egg recipes. The great master chefs—Taillevent, Cambacérès, Méot, Vatel and Carême—and the more modern masters—Dugléréz, Escoffier and Diat—all dealt imaginatively with eggs, although their attention centered chiefly on the omelet. Commentators on cuisine such as Dumas *père*, Brillat-Savarin, Montagné and others discussed methods and techniques of egg cookery, but often on a scale which is not practical in the home kitchen today. The recipes of the great chefs of the past must be tried and retried to discover the quantities and alterations needed to insure uniform results in today's kitchens.

Throughout history, in the kitchens of princes and popes, in the farm home as in the city apartment, the egg has occupied an important place. It was once indispensable to those observing fast-days, but its versatility suits it to be served at feasts, as well. It can be prepared to fit into the delicate diet of the invalid, or the robust fare of the workingman. The tiny child spoons up a soft-cooked egg with stubby fingers unaccustomed to handling a table utensil; the nurse helps the senile to eat one cooked in the same gentle fashion; the shuddering roisterer breaks a raw egg into a glass, sprinkles it with Tabasco and gulps it in an effort to quiet his unsure stomach. To paraphrase, if the egg did not exist, we would be forced to invent it.

Nothing can compete with the egg as a budget-stretcher, a combiner with bits and pieces left in the refrigerator. Read down the alphabet for proof, if proof is needed. A few stray stalks of asparagus, a sauce, and eggs produce Eggs Argenteuil, Alexandre Dumas, Beaumont, Chivry, Grand Duke, Ninon. Artichokes and eggs make Eggs Beauharnais, Carême, Elizabeth, Galli-Marie, Mascotte, Monselet. Bits and pieces of chicken combined with eggs bring to the table Eggs Auber, Belle-Hélène, Boiledeau, Daudet, Halévy, Jeannette, Princesse. Potatoes appear in Eggs Cécile, Duchesse, Jacqueline, Parmentier. Rice mixes with Eggs à l'Ancienne, Africaine, Milanese, Portuguese. A few slivers of tongue form the basis for Eggs Bamboche, Clarence, Edward VII, Palermitaine. Ham goes into Eggs Carmen, Coquette, Panetière, Lee, Virginia. A dabble of corn can result in a Kentucky Scramble, a few flakes of crab meat in Eggs Lorenzo. There is literally no meat, no vegetable, no fruit, from almonds and anchovies on through zucchini and zweiback, which is not used, gracefully and tastily, in egg dishes. You will meet many of the combinations and permutations in these pages.

In these days, when the complicated machinery of modern distribution intervenes between hen and consumer, most cooks are greatly concerned about the freshness of the eggs they buy. Their use is inhibited, their appetites diminished, by the fear that eggs bought at the store are damagingly less fresh than eggs taken from laying-nest to kitchen. They are only partly justified in their fears. There is no such thing today as a farm-fresh egg, unless you live on a farm and keep hens, but today's efficient processes of grading and refrigerated distribution do insure that the eggs you buy will be fresh within the acceptable use of the term. You will not get an egg warm from the hen unless the hand that gathers it is your own, but by sensible choice when you buy, you will get an egg so fresh that it is difficult indeed to tell the difference.

Sensible choice: confine your purchases to Grade AA or Grade A eggs, for the "A" designation denotes an egg unsullied by long storage; the difference between AA and A is one of size, not freshness. An egg cooled at once, placed immediately under refrigeration, gently handled in cool rooms during candling and packing and refrigerated during transportation, as is required of Grade A and AA eggs, will be as fresh when you buy it as will an unrefrigerated egg left unattended for 6 to 12 hours. Those first hours of an egg's life are the critical ones; if it is cooled at once and never allowed to go unrefrigerated thereafter until just before warming for the pan or mixing bowl, 3 to 4 days will not seriously damage its taste. Most eggs produced commercially receive this care; their producers arrange matters so that eggs go at once from hen to cooling room, then to refrigerated areas for inspecting and packing, and then in chilled trucks to the retailer's, usually the day they are laid.

Constant refrigeration is the key to the freshness of an egg which must, by the mechanics of today's living conditions, be laid many miles from the kitchen where it is to be cooked and the table on which it is to be served. In your own refrigerator, by the way, store eggs on the lowest shelf. Never mind those cunning little nests the manufacturer put on the top shelf; even inside a refrigerator, heat travels upward.

How can you tell a fresh egg? The shell, when the egg is absolutely fresh, will have a glossy bloom and feel slick to your fingers. Eggshells are porous and are covered on the outside with a membrane that is invisible to the naked eye. The shell and this outer membrane allow an egg to breathe through infinitesimally small pores; exposure to air brings a microscopic wrinkling of the outer membrane that destroys its gloss and gives the shell a rough texture. Dull shell, old egg. Refrigeration preserves freshness by retarding an egg's breathing, in much the same way that extreme cold retards and slows the metabolism of the human body. Washing removes an egg's outer membrane, allowing the egg to breathe faster and thus lose its freshness quicker. Never wash a fresh egg.

When an egg is opened the white albumen will be clear in direct ratio to its freshness; the tiny threadlike membranes that connect the yolk to the top and bottom of the eggshell are virtually invisible in a fresh egg. As aging progresses, these connectors increase in size and visibility, causing the albumen to lose its waterlike clarity. When broken into a dish, the yolk of a fresh egg will be smooth and glossy and will stand erect in a bravely rounded dome. Aging brings tiny wrinkles to the membrane enclosing the yolk, allowing it to sag flatly when the egg is broken into a dish. This is easier to see if a saucer is used instead of a cup; in a cup the albumen surrounds the yolk and makes this test for freshness almost impossible.

Shell color and fertility do not matter when the egg is fresh. Virtually all the eggs produced commercially today are infertile, and as for the color, a flock of hens will produce eggs with both brown and white shells; in the flock's production there will even be a variation in yolk colors, ranging from light lemon-yellow to tangerine-orange. The hen's individual metabolism reacting to her feed governs yolk shading. By selective feeding of the hens, egg yolks of green, blue, red, purple and other colors have been produced without affecting the taste of the egg itself, though it is somewhat disconcerting to be served a poached or fried egg with a blue or green yolk.

No matter how fresh you think an egg is, always break it into a saucer before cooking it or adding it to a batter, for the true test of freshness is the clarity of the white and the glossy erectness of the yolk.

Both egg yolks and whites may be stored, even frozen, though freezing eggs leaves them in a less than perfect state when thawed. For very short periods, a day or two or three, egg whites will hold in a tightly covered container in the refrigerator; a dash of water should be added to them before using. Yolks can be stored for the same length of time in a bowl with enough water to cover the yolks. To be frozen, egg whites must be in a sealed container; yolks must be covered with corn syrup or simple sugar syrup. Frozen whole eggs, both yolks and whites together, must have 1 tablespoon of sugar or corn syrup per cup added, or 1 teaspoon of salt; the eggs are then beaten and stored in sealed containers. But there is really no excuse for freezing eggs, unless you have an embarrassingly productive flock of hens. Avoid frozen eggs in any recipe you meet in this book, for it is impossible to assure uniform results with them.

In its raw state, after it has been deprived of the protection of its shell, the egg is not an appealing object. It looks naked and ashamed as its lone eye gazes up at you unwinkingly from its saucer. The egg starts to die from the moment its shell is cracked; from that instant it must be brought quickly to the pan or mixing bowl. Quickly, but without undue speed is the watchword of egg cookery, as will be seen in the recipes that follow. But restrain that eagerness to progress to the cooking; there are still a few house rules and admonitions before you are ready to place the egg in the pan.

2

House Rules

IF A RAW EGG in a saucer waiting to be cooked is a pathetic object, a cooked egg unadorned is almost equally so.

This doesn't imply that an egg alone is bad, far from it. A fresh egg cooked by any method, lightly sprinkled with salt and freshly ground white pepper, has a flavor of great delicacy indeed. But eggs unadorned soon jade the taste buds with their very mildness; the appetite sighs for a newer tang, a different texture. There are more imaginative things to do with eggs than merely to sprinkle them with salt and pepper. The whole purpose of this book is to help you to discover their possibilities, but before that help can be given, a few house rules must be agreed upon.

Many of the recipes you will meet in these pages share certain processes in common, and a lot of needless repetition will be saved if the reasons for these processes are explored right here. It isn't good enough for you to follow recipe instructions blindly. To be a creative cook, you should know the reasons behind those instructions. This not only applies to cooking processes, but to ingredients, kitchen hardware and all the other phases of food preparation. It certainly must include the ingredients on which the recipes are based, if you expect to duplicate the results of those recipes.

■ KITCHEN UTENSILS

With two or three exceptions, your kitchen should already have everything you will need in the hardware line to prepare any recipe in this book. There are only two special utensils that you may not have. One is the soufflé dish, the other is the *cocotte*. You are certainly familiar with the straight-sided soufflé dish. The *cocotte* is less often found in the average kitchen, or the name is applied to what is properly a ramekin. The true *cocotte* is a small deep cup of china or porcelain, sealed with a screw-on metal top; its only use is to cook eggs *en cocotte*. No other special cooking utensils or tools will be called for, though the third item you might not have is one that certainly should be in your kitchen if it isn't now: the heavy old-fashioned cast-iron skillet. No better utensil has ever been made for cooking eggs.

Used over any source of heat, the cast-iron skillet distributes the heat more evenly and will hold a desired temperature more reliably than any other type of pan. It is especially good at the low temperatures required for much egg cookery. Used regularly, the cast-iron skillet is as stick-free as Teflon; its bottom is tough, allowing a spoon or spatula to be used freely when mixing in the pan or serving up. Blending operations can be carried out with any tool, with no worry over scratching. It has no plastic handle to char, so it may be used as a casserole when desired. The new ceramic skillets come close to being as satisfactory; they are far better than pans pressed of thin metal for top-of-stove use. But for all-around versatility, the cast-iron skillet such as grandma used is still the winner.

Electric skillets and their companions, the table-top ovens and combination oven–skillets, are best avoided; they tend to heat unevenly on the bottom, and even their lowest setting is far too hot for best results in cooking eggs. Used as ovens, their heat distribution also presents problems in timing, since they are not true ovens that radiate an even heat from all sides. If the bottom of a dish cooked in them is done, the top is often uncooked; if the top is allowed to brown, the bottom is a tough crust and the insides of the dish are still raw. These shortcomings apply primarily to egg cookery; there are jobs these electric table-top cookers do well, so reserve them for those jobs and use your cast-iron skillet for eggs.

A lot of nonsense has been written about special omelet pans, so much that many cooks fear to cook an omelet without one. These attractively curved, special-purpose skillets look pretty, mark you as an expert cook and impress friends who see them hanging over your range. You don't really need an omelet pan, though. The iron skillet will cook one just as well. If you own an omelet pan, by all means use it. If you want to use this book as an excuse to buy one, then do so, remembering that the best are of solid copper, well tinned on the inside.

Special utensils such as omelet pans are nice to have, but not vital in the sense that a soufflé dish is. Also nice to have are individual shirring dishes in which eggs are oven-cooked *sur le plat;* they are doubly handy because the shirred egg is usually brought to the table in the dish in which it was cooked. But a shallow casserole, or the old standby cast-iron skillet, will work equally well. Ramekins of the kind called "custard cups" or "bean pots" will double as *cocottes* when their tops are sealed with aluminum foil; since many egg dishes are easiest to prepare and serve in an individual utensil containing a single portion, the ramekins will do double duty. If you plan to try your hand at soufflés, Chapter 8 explains why the special straight-walled soufflé dish is vitally necessary.

To be avoided along with the electric skillet is the chafing dish, unless eggs cooked in it are to be served at once. A chafing dish produces very fine scrambled eggs, but too often it is used only to store eggs already cooked, to keep them warm until they are served. When kept warm for extended periods, scrambled eggs overcook, dry out, lose flavor and acquire a texture that you would expect to find in a well-cooked suede glove. Keep your chafing dish for sauces, creamed hard-cooked eggs and similar dishes for which it is ideally suited. Since many chafing dishes are silver, a word of caution here: uncooked eggs and silver are enemies. The sulfur in raw eggs oxidizes silver on contact, resulting in darkened silver and, worse, evil-tasting eggs.

No matter how well equipped your kitchen is with power tools, it should have at least one hand-powered eggbeater. Preferably this will be the wire whisk resembling a small elongated birdcage; its correct name is the *fouet.* If you do not have one, the useful 10-inch size costs only about a dollar and will serve you well in dishes other than those containing eggs. A hand-operated rotary beater is second choice; if you must use a power mixer, the hand-held portable types have slower speeds than do the pedestal-mounted table models. They can also travel to the stove with you to stir and beat sauces as they simmer.

Using a hand beater is not a matter of clinging to old ways or traditions; there are good reasons. In beating egg whites, millions of tiny bubbles are trapped in the elastic albumen, and there comes a moment when the whites can hold no more bubbles. If beating continues beyond this time, a lot of the bubbles already formed will break; the albumen loses its elasticity and becomes like water. This moment arrives and passes quickly. Judging when it is about to arrive is much easier when egg whites are beaten by hand. With a power mixer, the moment may arrive and pass before you realize it, or before the mixer can be shut off.

Because of this critical moment, a blender should never be used to beat egg whites. It is simply too efficient a tool; its whirring blades whisk the eggs up to and past their peak of perfection before you know what has happened. It is a matter not of seconds, but of fractions of a second. The blender is an invaluable tool for grating, making purées and preparing some sauces, but as for beating egg whites —please don't risk it.

▪ TERMINOLOGY

Since French is the language of cooking, it's impossible to produce a cookbook without using the French names for many dishes and cooking processes; these are universally understood and accepted, on menus as well as in cookbooks. In this cookbook, dishes are listed by their best-known or most generally accepted names. If the name of the dish derives from that of a person or place, or has no precise English equivalent, no translation will be given. If the name refers to a style of service or method of cooking which has not by usage become part of the English language, or if the name's meaning is not apparent at a glance, it will be translated. Over the years most kitchen terms and cooking phrases have been transferred bodily from French to English, although some mean different things to different people. Following are the cooking terms you will meet in these pages and the meanings they will be given.

Bain-marie was once the name of a cooking utensil; it is used in this book only to describe a method of cooking, because that is easier than describing the process in those recipes using it. In this process, a small utensil containing the food to be cooked is placed in the oven inside of a larger utensil partly filled with water. *Beurre manié*, often abbreviated to *manié*, is a paste made by kneading equal parts of flour and butter; it is used to thicken a sauce or liquid by adding very small bits to the cooking pot. *Blanching* requires plunging raw ingredients into boiling water long enough to tenderize, but not to cook them. *Braising* is always used to describe brief steaming of a food in a tightly closed pan, usually with a tiny bit of water or fat in the pan. *Frying* refers only to deep-fat frying, for top-of-stove cooking the terms *sauté* or *sautéeing* are used; foods *sautéed* are seldom browned or cooked long enough to become crisp.

Many egg dishes are best when served as individual portions in a ramekin or a tartshell, or on a round of toast or pastry. But there's a wide area of confusion as to what is meant by this type of service. A tartshell is often called a *timbale*, which may be either a cup made of waffle-like batter, a small china serving dish or a little metal mold. Similarly, a *croustade* can mean a toast round, a round of baked pastry dough or a serving dish cut from a loaf of bread.

To keep things straight in the recipes that follow, a *tartshell* always means a small cup of thin pastry dough, baked in a mold. A *timbale* means a similar cup that is cooked by plunging a specially shaped iron mold into batter. A *ramekin* refers to a china or porcelain dish in which a portion is cooked or served. A *toast round* means just what it says, and a *croustade* means a flat round of baked pastry dough. Tartshells and *timbales* are often sold by bakeries or delicatessens; they may sometimes be found in the frozen food bins of the supermarket. Page 291 gives a recipe for a pastry dough that makes preparing your own very simple; they can be made in large batches and frozen to be used as needed.

▪ SUBSTITUTIONS

Tartshells and Bread

The use of individual containers or of a toast round as a platform isn't just a matter of blindly following a tradition, or trying to fancy-up a dish. As in so many aspects of cooking, there's a reason. Often a tartshell is needed to contain and control a soft or liquid dish; serving food on toast or a *croustade* is usually a way of providing something to retain and absorb the flavor of a sauce or gravy. The use of any of them might be necessary to provide texture and crispness to a frothy dish, or the reason might be the very down-to-earth one of making it easier to eat a soft dish with a fork. For whatever reason it is needed, the tartshell or the foundation of bread has a place in any recipe that calls for its inclusion. It also makes for a more attractive service of individual portions, especially with eggs.

Certainly no law keeps you from substituting a hollowed-out roll or bun or biscuit for a tartshell, or using toast instead of a *croustade*, or vice versa; the recipe simply gives the traditional method of service. And keep in mind what the great chef Prosper Montagné pointed out when discussing this type of service: half the joy of being served food in a crusty shell is in eating the container along with the food.

It's well to remember, though, that today's commercial loaf of bread is not the kind of loaf that was around when this method of service originated. The bakery loaf of even a few years ago was a much more solid product, with a firmer texture, than the fluffed-up loaf of today. Most of today's mass-produced bread becomes too crisp when toasted and simply melts away when it meets a liquid. A few nationally distributed specialty breads, most of them baked in regional centers, are firm and solid; so are English muffins; so are the French or Italian loaves from the smaller bakers. A substantial and quickly baked bread can be made from the Brioche recipe on page 290.

BUTTER AND OTHER SHORTENINGS

Prices being what they always are, and budgets limited, you may want to substitute margarine for butter; this can be done except when the recipe itself warns otherwise. The reason: almost all margarines and many of the solid hydrogenated shortenings now contain a silicone-based chemical designed to reduce foaming when food is placed in them. Many liquid shortenings also have this additive. Unfortunately, the chemical also keeps the treated fat from combining with some acid ingredients, especially lemon juice and vinegar, when used in recipes depending on this combination in the sauce or in the dish itself. On page 287 you will find out how to wash butter or margarine that is too salty.

Butter and margarine are the easiest fats to use in egg cooking, as they turn color when overheated and thus help you to judge the temperature of the fat. Solid hydrogenated shortenings melt at much higher temperatures, so eggs cooked in them are easily overdone; if you must use a solid shortening, pure lard is the best. Cooking oils are better, with peanut oil topping the list. It is unique among cooking oils in that it has no taste of its own, and so imparts no flavor to the food cooked in it. In addition, peanut oil does not retain the flavor of a food cooked in it, or become rancid when kept unrefrigerated. It does not deteriorate, can be reused, and is completely satisfactory over any range of temperatures, including the hot ones needed for deep frying.

Olive oil, once considered the superior cooking oil, is now very hard indeed to find in its best grade, which is a very pale, very light, delicately flavored oil. When available, it must usually be bought in gallon tins, which take so long to use up that the oil becomes rancid.

Most of the olive oil sold today is a mixture of this clear, top-run oil and the coarser greenish second-run product. It is all pure olive oil, as the label says, but with a much stronger flavor than a fine olive oil should have. Olive oil is specified in these recipes only when its flavor is required as part of the finished dish; this is also true of other fats such as bacon drippings. They are to be thought of as flavoring ingredients.

MILK

Milk is no problem; its quality is uniform and is the same in New York or California, Maine or Arizona. Evaporated milk can always be used in any recipe. Dilute three parts evaporated milk with one part water when very heavy cream is called for, and two parts milk with one part water for cream; use equal parts of evaporated milk and water when the recipe calls for milk. Powdered milk can be used, mixed according to label directions; remember that powdered milks are defatted and dishes prepared with them will taste less rich.

One substitution should never be made: the use of any of the aerosol-pressurized "toppings" or their packaged counterparts. These products are not sold as substitutes, but as imitations of whipped cream. They will not hold up under cooking.

CHEESE

Very free substitution may be made in recipes calling for cheeses, especially those specifying Gruyère. This is Europe's "mouse cheese"; it corresponds to the uncured (unaged) Cheddars known in the United States as Longhorns. Both cheeses are mild, without overpowering authority, for this comes only with age in a cheese. The Western cheese known as "Monterey Jack" or simply "Jack" may also be used freely as a substitute for Gruyère or Longhorn. Use of the "pizza cheese," Mozzarella, should be avoided; it is stringy when cooked, fine for pizza, but not happy with eggs. And when any cheese of strong character is specified, such as aged Cheddar or Emmenthaler, it should of course be used.

Parmesan, the grating cheese, presents a special problem. There is a great deal of it sold today, usually pregrated in a package or can, and what is in the package or can is almost always one part good aged Parmesan to nine parts young domestic white cheese. This packaged Parmesan is the only thing available in many areas; there is nothing really wrong with it except that it lacks the sharpness of a good imported Parmesan or Romano cheese. The lack can be cured by adding a quarter of a teaspoonful of finely grated Sapsago cheese to each cup of the packaged Parmesan. Sapsago has a mysterious character of its own; it is far too strong to be eaten alone, but when a small quantity is added to a milder cheese, it amplifies and reinforces the flavor of the mild cheese, much as monosodium glutamate acts with other foods. Using Sapsago as an amplifier for any cheese is a good habit to acquire; it grates easily, keeps well, and a little cone of it lasts a long time.

Whatever the cheese, avoid "process" cheeses as you would run from the plague. These products are merely milk curds flavored with a small quantity of good natural cheese, heated to pasteurize and blend them. The processing kills the life of the real cheese used, stops the ripening that brings flavor and gives the finished product many of the best characteristics of a good-quality library paste. Never mind what the ads say; they were all written by an employee of the company that makes the cheese. No recipe in this book contemplates the use of a processed cheese in its preparation.

WINE

This brings us to wine and eggs, as happy a marriage as any you will find, if the wine is right. First, use the same wine you would drink; avoid the "cooking wine" or "cooking sherry." Vast quantities of cheap wine are made on a base of alcohol from Thompson Seedless Grapes. Technically, the alcohol is a wine, but it is odorless, colorless and tasteless; it is colored and flavored in wine factories to produce anything the manufacturer desires, from "sherry" and "burgundy" to "sauterne."

Table wines worth cooking with—or drinking, for that matter—will almost always bear the names of the grapes from which they were pressed. There are a few exceptions, but not many. These wines are produced by good vintners who do not think of themselves as manufacturers, and who put on the labels of their wines the information you need to make a good choice. Fortified wines, sherry and Madeira, have no substitutes and cannot be interchanged. There are good domestic sherries; the ones you want will state on the label that they are made by the *solera* process; all imported sherry is made this way. There is no domestic Madeira.

Seasonings

All but one or two of the spices, seasonings and other ingredients called for by the recipes in this book are certain to be already in your pantry, or on your supermarket shelves. Some few of the recipes call for truffles, which are certainly not found in most supermarkets. They are stocked, however, in the specialty food sections that are now universal in big-city department stores; so is Truffle Essence, which substitutes in most recipes and is less costly than truffles. Aside from this item, nothing unusual in the line of seasonings, spices or ingredients will be required.

A word of caution, though. Quantities of seasonings called for in the recipes are based on using whole spices, ground or pounded or grated as used. Preground spices have a tendency to go flat, to lose strength and aroma when kept too long, since the cans they come in cannot really be sealed for shelf storage at home. Whole spices in the leaf, seed or berry can be stored in tightly sealed screwtop jars. The natural form of the spice or herb, the unbroken hull or the uncrushed leaf, helps to keep it fresh. Pepper and nutmeg are especially vulnerable to aging; compare those you have stored for a year with the freshly grated or ground spice to see the difference. White pepper, ground at the moment of using, not only has a more delicate flavor, but leaves no black specks in egg whites or in white sauces.

Glazing

A commonplace instruction met with in the recipes is to "glaze" a finished dish before serving, and there is good reason for this, too. That final minute under the broiler exposes a dish to an intense heat that marries its flavors into a unified whole. If it also adds attractiveness and insures the dish getting to the table at the proper temperature, that is a pleasant by-product.

Often the glazing is done with a sauce; the sauce is usually Espagnole, which is often referred to as "demi-glaze" because of its wide use for this purpose. Sauce Espagnole is given in "instant" and traditional form on page 275. The other most common glazes are formed from plain grated Parmesan or a mixture of Parmesan with an equal amount of breadcrumbs (page 291). The glazing process takes only a minute or two; it should not be omitted.

MEASUREMENTS

One of the charming peculiarities of egg cookery is that either one or two eggs may be served as a portion without having to adjust the quantities given in a recipe. Whether the egg is poached, shirred, soft-cooked or cooked *en cocotte*, the quantity of sauce or other ingredients will serve for one egg or two. But remember that this is based on the service of one portion, and must be multiplied by the number of portions to be served. When adjustment is needed, or when a recipe is based on serving more than one portion, it will be clearly stated.

The easy way to make adjustments for a larger or smaller number of servings than are given in the recipe is to change quantities in ratio to the number of eggs added or subtracted. This isn't as complicated as it sounds; a recipe calling for 4 eggs and 2 cups of ingredient X will need only 1 cup of X if it is to be made up for 2 eggs, 3 cups if it is to be made for 6 eggs. All other ingredients are similarly adjusted. Even seasonings usually respond to this kind of simple adjustment, though in the final analysis the seasoning of a dish must be a matter of the cook's judgment.

Giving strictly precise measurements for seasonings in a recipe is always tricky. In spite of the efforts of generations of teachers and exhorters, cooking remains an art instead of a science because no foolproof way has been found to measure the strength of seasonings. The pepper Agatha uses may be dulled by long exposure to air in an unsealed can; Clementine grinds pepper into the measuring spoon from her own little pepper mill. Mary's thumb is twice as big as Bertha's, so her pinch of salt is twice as large. No written recipe can do more than offer guidelines; you must decide how closely to follow them.

This is also true of temperatures and oven settings. Betty's skillet is pressed from thin aluminum, Thelma's is of heavy cast aluminum, and Joanne's is cast iron; all three are different sizes and their temperatures over low or high heat will vary significantly. Cora uses a thick earthenware casserole; Martha likes one made from thin enameled steel. What's cooked in Martha's casserole is going to be finished sooner than it would in Cora's. Even the most precise adjustment of an oven thermostat at a factory will not hold forever; between two kitchen ranges there will be a wide variation of actual temperatures even when both thermostats are set at 300 degrees. So do not feel enslaved by either the quantities or the cooking times given by writers on cooking.

▪ ORGANIZATION OF THE BOOK

To help you find your way around this book, here's how it was laid out. Four chapters are devoted to general egg recipes, grouped according to how the eggs are cooked. Each chapter moves to a little higher plateau; first the *simple* dishes, containing the egg and one or two additional ingredients. After that come the *substantial* egg dishes, the kind you might serve at a family meal; these stick to commonplace ingredients, in many cases the bits you will have left in the refrigerator.

Following these is the *special* group, for use when you want to give the family a treat or serve an egg dish to guests; in this group the components and preparation are both more elaborate. Then come the *surprising* dishes, some of which might not appeal to every taste; they offer journeys for the adventuresome eater, involve offbeat ingredients, or contain an element of novelty in presentation that causes guests to sit up straighter and adds great luster to your reputation as a cook.

Omelets and soufflés occupy their own chapter, which is subdivided into recipes simple, special and surprising. Then come the *sweets*, the egg as dessert, and a short chapter on the egg as a beverage, for *sipping*. At the end there is a chapter on *sauces and auxiliaries*. This may help you to see saucing in a new light, for it contains shortcuts to reduce what used to be long, tedious preparations. Until you lose all fear of sauces, you will be an inhibited cook. Finally, there is a brief chapter that may help you to face leftovers with fewer furrows in your brow, since it contains a Thrifty Cook's Index, which keys many of the recipes to their chief ingredient in addition to eggs. This will allow you to make economical, tasty use of dabs of food left over in the refrigerator or freezer. This chapter also has hints on how to decorate Easter eggs, as well as suggestions for serving the eggs themselves.

Now we give you the two most important house rules of all, the first of which can be stated in two words: Have Confidence.

Have confidence in your judgment; just because you read it in a magazine or book (even this book), it ain't necessarily so. Have confidence when your taste tells you that a dish is right. If you have a habitual guest or family member who spoils your good cooking by pouring on salt and pepper, hide the salt and pepper and "regret" that you just ran out of both. Do this for a few meals, and the offender will learn again how food should taste. The place for salt and pepper is in the kitchen, not on the dining table.

Have confidence in your judgment; let it give you the courage to question. If it seems logical to you to substitute an ingredient and change a quantity, go ahead and do it. That's how good cooks are made. If the result is bad, admit it, and try something else. That's how experienced cooks are made. Have the confidence to abandon a recipe and take off on your own to make something different. That's how creative cooks are made.

And the last house rule: Don't make a hard job out of cooking. Cooking is fun. Enjoy yourself!

3

The Basic Egg

FROM THIS POINT ON, we'll be escalating each chapter, moving to higher plateaus. In each chapter the recipes are arranged alphabetically within sections, which themselves are divided by method of cooking the eggs. There is an exception: when there are two or more recipes bearing a strong family resemblance, they are grouped to follow one another so that the resemblances and differences can quickly be seen. Now, go ahead and cook an egg.

■ SOFT-COOKED EGGS

Since a "boiled" egg can be of any degree of consistency from almost liquid to completely solid, we will use the term "soft-cooked" to describe the egg that is just passed through the water lightly, and is served very, very fluid. The soft-cooked egg should show only a slight congealing of yolk and albumen. In this state it does not lend itself to further cooking, but is complete, and must be eaten from shell or cup with a spoon after it has received the blessing of a dollop of butter and a touch of salt and pepper.

To soft-cook eggs in the shell, take them out of the refrigerator at least a half-hour before they are to be cooked. Bring to a rolling boil enough water to cover the eggs completely and lower them into it. The boiling will stop momentarily, or at least hesitate, as the eggs go in; timing should start the moment boiling resumes. Two and a half minutes at sea level results in an egg which is cooked, but still largely liquid.

This brings up the question of altitude and its effects on cooking. Eggs are as sensitive as cakes in this respect; cooking times for eggs in the shell must be adjusted for altitude if you expect uniform results. As you go higher, the atmospheric pressure is lowered and the boiling point of water becomes lower in turn. A 3-minute egg cooked on top of a 5,000-foot mountain will still be raw when removed from the water. When cooking eggs in the shell, add 30 seconds' cooking time for each 1,000 feet of altitude above sea level. At sea level, then, a 2½-minute egg timed as described will have its albumen milky-white but cooked, and its yolk cooked but liquid. At 4 minutes the white begins to turn to jelly and the yolk starts to set. At 5 minutes the white is virtually solid and only a tiny core of liquid remains in the yolk's center. An egg cooked longer than 5 minutes in the shell is not a soft-cooked egg. There are no recipes using soft-cooked eggs.

▪ CODDLED EGGS OR EGGS *MOLLETS*

The use of the word "coddled" is terribly inexact. To some a coddled egg is a shirred egg; to others it means an egg *en cocotte;* to still others an egg cooked soft in the shell. The last is correct; a coddled egg cooked in its shell should be of the consistency described in French as *mollet;* since *mollet* is a word with a precise meaning, let's use it from this point on.

Eggs *mollets* are cooked by plunging room-temperature eggs into enough briskly boiling water to cover completely and at once removing the pan from the heat. The pan is covered and allowed to stand 5 to 8 minutes, depending on the altitude and the degree of firmness you want in the eggs *mollets.* After the allotted time, remove the eggs from the hot water and plunge them into a large quantity of very cool water for 5 minutes. Shell them at once, and if they are not to be served immediately, put them back into cool water to stand until ready.

An egg *mollet* should be of jellylike consistency throughout, yolk and white alike, but should be firm enough to be handled unshelled. When put on a dish, a properly cooked egg *mollet* will sag gently but still retain its egg shape; as it cools it will gain slightly in firmness, but will never lose the interior softness that is the distinguishing characteristic of an egg cooked in this manner. In the recipes calling for poached eggs, eggs *mollets* can be freely substituted.

▪ HARD-COOKED EGGS

Plunge room-temperature eggs into briskly boiling water to cover completely and time 7 to 10 minutes, depending on altitude, from the moment boiling resumes. Remove the eggs and place in cool water; this does nothing for the cooking, but makes them easier to shell.

To shell a hard-cooked egg or an egg *mollet* easily and quickly, crack the shell in several places by tapping with the bowl of a spoon, then roll the egg under your hand on a firm flat surface, using just enough pressure to crack the shell into dozens of tiny pieces. Pinch up the shell and inner membrane at the egg's large end, where the air bubble has formed, and use the membrane to strip away the shell.

▪ POACHED EGGS

A poached egg is one that has been simmered in a liquid after being removed from its shell. The liquid should cover the egg completely. So-called American-style poaching is done in plain water; French-style poaching is done in water to which a few drops of vinegar are added. The vinegar brings the whites to firmness faster and reduces the froth that always rises from the eggs as they are poached; this foam should be skimmed off with a slotted spoon. Eggs may be poached in any liquid: broth, stock, soup, gravy, sauce, wine, even in butter; they are still poached eggs.

When poaching, the liquid should be simmering gently, not boiling briskly, and the simmering should be constant throughout the cooking. When several eggs are to be poached it is better to use a number of small pans; if one large pan is used, the aluminum or stainless-steel circles designed to keep the eggs from joining are very handy. Grease the circles lightly before putting them in the water and take them off the eggs as soon as the whites will hold their shape. In small pans, create a little whirlpool by stirring the liquid with a circular motion and drop the egg into the center of the whirl; this reduces its tendency to disperse. All poached eggs should drain for a moment on an absorbent cloth or paper towel before serving.

There is a widespread misconception that the little cuplets pressed in a circle of metal and designed to fit into a large water-filled skillet will produce poached eggs. They do not; an egg is poached only when cooked in contact with and surrounded by liquid. Using these cuplet devices results in an egg more shirred, or even sautéed, than poached; there is certainly nothing wrong with them, and the eggs do come out in neat rounds. However, they are not poached eggs in either taste or texture. Eggs cooked in this fashion can be used in all recipes except those calling for the egg to be poached in a liquid other than water.

▪ SCRAMBLED EGGS

There are three methods of scrambling eggs, and each results in a different taste and texture in the completed dish.

Soft-scrambled eggs are beaten with 1 tablespoon of milk or cream to each egg; salt and pepper are added as the eggs and milk are beaten together. The eggs are cooked at the very lowest heat in a lightly buttered skillet while being stirred constantly. The spoon or spatula must be kept busy removing from the pan's bottom and sides the bits of egg that congeal from the heat; the result is a moist, very fine-textured dish. Eggs cooked this way hold better for deferred serving than any other scrambled eggs.

Firm-scrambled eggs are beaten with their seasonings and 1 teaspoon of water per egg, and are stirred intermittently as they cook over lowest heat. It is important to serve firm-scrambled eggs at once, since they quickly become leathery in texture and drab in taste. This is the egg most frequently served at the average restaurant, where the cook is too busy to attend to soft-scrambled eggs with the constant stirring they require.

Farm-scrambled eggs, or country-scrambled eggs, are broken into the pan without being beaten and with no added liquid. They are cooked over medium heat and are stirred only three or four times as they cook. When done, the eggs will have a streaked appearance, with distinct strands of white and yolk. Eggs scrambled this way should be served while still moist, since they have no added liquid and continue to cook for a moment on the serving plate. They also become leathery if allowed to stand too long.

▪ SHIRRED EGGS

Shirred eggs are oven-cooked on a shallow heatproof dish or *plat*, and are customarily served on the dish in which they have been cooked;

they are often referred to as eggs *sur le plat*. When other ingredients are called for in a shirred egg recipe, they are generally cooked on the dish with the egg, which is placed on top of them.

Only your taste can guide you as to the cooking time for a shirred egg, for only you know how firm or soft you prefer the finished egg to be. Six to 10 minutes in a 375-degree oven is the usual range, but when other ingredients are on the *plat*, longer cooking and a lower temperature may be necessary. This is especially true when the eggs are covered with a liquid such as a sauce or a purée, or with cheese, preventing heat from reaching the egg. Avoid trying to cook eggs quickly by putting them under the broiler; this only forms a stubborn film on the egg's surface. Only after a shirred egg has been cooked should it be put under the broiler, and then it should be covered with a sauce or glaze.

■ SAUTÉED OR FRIED EGGS

Sautéed and fried eggs are not necessarily the same thing, though produced by the same cooking process. Only a fried egg cooked at the right temperature with the properly scanty quantity of fat in the skillet is a sautéed egg. Just enough fat should be used to cover the pan's bottom, and the heat should never be raised past medium. The egg should still be tender and pliable even if cooked until very well done.

Customs vary in the presentation and finishing of a sautéed or fried egg. The American technique uses more fat, the white being solidified by basting it with the hot fat during cooking. The European method is to fold opposite sides of the egg white over the yolk as soon as the bottom becomes firm, and then to extend the cooking time until the interior is firm. The American egg is served as a round, the European as a rectangle.

Any manner of finishing that suits you best, even flipping the egg to cook on both sides, is naturally the one you should use. But do avoid having too much fat in the pan, or setting the heat so high that the whites sizzle into brown lace the instant the egg is dropped into the pan; this only results in a very tough-bottomed egg with a yolk like a stone.

■ EGGS *EN COCOTTE*

En cocotte correctly describes only one manner of cooking. It is applied to an egg broken into a cuplike container with a screw-on top, which is tightly closed and then plunged into a *bain-marie*. Usually, butter, seasonings and any other desired ingredients are put in the *cocotte* with the egg and are cooked or heated at the same time. The result is a blend of poaching, in-shell cooking and shirring; it is a unique cooking method.

Frequently the term *en cocotte* is incorrectly given to eggs cooked in open ramekins, but this is properly a shirring process. Only when a sealed container is used, allowing steam to work its seasoning through the egg white, is an egg cooked *en cocotte*.

The timing for cooking *en cocotte* is extremely variable, for it depends on the size and wall-thickness of the container used, the efficiency with which it is sealed, and whether other ingredients have been added. There is also the question of taste: How firm or how soft do you prefer your egg to be? Generally, with a prewarmed *cocotte*, 8 to 10 minutes is right for an egg cooked in a waterbath in a 350-degree oven, with only butter added to its container. When the *cocotte* is placed in a waterbath simmering on top of the stove, 5 to 8 minutes is usually about right.

Within the past few years, the charming *cocotte*, which was becoming an item for antique collections, has again appeared in quantity on the market. Invented and first produced by the Sèvres porcelain-makers around 1760 as a novelty for the king's kitchen, the *cocotte* evolved over the years into a unique and efficient utensil. Today it is a china or porcelain cup, usually decorated, with a tightly fitting screw-on top of heavy nickel-plated metal; the top has a large ring rising from it by which the *cocotte* is lowered into and removed from the water. The best today are produced in England, are often sold in jewelry stores as well as housewares firms, and are available in two sizes. If you buy, choose the larger size. Custard cups or deep ramekins may be substituted for *cocottes*, their tops sealed with a double fold of tightly pressed aluminum foil. But an egg cooked in an unsealed container outside a *bain-marie* is a shirred egg, not an egg *en cocotte*.

These, then, are the eight basic ways of cooking an egg. There are really two more, bringing the total to ten. The missing pair are the omelet and the soufflé, both of which will be covered in a later chapter, along with a galaxy of recipes for their preparation.

4

Simple Egg Dishes

BEFORE YOU BEGIN using the recipes that follow, about half of which are sauced, you might find it helpful to read all about sauces in Chapter 11. You will find that there's surprisingly little difference among the most common white sauces, that you can modify Béchamel with onions to produce Soubise or with a little tomato flavor for Aurore. And you will find, too, that you're free to substitute almost any of the white sauces among members of their own family group.

One more reminder: Quantities called for are based on the service of one portion containing one egg, but adding an extra egg to the portion does not necessarily require an increase in the other ingredients. This is true except for the scrambled egg recipes, which are based on serving four.

■ POACHED EGGS OR EGGS *MOLLETS*

■ *EGGS AMANDINE (Eggs with Almonds)*

> 1 *tablespoon butter*
> ¾ *tablespoon blanched, slivered almonds*
> 1 *poached egg or egg* mollet

Heat butter to a rich brown, sauté almonds until crisp and pour over egg that is drained and waiting on a warm plate. (There is no reason why unsalted peanuts couldn't be used instead of almonds; the interest of the dish is in the contrasting texture of the crisp nutmeats and the smooth egg.) Makes 1 portion.

■ *EGGS À L'ANCIENNE*

> *¾ cup rice, cooked in meat broth*
> *1 tablespoon Sauce Velouté (page 279)*
> *1 poached egg or egg mollet*

Arrange the rice on a serving plate in a patty shape and put a little of the sauce on it. Add the egg on top of the rice and cover with the remaining sauce. Makes 1 portion.

■ *EGGS AURORE* (*Rosy Eggs*)

> *1 lightly buttered toast round*
> *2 tablespoons Sauce Aurore (page 280)*
> *1 poached egg or egg mollet*

Spread the toast round with a little of the sauce and cover it with the egg, trimming it neatly. Add the remaining sauce and glaze the dish under the broiler a minute before serving. Makes 1 portion.

■ *EGGS BONVALET*

> *1 double-thick toast round*
> *2 tablespoons Sauce Béarnaise (page 282)*
> *1 poached egg or egg mollet*
> *2 tablespoons Tomato Sauce (page 278)*

Scoop a hollow in the toast round, spoon in a coating of the Sauce Béarnaise, put in the egg and cover with the remaining Béarnaise. Surround the toast round with Tomato Sauce. If you have a few ripe olives handy, chop one or two coarsely and sprinkle over the top. Makes 1 portion.

■ *EGGS À LA BRUXELLOISE* (*Brussels Eggs*)

> *1 large sprig fresh endive*
> *1 teaspoon butter*

1½ *tablespoons Cream Sauce* (*page* 281)
Pinch salt
Pinch pepper
1 *toast round*
1 *poached egg or egg* mollet

Braise the endive with the butter and a little water, chop very coarsely, moisten with Cream Sauce, add salt and pepper and cover the toast round with the endive. Place the egg on the endive and spoon on the remaining sauce. Makes 1 portion.

Eggs à la Flamande is another name for this dish.

▪ *EGGS COLBERT*

Any dish with Colbert Butter (page 288) bears the name of the famed finance minister of Louis XIV, who skillfully juggled the royal treasury to keep France afloat. The butter itself was the creation of Louis' chef, Vatel.

2½ *tablespoons Colbert Butter* (*page* 288)
1 *toast round*
1 *poached egg or egg* mollet

Melt the Colbert Butter; pour a small quantity on the toast round, add the egg, then cover with the remaining butter. Makes 1 portion.

▪ *EGGS CRÉCY*

1 *toast round or shallow tartshell*
¼ *cup puréed carrots*
1 *poached egg or egg* mollet
1 *tablespoon Sauce Velouté* (*page* 279)

Spread the toast round or tartshell with the puréed carrots, making a small hollow for the egg. Add the egg and spoon on the sauce, then glaze under the broiler a moment before serving. Makes 1 portion.

▪ *EGGS CRESSONIÈRE* (*Eggs with Watercress*)

2 *tablespoons chopped blanched watercress*
1½ *tablespoons Cream Sauce* (*page* 281)
1 *toast round*
1 *poached egg or egg* mollet

In a blender or a sieve, purée the watercress with ½ tablespoon of the Cream Sauce. Spread the purée over the toast, add the egg and cover with the remaining sauce. Makes 1 portion.

■ *EGGS ESAU*

> ¼ *cup puréed cooked lentils*
> 1 *toast round or* croustade
> 1 *poached egg or egg* mollet
> 1 *tablespoon veal gravy*

Spread the puréed lentils over the toast or *croustade*, top with the egg and spoon on the gravy, which should be very warm. Makes 1 portion.

■ *EGGS LUCETTE*

> 1 *egg*
> 1 *cup milk*
> *Dash salt*
> *Dash pepper*
> 1 *toast round*
> ¼ *tablespoon Anchovy Butter* (*page* 288)
> 1½ *tablespoons Béchamel Sauce* (*page* 280)

Poach the egg in the milk, seasoning it with salt and pepper. Spread the toast round with Anchovy Butter, add the egg on top and spoon on the sauce. Makes 1 portion.

■ *EGGS LYONNAISE*

> 2 *tablespoons butter*
> ½ *cup chopped onions*
> 1 *toast round*
> 1 *poached egg or egg* mollet

Using half the butter, sauté the onions until very tender, then drain them. Sauté the toast round in the remaining butter until crisply golden. Cover the toast with the onions and put the egg on top. Makes 1 portion.

■ *EGGS ARCHDUKE* uses this recipe, but the egg is covered with Sauce Suprême (page 282) and dusted heavily with paprika. Makes 1 portion.

▪ *EGGS MAINTENON*

Count Benjamin Soubise, a Huguenot in the court of Louis XIV, is the man for whom the classic onion-flavored white Sauce Soubise was named, and for whom this egg dish was originally called. The Marquise de Maintenon pre-empted it, which is the prerogative of kings' mistresses, but the dish is often called Eggs Soubise, especially when eggs *mollet* are used.

> 2 *tablespoons Sauce Soubise (page* 281)
> 1 *toast round or shallow tartshell*
> 1 *poached egg or egg* mollet
> 1 *teaspoon grated Parmesan cheese*

Spoon a little of the sauce into the tartshell or over the toast; add the egg and cover with remaining sauce. Sprinkle with grated Parmesan and glaze under the broiler for a minute. Makes 1 portion.

▪ *EGGS BÉRANGÈRE* is the same dish with Sauce Mornay (page 281) used instead of Sauce Soubise.

▪ *EGGS STANLEY* is the same dish with curry powder added to the sauce and the Parmesan glazing step omitted.

▪ *EGGS MORNAY*

> 1 *toast round*
> ½ *teaspoon olive oil*
> 1½ *tablespoons Sauce Mornay (page* 281)
> 1 *poached egg or egg* mollet
> 2 *teaspoons Breadcrumb–Cheese Glaze (page* 291)

Fry the toast round in olive oil until very crisp, spread it with the sauce and top with the egg. Cover with the remaining sauce, sprinkle with the glazing mixture and place under the broiler a minute before serving. Makes 1 portion.

▪ *EGGS NINON*

There is only one Ninon for whom this could have been named: Ninon d'Lenclos, perennial beauty and mistress of kings and nobles, who took her last lover in 1705 and died a year later at the age of 90.

> *3 or 4 cooked asparagus tips*
> *1 toast round or* croustade
> *1 poached egg*
> *1½ tablespoons Hollandaise Sauce (page 284)*

Arrange the asparagus tips on the toast round or *croustade*, put the egg on top of them and cover with Hollandaise Sauce. Makes 1 portion.

▪ EGGS D'ORSAY

> *1 toast round*
> *½ tablespoon butter*
> *1½ tablespoons Chateaubriand Sauce (page 277)*
> *1 poached egg or egg* mollet

Sauté the toast round in butter; it should be firm but not brown. Spread a portion of the sauce on the toast, add the egg and cover with the remaining sauce. Makes 1 portion.

▪ EGGS SÉVIGNÉ

A delicate taste in eggs is indicated for the letter-writing Marquise de Sévigné, whose salon flourished in the years after 1650, but coffee-lovers will never forgive her for refusing to serve coffee to her guests or for her prediction that the beverage, being suited only to the coarser tastes of peasants, would never have enduring popularity.

> *3 or 4 small, tender lettuce leaves*
> *1 teaspoon butter*
> *2 thin toast rounds*
> *1 poached egg or egg* mollet
> *2 tablespoons Sauce Velouté (page 279)*

Braise the lettuce leaves in the butter with a few drops of water, then put them on one toast round and trim neatly. Lay the second toast round on top of the lettuce and cover it with the egg. Top with warm sauce. Makes 1 portion.

▪ EGGS WALDORF

There are a number of variations of this classic version of eggs and mushrooms, but basically they are the same.

> 1 *large mushroom cap*
> 1 *tablespoon butter*
> 1 *toast round or shallow tartshell*
> ¼ *cup puréed mushrooms*
> 1 *poached egg or egg* mollet

Sauté the mushroom cap very lightly in the butter. If a toast round is used, sauté it in the same butter; if a tartshell, thin down the puréed mushrooms with the remaining butter. Spread the puréed mushrooms on the toast or line the tartshell with them, slide on the egg and top with the mushroom cap. Glaze a moment before serving. Makes 1 portion.

▪ *EGGS APICIUS* uses a purée of shrimp or crayfish instead of mushrooms; otherwise the dish is the same.

▪ *EGGS BRILLAT-SAVARIN* uses a mushroom purée, adds minced truffles and a coating of Sauce Velouté (page 279) reinforced by stirring in a little sherry.

▪ *EGGS BRIMONT* is Eggs Waldorf in a tartshell covered with Sauce Velouté (page 279).

▪ *EGGS DAUMONT* is identical with Eggs Apicius except that Shrimp Butter (page 288) is spread over the top of the mushroom cap before glazing.

▪ *EGGS DEMI-DEUIL* (*Eggs in Half-Mourning*) fills the tartshell with minced mushrooms and ham instead of a purée and covers the egg with Madeira Sauce (page 277).

▪ *EGGS MARIVAUX* uses a deep tartshell with the egg put in first; the shell is then filled with chopped creamed mushrooms, topped with the mushroom cap and garnished with Madeira Sauce (page 277).

▪ *EGGS MONTROSE* is a simplified version of Eggs Marivaux: the sauce is omitted and the mushroom cap dusted with coarsely ground pepper.

▪ *EGGS TROUBADOR* is identical with Eggs Brimont except that an egg *mollet* is specified.

▪ *EGGS WINDSOR* calls for chopped sautéed mushrooms on a toast round, the egg topped with the mushroom cap and Sauce Allemande (page 279) spooned over; the dish is then glazed.

■ SCRAMBLED EGGS

A good rule of thumb is to use one more egg than the number of people to be served, when the number is fewer than five; six eggs are usually considered to be sufficient for six, and above that number one egg per person can safely be used. But you know best how hearty are the appetites of those for whom you cook. All the recipes for scrambled eggs are based on five eggs, serving four persons.

■ *EGGS ALEXANDRE DUMAS*

As prolific a creator of dishes as he was a creator of swashbuckling romances, Dumas *père* claimed that the broth used in this recipe would make a smoother, more toothsome dish.

> 1 *cup precooked asparagus tips*
> 2 *tablespoons heavy cream*
> 5 *eggs*
> 5 *tablespoons warm chicken broth*
> *Dash salt*

Soak the asparagus tips in the cream for 15 minutes. Beat the eggs and chicken broth together, adding a dash of salt but no pepper. Begin scrambling the eggs at lowest heat in a lightly buttered pan, stirring constantly. Lift the asparagus tips from the cream and add them one at a time as the eggs are stirred. Pour in the remaining cream during the last few seconds of cooking; the dish should be soft rather than firm. Serves 4.

■ *AMERICAN SCRAMBLED EGGS*

In European minds, Americans ordering eggs expect to be served ham or bacon as part of the dish. Unless you specify differently, this is what you will be served in a café in Europe.

> 5 *eggs*
> 5 *teaspoons milk or water*
> *Dash salt*
> *Dash pepper*
> ½ *cup diced sautéed ham or bacon*

Beat the eggs with the liquid and the salt and pepper. Strew the bottom of a lightly buttered skillet with the diced meat and pour the eggs over it. Cook over lowest heat, stirring occasionally. Serves 4.

■ *CURRIED SCRAMBLED EGGS*

Obviously the amount of curry powder used is going to depend on your taste and the strength of the curry powder you prefer. If you are a curried-food addict, you will know; if you are a stranger to this Eastern condiment, experiment. Incidentally, the addition of minced chicken, veal or lobster or a few flakes of crab meat lift this dish out of the "simple" category.

> *5 eggs*
> *5 tablespoons cream*
> *Curry powder (to taste)*
> *½ tablespoon butter*

Mix the eggs, cream and curry powder. Melt the butter and soft-scramble over lowest heat. Serves 4.

■ *SCRAMBLED EGGS AUX FINES HERBES*

Traditionally the "fine herbs" used are parsley, chives, chervil and tarragon in equal parts, chopped fine. Shallots are often substituted for chives.

> *5 eggs*
> *5 tablespoons cream*
> *2 tablespoons* fines herbes
> *Dash salt*

Mix the eggs, cream, herbs and salt. Soft-scramble over lowest heat in a lightly buttered skillet. Serves 4.

■ *SCRAMBLED EGGS AU FROMAGE* (*Eggs with Cheese*)

> *5 eggs*
> *5 tablespoons cream*
> *Dash salt*
> *Dash pepper*
> *3 tablespoons grated mild cheese*
> *2 cups crisp buttered croutons*

Beat the eggs, cream, seasonings and cheese. Scramble in a lightly buttered skillet over lowest heat. Serve over the croutons. Serves 4.

■ GRANDMOTHER'S SCRAMBLED EGGS

> 1½ *cups of ½-inch bread cubes*
> 2 *tablespoons butter*
> 5 *eggs*
> 5 *tablespoons cream*
> *Dash salt*
> *Dash pepper*

Fry the bread cubes in butter until crisply golden, then drain them. Beat the eggs with the cream and seasonings, and begin scrambling in a buttered skillet over lowest heat. As the eggs begin to set, add the fried bread cubes a few at a time. Stir constantly so that they will be well distributed through the finished dish. Serves 4.

Eggs Pauvre Femme is the name given these scrambled eggs in France.

■ SCRAMBLED EGGS WITH MUSHROOMS

Not even the marriage of the egg with ham has been celebrated so often or consummated with such fervor as that of the egg with the mushroom. When mushrooms meet scrambled eggs, the resulting dish is usually given the name of the mushroom: cèpes, morels, or whatever type is used or available.

> 3 *tablespoons chopped mushrooms*
> 1 *tablespoon butter*
> 1 *tablespoon sherry*
> 5 *tablespoons cream*
> 5 *eggs*
> *Dash salt*
> *Dash pepper*

Sauté the mushrooms very lightly in the butter, adding the sherry during the last moments of cooking. (If canned mushrooms are used, heat them in the melted butter until warm.) Spoon into the pan 1½ tablespoons of the cream and at once remove from the heat. Beat the eggs with the remaining cream and seasonings. Replace the pan on the heat, pour in the eggs and soft-scramble. Serves 4.

▪ *NEAPOLITAN SCRAMBLED EGGS*

> 1 *tablespoon olive oil*
> 2 *teaspoons grated Parmesan cheese*
> 5 *eggs*
> *Dash salt*
> 1 *tablespoon tomato paste*

Heat the oil in a skillet over low heat and sprinkle 1 tablespoon of the cheese evenly over the surface of the oil. Break the eggs directly into the skillet, stirring each one as it is added. Stir in the salt, then stir occasionally until the eggs are set. Remove to a warm platter or service plates. Blend the remaining Parmesan with the tomato paste and brush thickly over the eggs. Place under broiler a minute to form glaze. Serves 4.

▪ *EGGS PÈRE DOUILLET*

Another of Dumas' egg dishes; who Father Douillet is or was has been lost to history except for this recipe.

> 5 *eggs*
> 5 *tablespoons chicken broth*
> *Dash salt*
> *Dash pepper*
> 1 *tablespoon butter*

Beat the eggs very briskly with the broth and seasonings; strain and set aside to stand for 15 minutes. Butter a shallow casserole and put in a 350-degree oven until the butter melts; tilt the casserole to distribute the butter on its inner surface. Pour the eggs into the casserole and cook 10 to 12 minutes in a 350-degree oven. Do not overcook it. Dumas warns us that the dish should tremble gently when removed from the oven; its cooking will be completed during the few moments between removal from the oven and serving. Serves 4.

▪ *SPRING SCRAMBLED EGGS*

This dish was once restricted to the first days of spring, when the tender tops of young growing onions appear. There are now green onions on the market all year around, so enjoy it whenever you feel the urge.

5 eggs
1½ cups tender green onion tops, chopped
1 tablespoon butter
3 tablespoons milk
Dash salt
Dash pepper

Beat 1 egg and stir the onion tops through it until they are lightly coated. Heat the butter in a skillet, and very lightly sauté the onion tops over lowest heat; in 2 or 3 minutes they will become soft but will still retain an inner crispness. Beat the remaining eggs with the milk and seasonings (adding any of the first egg remaining) and pour them into the skillet over the onion tops. Stir frequently until the eggs set. Serves 4.

■ SHIRRED EGGS

Of all egg dishes, those involving shirring are easiest to prepare and serve. The eggs can be watched or peeked at occasionally, as they are not harmed if the oven door is opened briefly while they cook. All ingredients usually go on the same *plat*, and the cooked eggs hold well while waiting to be served; indeed, they cannot be served too soon from the oven or burned lips will result, and this should be taken into consideration when timing their cooking.

Again, the shirred egg recipes take for granted that one or two eggs may make a single portion, and are based on quantities required for one *plat*.

■ *AMERICAN SHIRRED EGGS*

1 slice ham or 2 slices bacon
1 teaspoon butter
1 egg
Dash salt
Dash pepper

Sauté the ham or bacon lightly in the butter; if not precooked it will not be done at the same time as the egg. Pour the butter from the skillet into a shirring dish, slide in the egg and season it. Lay the ham slice cut in halves on either side of the egg, or put a slice of bacon on each side. Cook 6 to 10 minutes in a preheated 375-degree oven. Makes 1 portion.

■ *ANCHOVY SHIRRED EGGS*

> 1½ *teaspoons Anchovy Butter* (*page* 288)
> 1 *egg*

Spread Anchovy Butter evenly on the shirring dish, and slide on the egg. Cook 6 to 10 minutes in a preheated 375-degree oven. Usually, no seasoning besides the pungent Anchovy Butter is required. Makes 1 portion.

■ *SHIRRED EGGS ARCHDUKE*

> 2 *tablespoons chopped onions*
> ½ *tablespoon butter*
> *Dash salt*
> *Dash pepper*
> 1 *egg*
> *Pinch paprika*

Sauté the onions in the butter until they begin to become transparent at the edges, spread them in a layer over the shirring dish and sprinkle with salt and pepper. Slip the egg atop the onions and cook 6 to 10 minutes in a preheated 375-degree oven. Dust liberally with paprika before serving. Makes 1 portion.

■ *EGGS LYONNAISE* merely omits the paprika.

■ *EGGS CÉCILE*

No shirring dish is needed for this recipe or the one that follows.

> ¾ *cup cooked mashed potatoes*
> ½ *teaspoon milk*
> *Dash salt*
> *Dash pepper*
> ½ *whole egg, beaten, per portion*
> ½ *teaspoon butter*
> 1 *egg*
> ½ *teaspoon grated Parmesan cheese*

Beat the potatoes, milk, salt and pepper with the ½ egg until a smooth doughlike paste is formed. Shape into a cuplet and bake 5 minutes on a greased cookie sheet in a preheated 350-degree oven.

Remove, drop the ½ teaspoon butter into the cuplet and slide in the other egg. Sprinkle the top with the grated Parmesan. Bake 8 to 12 minutes in a preheated 375-degree oven. For extra garnish, sprinkle with paprika or cayenne before serving. Makes 1 portion.

■ *EGGS À CHEVAL* (*Eggs on Horseback*)

A house specialty of the 1930s at the Café Régence in Paris, the original recipe called for a light-textured French bread, *pain mie*, for which the best substitute is an English muffin.

> 1 *English muffin*
> 1 *egg*
> *Dash salt*
> *Dash pepper*
> *Pinch cayenne*
> 1 *thick slice Gruyère or other mild cheese*

Slice a thin sliver from the top of the muffin and pull out the inner crumbs to leave a case. Slip the egg into the case and dust with salt, pepper and cayenne. Cover the top of the muffin with the slice of cheese, trimming it so that the muffin is neatly covered. On an un-greased cookie sheet, cook 20 to 25 minutes in a preheated 350-degree oven.

A word of caution: Do not be too impatient to begin eating, for the dish holds heat a surprisingly long time. Makes 1 portion.

■ *ENGLISH-STYLE SHIRRED EGGS*

> 1 *large, thick slice bacon*
> 1 *egg*
> *Dash salt*
> *Dash pepper*

Blanch the bacon by plunging it for 2 minutes into boiling water. Trim it to cover the bottom of a shirring dish. Slide the egg on the bacon and dust with seasonings. Cook 6 to 10 minutes in a preheated 375-degree oven. Makes 1 portion.

■ *EGGS AU GRATIN*

This is the classic dish of shirred eggs.

> 1 *egg*
> 1 *tablespoon milk*
> 2 *tablespoons grated Gruyère or other mild cheese*
> *Dash salt*

Slide the egg onto a lightly greased shirring dish, pour on the milk and sprinkle the grated cheese and salt over the egg in an even coating. Cook 8 to 12 minutes in a preheated 375-degree oven; if you enjoy the cheese soft rather than crusted, decrease the oven temperature and extend the cooking time. Frequently a sprinkling of Breadcrumb–Cheese Glaze (page 291) is used on this dish, or a sprinkling of either paprika or cayenne. Makes 1 portion.

▪ *EGGS À LA MIDINETTE* (*Seamstress' Eggs*)

> 1 *egg*
> ¼ *cup sautéed mushrooms, chopped fine*
> 1 *tablespoon Breadcrumb–Cheese Glaze* (*page* 291)
> 1 *teaspoon butter*
> *Dash salt*
> *Dash pepper*

Butter the shirring dish and slide in the egg. Cover with a thick layer of mushrooms and spread the glaze mix over the mushrooms, dotting with butter. Sprinkle on the seasonings and cook 8 to 12 minutes in a preheated 375-degree oven. Makes 1 portion.

▪ *EGGS MONTROUGE*

> ½ *cup mushroom purée*
> 1 *egg*
> *Breadcrumb–Cheese Glaze* (*page* 291)
> *Dash salt*
> *Dash pepper*

Make a ring of the mushroom purée on a buttered shirring dish and slide the egg into it. Cover with the glaze mix and seasonings. Cook 6 to 10 minutes in a preheated 375-degree oven. Makes 1 portion.

▪ *EGGS SOUBISE*

> ¼ *teaspoon butter*
> 1 *egg*

> *½ cup Sauce Soubise* (*page* 281)
> *½ teaspoon Sauce Espagnole* (*page* 275)

A deep shirring dish or ramekin is required. Butter it generously, put in the egg, and cover it with the Sauce Soubise. Cook 8 to 12 minutes in a preheated 375-degree oven. Warm the Sauce Espagnole with a little butter, spread it on top and place the dish under the broiler for a minute to glaze before serving. Makes 1 portion.

▪ SHIRRED SWISS EGGS

> *2 tablespoons grated Emmenthaler cheese*
> *1 egg*
> *½ tablespoon minced parsley*
> *½ tablespoon minced onion*
> *Dash salt*
> *Dash pepper*
> *¼ tablespoon butter*

Sprinkle the bottom of the shirring dish with one-fourth of the cheese and slide on the egg. Mix the remaining cheese with the parsley, onion and seasonings, and spread over the egg. Dot the top with flakes of butter. Cook 8 to 12 minutes in a preheated 350-degree oven. Makes 1 portion.

Prepare in a shallow casserole if multiple servings are desired, making indentations to cup each egg in the cheese lining the casserole's bottom.

▪ VIRGINIA-STYLE EGGS

In its original plantation form, special oversized biscuits were baked the night before this dish was to be served for breakfast. If you use biscuits, make them really big, 4 to 5 inches in diameter and proportionately thick.

> *1 roll, bun or English muffin*
> *¼ teaspoon dried mustard*
> *½ teaspoon vinegar*
> *Pinch sugar*
> *¼ cup minced Virginia ham*
> *1 egg*
> *Dash cayenne*

Slice the top from the bun or muffin and scoop out the crumbs to form a case. Mix the mustard, vinegar and sugar into a paste, bind the ham with it and line the case with the seasoned ham. Slide the egg on top of the ham, and dust with cayenne. Bake 10 to 12 minutes on a buttered cookie sheet in a 350-degree oven. (A thick coating of canned deviled ham can be used in place of the sturdily flavored natural Virginia ham.) Makes 1 portion.

▪ SAUTÉED OR FRIED EGGS

▪ *AMERICAN-STYLE HAM AND EGGS*

> 1 *egg*
> 1 *slice ham or 2 slices bacon*
> *Dash salt*
> *Dash pepper*

In most American kitchens the eggs to be served with ham (or bacon; for all practical purposes the two are interchangeable) are sautéed in the pan juices of the meat used, seasoned only with salt and pepper. Makes 1 portion.

▪ *EGGS BAYONNE* is the same dish with a French accent, though generally the menu specifies the type of ham or the region from which it comes; in this case, the hard, salty Orthez ham, very like an American Virginia or Smithfield ham.

▪ *EGGS PARMA* uses the prosciutto or capocollo (ham-cured pork tenderloin); these are so dry that they must usually be sautéed with a little fat or butter.

▪ *ENGLISH-STYLE EGGS*

> 1 *thick slice toast*
> 2 *tablespoons veal gravy*
> 1 *egg*

Soak the toast in the gravy, allowing it to absorb all it will hold without becoming soggy. Sauté the egg and serve it on the soaked toast. Makes 1 portion.

▪ *TOAD-IN-THE-HOLE*

If you ordered English-style eggs on the Continent you would probably be served the preceding recipe. If you ordered the same dish in an English restaurant catering to the lower- or middle-class trade, you would probably get this one. Only the British could come up with such an unattractive name!

> 1 *slice bread, 1½ inches thick*
> 2 *tablespoons bacon drippings*
> 1 *egg*

Trim the crust from the bread and use a large cookie or biscuit cutter to remove a round from the center of the slice. Have the bacon fat very hot, though not smoking. Fry the bread slice until crisp on one side, turn and immediately slide the egg into the hole. When the egg is firm, lift the bread slice and egg to a paper towel and allow it to drain a moment before serving. The bacon fat should be salty enough so that no additional seasoning is needed. Makes 1 portion.

▪ EGGS *EN COCOTTE*

Keep in mind that *cocottes* are designed to be sealed; if custard cups or bean pots are used, cover them with a double thickness of aluminum foil pressed tightly down around the sides. It is the action of the steam generated as the *cocotte's* contents cook that gives this type of cooking its character.

If two eggs are to be cooked, and solid ingredients are called for in the recipe, always divide the solids into two halves; put half in the *cocotte's* bottom, slip in one egg, then the other half of the solids, then the second egg.

▪ *EGGS BENÊCHE*

> 1½ *tablespoons tomato catsup*
> ¼ *teaspoon curry powder*
> 1 *egg*

Blend the catsup and curry powder and place them in the buttered *cocotte;* add the egg. Seal and poach in a *bain-marie:* if in the oven, 10 to 12 minutes at 350 degrees; if on top of the stove, 6 to 10 minutes in gently simmering water. Makes 1 portion.

▪ *EGGS COQUETTE*

> *Dash pepper (add dash salt if ham is very mild)*
> 2 *tablespoons cream*

> 1 *egg*
> 1 *tablespoon minced ham*

Mix the pepper with the cream, put in a *cocotte*, drop in the egg and cover with the minced ham. Seal and poach in a *bain-marie* 12 to 14 minutes in a 350-degree oven; or 5 to 8 minutes in simmering water on top of the stove. Makes 1 portion.

▪ *EGGS JEANNETTE* substitutes minced breast meat of chicken in place of the ham; it will require salt added to the seasoning.

▪ *EGGS* EN COCOTTE *WITH CREAM*

> ½ *tablespoon butter*
> *Dash salt*
> *Dash pepper*
> 1½ *tablespoons rich cream*
> 1 *egg*

Put the butter in the bottom of a *cocotte*, add the seasonings, cream and egg. Seal; poach in a *bain-marie* 10 to 12 minutes in a 350-degree oven; or 6 to 10 minutes on top of the stove in simmering water. Makes 1 portion.

▪ *EGGS* EN COCOTTE AU JUS

This recipe and the one just preceding are the two classics of *cocotte* egg cookery, severely simple yet thoroughly delightful.

> 1½ *tablespoons pan juices from roasted meat*
> *Dash pepper*
> 1 *egg*

Put pan juices and pepper in a buttered *cocotte*, add the egg and seal. Cook in a *bain-marie* 8 to 12 minutes in a 350-degree oven; or 5 to 8 minutes on top of the stove in simmering water. Makes 1 portion.

The pan juices used in this recipe should contain very little fat; if they are refrigerated overnight the fat can be lifted off easily. The juices from beef, pork, veal, chicken and turkey are all good. So are many gravies thinned with a little broth or stock; for that matter, broths and stocks reduced in volume and seasoned to taste work as well as do pan juices.

▪ HARD-COOKED EGGS

There are few really simple dishes involving hard-cooked eggs, as most of the recipes involve stuffing the egg and recooking; these will be found in the following chapters according to their degree of involvement with additional ingredients.

▪ *EGGS GOLDENROD*

Certainly nothing could be simpler than this recipe, beloved of home economists teaching their first class of novice cooks.

> 1 *hard-cooked egg*
> ½ *cup Cream Sauce (page* 281)
> 1 *slice toast cut in triangles*

Remove the yolk from the egg, chop the white coarsely, heat the Cream Sauce and stir in the chopped egg white. Pour the sauced white over the toast, and grate the yolk over the top. Makes 1 portion.

▪ *EGGS HUNTINGTON*

A kissing cousin to Eggs Goldenrod is this specialty of the house from Pasadena's Hotel Huntington.

> 1 *hard-cooked egg*
> ½ *cup Cream Sauce (page* 281)
> ¼ *cup milk*
> *Breadcrumb–Cheese Glaze (page* 291)

Chop the egg coarsely, thin the sauce with the milk and stir in the egg. Place the sauced egg in a ramekin, cover the top with the glaze and put it under the broiler for a moment. Makes 1 portion.

▪ *EGGS MAYONNAISE*

> 1 *hard-cooked egg*
> 2 *toast rounds*
> 1½ *teaspoons Mayonnaise (pages* 285-286)
> 3 *or* 4 *drops Worcestershire sauce*
> ½ *teaspoon red wine*

Halve the egg lengthwise and place each half cut side down on a toast round. Blend the Mayonnaise, Worcestershire sauce and wine, and spoon over the egg halves. Makes 1 portion.

■ UNCLASSIFIED EGG DISHES

In every chapter you'll meet a few recipes that defy any category; often the dishes aren't as simple as this undeniable classic.

■ *FRENCH TOAST*

> 2 *eggs*
> 1 *teaspoon milk*
> *Dash salt*
> 2 *slices bread*

Beat the eggs with the milk and salt. Dip the bread on both sides in the milk, but do not soak. Sauté over medium heat, turning when the bottom browns lightly. Makes 1 portion.

No dressing is given for French Toast, for everyone has his own idea of what makes a suitable accompaniment. Some choose to douse the slices with catsup, some with syrup or honey. Many like jams or jellies, some prefer it plain with a little fresh-ground pepper and additional salt, and many sprinkle the still-warm slices with brown sugar or confectioners' sugar. To each his own.

5

Substantial Egg Dishes

IN THEIR MENU PLANNING too many housewives overlook the egg. With a minimum of fuss, muss and bother, the egg in combination with other foods produces substantial dishes for any meal: casseroles, chowders, egg pies. A number of them are good served cold; others can be prepared in advance and finished in a few final minutes just before mealtime. Egg dishes are also overlooked in their role of budget-stretchers; they are ideally designed to use up embarrassing bits and pieces of leftovers and re-serve them in disguise. This is the kind of dish you will be meeting in this chapter, as well as the sandwiches that have become standbys in the United States and abroad.

▪ POACHED EGGS

▪ *EGGS AMALIE*

> 1½ *tablespoons mixed vegetables*
> 1 *toast round or* croustade
> 2 *tablespoons Madeira Sauce (page 277)*
> 1 *poached egg or egg* mollet

Arrange the vegetables on the toast round by binding with a small quantity of the sauce. Place the egg on the vegetables and spoon over it the remaining sauce. Makes 1 portion.

▪ *EGGS ANVERSOISE* (*Eggs with Hop Shoots*)

Granted that you'll seldom acquire the key ingredient for this one, doesn't it lead you to think of new combinations you can create yourself?

> 2 *tablespoons chopped tender hop shoots*
> 1 *teaspoon butter*
> 1½ *tablespoons Cream Sauce* (*page* 281)
> 1 *toast round*
> 1 *poached egg or egg* mollet

Sauté the hop shoots very lightly in the butter; pour the Cream Sauce over them in the pan and allow it to warm, stirring frequently. Spoon a portion of the sauced shoots over the toast round, add the egg and put the remaining sauced shoots over it. Makes 1 portion.

▪ *EGGS ARGENTEUIL*

When Paris was a young town it was surrounded by tiny farming communities whose products appeared daily at Les Halles, the great city marketplace. Over the years, many of the towns came to be famed for a certain kind of vegetable or fruit: Argenteuil for asparagus; Crécy for carrots, Clamart for green peas, and so on. Most of these Seineside towns are now part of the city, but their original claims to fame are recalled by recipes based on the foods for which they were originally noted.

> 6 *stalks cooked asparagus*
> 2 *tablespoons Cream Sauce* (*page* 281)
> 1 *large toast round or* croustade
> 1 *poached egg or egg* mollet
> *Paprika*

Cut the asparagus into thirds and reserve the tips. Finely chop the middle section. Purée the bottom section with a little of the Cream Sauce. Spread the toast round with the chopped asparagus; outline it on the serving plate with a ring of the purée. Place the egg on the chopped asparagus and arrange the tips to radiate like a star from the yolk. Cover with the Cream Sauce and sprinkle a light dusting of paprika on top. Makes 1 portion.

▪ *EGGS CHIVRY* is identical except that the sauce is modified by the addition of a small amount of sherry.

▪ *EGGS GRAND DUKE* substitutes Sauce Mornay (page 281) for the Cream Sauce and is traditionally garnished with a truffle sliver.

▪ *EGGS ARMENONVILLE*

Any dish in which the combination of tiny, tiny carrots and the small *petits pois* appears is called Armenonville.

> 1 *tablespoon parboiled tiny carrots*
> 1 *tablespoon parboiled tiny green peas*
> 2 *tablespoons Sauce Velouté* (*page* 279)
> 1 *poached egg or egg* mollet
> 1 *tartshell*
> 3 *or* 4 *cooked asparagus tips*

Warm the carrots and peas in the sauce. Place the egg in the bottom of the tartshell, fill it with the sauced vegetables and garnish with asparagus tips. Or, if you prefer, place the egg on top of the filled shell. Makes 1 portion.

▪ *EGGS BAGRATION*

Now, there are two recipes for Eggs Bagration. This is the easy one; the other involves lining a round mold with a symmetrical layer of macaroni and poaching the eggs inside the mold in a *bain-marie*. The dish is served upright on a large *croustade*, or is used to garnish a roast of beef or veal. Though both bear the name of the Russian general who fell at the Battle of Borodino, the preparation of the more elaborate recipe is an exercise in frustration, so be warned and stay with this easy one.

> 1 *teaspoon butter*
> 2 *tablespoons cream*
> ¾ *cup cooked macaroni*
> 1 *tartshell*
> 1 *poached egg*

Warm the butter, cream and macaroni together; if the macaroni has been cooked in salted water no additional seasoning should be needed. Fill the tartshell with the macaroni, and top with the egg. Makes 1 portion.

If service for several is desired, serve the dish in a large pie shell with the eggs spaced on top.

▪ *EGGS À LA BEAUHARNAIS*

> 1 *large or* 3 *small artichoke hearts*
> 1 *tablespoon butter*
> 1 *poached egg or egg* mollet
> 1½ *teaspoons Sauce Espagnole* (*page 275*)

Sauté the artichoke hearts in the butter; arrange them on a warm service plate to support the egg. Place the egg on top, brush with the Sauce Espagnole and glaze for a minute under the broiler. Makes 1 portion.

▪ *EGGS BANVILLE* calls for the artichoke hearts to be spread with minced breast meat of chicken before adding the egg.

▪ *EGGS BEAUMONT*

> 1 croustade
> 1½ *tablespoons puréed artichoke*
> 1 *poached egg or egg* mollet
> 2 *tablespoons diced, sautéed artichoke*
> 3 *or* 4 *cooked asparagus tips*
> 1 *tablespoon Béchamel Sauce* (*page 280*)

Spread the *croustade* with the artichoke purée and put the egg on top. Garnish around the sides with the diced artichoke spaced between the upright asparagus tips. Spoon the sauce over the egg. Makes 1 portion.

▪ *EGGS BENEDICT*

This is another of the timeless, classic egg dishes. The legend is that it was created in the Vatican kitchens about 1760 for Pope Benedict XIII.

½ English muffin
1 slice ham, lightly sautéed
1 poached egg
1½ tablespoons Hollandaise Sauce (page 284)

Toast the muffin lightly, place the ham on the cut side, then the egg on the ham, and cover with Hollandaise Sauce. Makes 1 portion.

▪ *EGGS ZINGARA* (*Gypsy Eggs*) is a Hungarian version of the same dish, served on a thick toast round and covered with Sauce Zingara, which is made by adding minced ham, truffles and paprika to Sauce Espagnole (page 275).

▪ EGGS BÉNÉDICTINE

2 tablespoons cooked, flaked codfish
1 teaspoon cream
1 teaspoon olive oil
3 or 4 capers
1 toast round
1 poached egg or egg mollet
1½ tablespoons Cream Sauce (page 281)

Pound the codfish with the cream, olive oil and capers into a smooth paste. Spread this paste on the toast round, top with the egg and cover with sauce; glaze under the broiler a minute before serving. Makes 1 portion.

▪ EGGS EN BERCEAU (Eggs in a Cradle)

½ baked potato in jacket
2 tablespoons minced chicken meat
¼ tablespoon cream
1 poached egg or egg mollet
Breadcrumb–Cheese Glaze (page 291)

Scoop out the pulp of the baked potato to leave a thin shell or cradle. Bind the chicken with the cream and line the potato shell; put the egg on this lining. Sprinkle it with the glaze and place it under the broiler; by the time the glaze sets, the dish will be warmed. Makes 1 portion.

▪ *EGGS BERNIS* uses a tartshell for a cradle instead of the baked potato half and garnishes it with Sauce Suprême (page 282) before glazing. An additional garnish of 3 or 4 asparagus tips is often added before the dish is sauced and glazed.

■ *BOSTON EGGS*

> 2 *thin slices raw mushroom*
> 1 *teaspoon butter*
> 3 *tablespoons heavy cream*
> 1 *slice toast, 3/4 inch thick*
> 1 *poached egg*
> *Breadcrumb–Cheese Glaze* (*page* 291)

Sauté the mushroom slices gently in the butter for 1 minute, then add the cream and simmer until the mushroom slices are tender. Remove the mushrooms, and slowly spoon the cream over the toast on a warm serving plate, allowing the toast to absorb all it will hold before becoming mushy. Arrange the mushroom slices on the toast, slip the egg on top and pour the remaining cream over the egg. Sprinkle with the glaze and set under the broiler for a minute. Makes 1 portion.

■ *BRETON EGGS*

> 1 *thick toast slice*
> 1/2 *cup thick purée of white beans*
> 1 *poached egg or egg* mollet
> 2 *tablespoons veal gravy*
> 1/2 *teaspoon butter*
> *Dash salt*
> *Dash pepper*

Spread the toast slice thickly with the bean purée, making an indentation to hold the egg. Heat the veal gravy with the butter and seasonings; it should be very hot. Put the egg on the bean purée, the gravy over the egg. Makes 1 portion.

Close cousins, handy to know about if getting rid of leftover beans is a problem, are Eggs Esau (page 42); Condé (page 84); Conti (page 85); and for green beans, Chevreuse (page 83).

■ *EGGS CARDINAL*

> 1 *tartshell*
> 1/2 *cup chopped lobster meat*

1 *poached egg or egg* mollet
1½ *tablespoons Béchamel Sauce* (*page* 280)

Spread the tartshell with the lobster meat, and slide on the egg. Spoon the sauce over the egg, then glaze for a moment before serving. Makes 1 portion.

A much fancier version of this dish calls for Cardinal Sauce, which is based on Sauce Velouté made with fish stock. The sauce involves adding the lobster's coral and reducing to thicken; cayenne is used for seasoning.

▪ *EGGS CARMELITE*

2 *tablespoons cream or rich milk*
2 *tablespoons dry white wine*
½ *cup raw chopped mussels*
1 *tartshell*
1 *poached egg or egg* mollet
1½ *tablespoons Shrimp Butter* (*page* 288)

Mix the cream and wine and simmer the mussels over low heat. Fill the tartshell with this mixture, place the egg on top and spread thickly with the Shrimp Butter. Place under the broiler until the butter has melted and the cream is bubbling. If additional flavor is desired, dust with cayenne or paprika. Makes 1 portion.

▪ *EGGS CARNAVELET*

½ *cup cooked, chopped spinach*
½ *cup mixed vegetables*
1½ *tablespoons Béchamel Sauce* (*page* 280)
1 *poached egg or egg* mollet
1½ *teaspoons grated Parmesan cheese*

Mix the spinach and vegetables, using a little of the sauce to bind them, and form a flat patty on which to slide the egg. Spoon over the remaining sauce, sprinkle on the cheese and glaze under the broiler for a minute before serving. Makes 1 portion.

▪ *EGGS CHORON*

1 *tablespoon green peas*
3 *tablespoons Sauce Choron* (*page* 283)

¾ cup toasted, buttered croutons
1 poached egg or egg mollet

Warm the peas in the sauce. Arrange the croutons to receive the egg, spooning a little of the liquid from the saucepan over them. Place the egg on top, and cover with sauced peas. Makes 1 portion.

▪ *EGGS CLAMART*

Clamart is in the same class with Argenteuil, Crécy and the other towns whose farms produced a specialty that identifies most dishes in which it is used; in this case, green peas.

½ tablespoon finely shredded lettuce
1 tablespoon parboiled green peas
1½ tablespoons Sauce Velouté (page 279)
Dash of salt
1 tartshell
1 poached egg or egg mollet

Warm the lettuce and peas in the sauce until the lettuce grows tender, but not soft; since the lettuce will absorb some of the salt from the sauce, a dash of salt may be required. Lift the peas and lettuce with a slotted spoon from the sauce into the tartshell, slide the egg on top of them and pour on the remaining sauce. Glaze for a moment before serving. Makes 1 portion.

▪ *EGGS DUCHESSE*

Included here is a bonus recipe for the Potatoes Duchesse needed to prepare this dish. They stand in esteem with French Fries as one of that nation's great contributions to the potato.

1 cup Potatoes Duchesse
1 poached egg or egg mollet
2 tablespoons veal or chicken gravy

Form the potatoes into a cup large enough to hold the egg, then bake 5 to 8 minutes in a preheated 350-degree oven on a greased cookie sheet. Transfer to a warm service plate, put the egg into the potato cup and pour over the hot gravy. Makes 1 portion.

▪ *Potatoes Duchesse:* Beat 3 cups mashed potatoes into a bowl in which a whole egg has been beaten with ¾ cup of milk. While beating, add a generous dash of salt, a scant pinch of pepper and a large dash of nutmeg.

▪ *EGGS BERLIOZ* is also served in cuplets made of Potatoes Duchesse, with the gravy replaced by Madeira Sauce (page 277), and with a spoonful of shredded, sautéed mushrooms sprinkled over the egg before saucing.

▪ *EGGS DUXELLES* (*Eggs with Ham and Mushrooms*)

A *duxelles* is a hash of mushrooms, chopped fine and sautéed in butter; sometimes a few shreds of ham are added.

> 1 *tablespoon diced mushrooms*
> 1 *tablespoon diced ham*
> ½ *tablespoon butter*
> 1 *toast round*
> 1 *poached egg or egg* mollet
> 1 *tablespoon Sauce Espagnole* (*page 275*)

Sauté the mushrooms and ham in the butter, and spread over the toast round. Place the egg on top, brush with the sauce and glaze for a moment before serving. Makes 1 portion.

▪ *EGGS À LA FORESTIÈRE* (*Forester's Eggs*) specifies that field mushrooms be used and replaces the ham with bacon; otherwise it is the same dish.

▪ *EGGS LEE* requires cooking the mushrooms and ham separately, covering the toast round with the ham sliced and trimmed to fit, then spreading on the mushrooms and topping with the egg; the dish is glazed.

▪ *EGGS HALÉVY*

> ½ *cup diced cooked breast meat of chicken*
> 2 *tablespoons White Wine Sauce* (*page 283*)
> 1 *shallow tartshell*
> 1 *poached egg or egg* mollet
> *Breadcrumb–Cheese Glaze* (*page 291*)

Warm the chicken in the sauce, lift out with a fork into the bottom of the tartshell and top with the egg. Pour the remaining sauce into the shell, sprinkle with the glaze mix and put the egg under the broiler for a moment until the glaze sets. Makes 1 portion.

▪ *SCOTCH EGGS*

You will have noticed by now that dishes bearing a family name share common ingredients, but not so with the three "Scotch" egg recipes you will find included in this book. All they have in common is the eggs.

> 1 *tartshell or* croustade
> 1½ *tablespoons Shrimp Butter (page* 288) *or Salmon Butter*
> ¾ *cup salmon, poached or baked*
> 1 *poached egg or egg* mollet

Spread the inside of the tartshell with a thin coating of the butter and line it with the salmon, flaked. (If canned salmon is used, drain the meat well to remove excess oil.) Slide the egg onto the salmon, dot generously with the remaining butter and place under the broiler until the butter bubbles. Makes 1 portion.

▪ *SHERRIED POACHED EGGS*

Because sherry is a wine of such infinite gradations, and because taste is such an individual thing, the choice of your cooking sherry must be up to you. As a suggestion, try one of the excellent *solera*-run domestic cream sherries. If you choose an import, the Olorosa group best meets most tastes in cooking. You might start in the middle of the Olorosas and work in both directions, first to the sweeter, heavier cream sherries, then if you're not pleased, up the dryness scale to the Finos and Manzanillas, until you find the combination that makes your taste buds sing.

> 2½ *tablespoons butter*
> 1 *egg*
> 2 *tablespoons sherry*
> *Tiny pinch pepper*
> 1 *toast round*

Melt the butter in a heavy skillet over lowest heat and slide in the egg the moment it is all melted. Poach for 1 minute and slowly add the sherry, rolling the pan to blend the wine with the butter. Cover the skillet and poach 2 to 3 minutes longer. Dust the egg with the pepper and lift it with a slotted spoon to drain the liquid back into the pan. Spoon part of the sherry over the toast round, place the egg on top and pour the remainder of the sherry–butter mixture over the egg. Makes 1 portion.

Not all margarines can be substituted for butter in this recipe; those containing a foam-retardant will not marry with the wine. To be sure of good results, use butter.

■ *EGGS SUZANNE*

> 1 *egg*
> 3 *tablespoons tomato juice*
> *Dash salt*
> *Dash pepper*
> 1 *slice ham*
> 1 *slice eggplant*
> 1 *tablespoon Hollandaise Sauce* (*page* 284)

Poach the egg in the tomato juice, season with salt and pepper and drain, but allow some of the poaching liquid to cling. Sauté the ham in a lightly greased skillet, then sauté the eggplant until it is well done but neither crusty nor mushy. Place the eggplant on a warm serving dish, cover with the ham slice, add the egg and spoon the sauce over the egg. Makes 1 portion.

■ SCRAMBLED EGGS

■ *EGGS ARLÉSIENNE*

> 2 *small zucchini* (*about 7 inches long*)
> 2 *tablespoons butter*
> 5 *eggs*
> 3 *tablespoons milk*
> *Dash salt*
> *Dash pepper*
> 1/4 *teaspoon cayenne*
> 1 *tablespoon Sauce Espagnole* (*page* 275)

Split the zucchini lengthwise and sauté them cut side down in the butter in a covered pan until they are tender but still firm. Remove from the pan and scoop out most of the pulp, leaving only a thin shell within the skin; reserve both skin-shells and pulp. Mix eggs, milk, salt and pepper; scramble very soft. Blend the eggs with the zucchini pulp, adding the cayenne. Stuff the skin-shells with this mixture, coat the tops well with Sauce Espagnole and glaze for a moment under the broiler. Serves 4.

▪ *EGGS ARMORICAINE (Brittany Eggs)*

In its original form, this recipe calls for Sauce Armoricaine, a fairly complex thing in itself, involving lobster coral, wine, herbs and tomatoes. The mock-Armoricaine sauce given works equally well, and takes only about 5 minutes to prepare.

> ¼ *cup white wine*
> 1 *tablespoon Madeira*
> ⅛ *teaspoon onion salt*
> ¾ *cup Tomato Sauce (page 278)*
> 1½ *cups cooked chopped lobster meat*
> 5 *soft-scrambled eggs*
> 4 *deep tartshells*

Add the wines and onion salt to the Tomato Sauce and simmer for a moment. Place the lobster in the sauce and allow it to stay until warmed; beware of overcooking any shellfish, for toughness results. Remove the lobster, raise the heat under the sauce and stir briskly until it is reduced one-third. Place the lobster and scrambled eggs in alternate layers in the tartshells, and pour the bubbling hot sauce over the filled shells. Serve at once. Serves 4.

▪ *EGGS BORDEAUX*

Along the banks of the Garonne River, where the vineyards lie which give us the great Sauternes, Graves and Barsacs, these wines are added to many dishes, including scrambled eggs.

> 2 *tablespoons butter*
> 1 *tablespoon grated Parmesan cheese*
> *Dash salt*
> *Dash cayenne*
> 5 *eggs*
> ½ *cup white wine*
> ½ *cup grated Gruyère or other soft white cheese*
> 4 *slices dry toast*

Melt the butter over lowest heat, stir in the Parmesan, add salt and cayenne and stir until smooth. Beat the eggs with the wine and Gruyère, pour over the mixture in the pan and scramble until fairly firm. Serve over toast. Serves 4.

▪ *EGGS SCRAMBLED WITH BRAINS*

> 1 *brains*
> 2 *tablespoons butter*
> 1 *teaspoon lemon juice*
> 5 *eggs*
> 3 *tablespoons milk or light cream*
> *Dash salt*
> *Dash pepper*

Soak the brains in cold water, removing all outer membrane. Melt the butter over medium heat and add the brains when it begins to bubble, breaking them up with a fork in the pan as they cook. As they begin to brown, sprinkle them with lemon juice. When the brains are lightly browned, beat the eggs with milk, salt and pepper, and pour them over the brains. Stir occasionally as the eggs cook; the dish should be fairly firm. Serves 4.

▪ *EGGS CHÂTILLON*

> 5 *eggs*
> 5 *tablespoons cream*
> 3 *tablespoons chopped mushrooms*
> *Dash salt*
> *Dash pepper*
> 4 *tartshells with extra dough to cover* (*page* 291)
> 4 *teaspoons Maître d'Hôtel Butter* (*page* 288)

Beat the eggs with all but 1 teaspoon of the cream; set aside to stand 15 minutes. Sauté the mushrooms in a lightly buttered pan for 1 to 2 minutes. Add the seasonings to the beaten eggs and stir briskly once or twice, adding the mushrooms and the reserved cream. Coat the insides of the tartshells with the seasoned butter, fill them two-thirds full of the egg–mushroom mixture and seal the tops of the shells with a thin crust of dough, slashing it to allow the steam to escape. Put in a preheated 325-degree oven on a lightly greased cookie sheet and bake for 20 to 25 minutes. Brush the outsides of the shells with melted butter just before serving. Serves 4.

▪ *CUBAN SCRAMBLED EGGS*

> 4 *small sausages ("little pig" type)*
> 2 *tablespoons minced onion*
> 1 *teaspoon olive oil*
> 5 *eggs*
> 1 *tablespoon tomato juice or 2 teaspoons tomato*
>   *purée*
> *Dash salt*
> *Dash pepper*

Parboil the sausages in water for about 2 minutes, drain, split lengthwise and cut each half into 2 or 3 pieces. Sauté the onions in the oil until they begin to become transparent; add the sausage pieces. Beat the eggs with the tomato juice, salt and pepper, and pour into the pan over the onions and sausage. As they cook, stir only enough to mix thoroughly. Serves 4.

▪ *EGGS GEORGETTE*

> 2 *baked potatoes*
> 5 *soft-scrambled eggs*
> 4 *teaspoons Shrimp Butter (page 288)*

Scoop out the pulp from the baked potatoes after cutting them in half to form cups; the shell left should be about ¼ inch thick. Fill the potato shells with the very soft eggs and put a teaspoon of the Shrimp Butter on top. Bake in a casserole or on a cookie sheet for 10 to 12 minutes in a preheated 325-degree oven. Serves 4.

▪ *HANGTOWN FRY*

By an alphabetical accident, two of the most famous egg dishes of purely American origin come next. The first, so legend tells us, is a product of the California Gold Rush, originating in the town which changed its name to Placerville after the vigilantes stopped using the hanging oak on its plaza. A grizzled forty-niner celebrating his first rich strike demanded of a Hangtown chef the most expensive dish he could cook up. With eggs $1 apiece and oysters $25 a dozen, the chef came up with the following. Technically, it is an omelet; it is named a "fry" even though composed of scrambled eggs. Regardless of these discrepancies, it is always correctly called a Hangtown Fry.

5 eggs
8 oysters
Flour for dredging
½ cup very fine cracker crumbs
2 tablespoons butter
Dash salt
Dash pepper

Break 1 egg into a small bowl and beat lightly. Dip each oyster in flour, then into the beaten egg; roll in the cracker crumbs and sauté in a buttered skillet at lowest heat. Beat the eggs with salt and pepper, turn the oysters and pour the eggs over them. Stir once or twice as the eggs set. Serves 4.

Incidentally, the oysters used in the original Hangtown Fry were probably the coppery-tasting natives that pollution has now killed out of San Francisco Bay. They would have had the verdigris flavor common to oysters from the iodine-rich Pacific waters, a taste akin to that of the Portugaises Vertes harvested from France's Vendée coast.

▪ *KENTUCKY SCRAMBLE*

This traditional American egg dish dates back to the days when Bourbon was a regional whiskey, made in the Bluegrass region from locally grown corn. And do not call it "Kentucky Scrambled Eggs"; the dish is always referred to as a "Kentucky Scramble."

1 cup fresh boiled corn cut from the cob (or drained canned whole-kernel corn)
¼ cup bacon drippings
5 eggs
Dash salt
Dash pepper

In a skillet over medium heat, sauté the corn in bacon fat until a light crust forms on each grain; stir well as it cooks. Beat the eggs with the seasonings and pour over the corn, stirring often as they set. Serves 4.

▪ *EGGS MASSENET*

½ cup minced, raw artichoke hearts
1 tablespoon butter
5 eggs

> *5 tablespoons cream*
> *Dash salt*
> *Dash pepper*
> *4 tartshells*
> *¾ cup veal gravy*

Over lowest heat, sauté the minced artichoke hearts in the butter. Beat the eggs with the cream and seasonings, pour over the tender mince and scramble until medium-firm. Fill the tartshells, and pour a portion of the hot gravy into each one. Serves 4.

An asparagus-tip garnish is generally used, 3 or 4 tips laid symmetrically on the tops of each serving.

▪ *EGGS PALERMITAINE*

This is actually a one-dish meal, designed for platter service when a group of ladies gather at lunch.

> *6 eggs*
> *½ cup cream*
> *Dash salt*
> *Dash pepper*
> *8 very thin slices boiled tongue*
> *1½ to 2 cups cooked macaroni*
> *2 tablespoons chopped ripe olives*

Beat 1 egg with the cream and seasonings. Line a ring mold with the tongue slices and fill with the macaroni; pour the beaten egg–cream mixture into the mold. Poach in a *bain-marie* for 20 minutes in a preheated 275-degree oven; during the last few minutes that the mold is poaching, soft-scramble the 5 remaining eggs. Turn out the mold on a large round service plate or platter. Fill the center of the mold with the eggs, and strew the chopped black olives over them. Serves 4.

▪ *EGGS PANETIÈRE* (*Eggs in Bread Nests*)

> *2 long rolls (or loaf of French bread)*
> *2 teaspoons Anchovy Butter (page 288)*
> *5 eggs*
> *3 tablespoons milk*
> *Dash salt*
> *Dash pepper*
> *2 tablespoons chopped ham*

2 tablespoons chopped mushrooms
Breadcrumb–Cheese Glaze (page 291)

Slice the rolls or bread lengthwise and scoop out most of the crumbs to form a case. Spread the insides with Anchovy Butter, then toast for a moment. Beat the eggs, milk and seasonings. Sauté the ham and mushrooms in a lightly greased skillet, add the eggs and soft-scramble. Fill the bread cases with eggs, sprinkle with the glaze mix and place under the broiler until the glaze is browned. Serves 4.

■ *ANCHOVIED EGGS* substitute drained, chopped anchovy fillets for the ham and mushrooms; otherwise the dishes are identical.

■ *PORTUGUESE SCRAMBLED EGGS*

2 medium tomatoes, peeled and drained
1 tablespoon butter
5 eggs
2 tablespoons cream
½ cup flaked boiled codfish
Dash salt
Dash pepper
Generous pinch freshly chopped parsley

Chop the tomatoes coarsely and sauté very lightly in butter over lowest heat. Beat the eggs, cream, codfish and seasonings, pour into the skillet over the tomatoes and scramble until firm. Sprinkle with parsley just before serving. Serves 4.

■ *EGGS PRINCESSE*

While this recipe calls for individual service, it is equally as useful cooked in a single mold for group serving.

1 egg white
5 tablespoons milk or cream
2 cups ground white meat of chicken
Dash salt
Dash pepper
Generous dash nutmeg
5 eggs
4 toast rounds
¾ cup Sauce Velouté (page 279)

Beat the egg white with ½ tablespoon milk or cream and use it to bind the chicken meat into a paste; season lightly with salt, pepper and nutmeg. Line small molds with this paste, buttering the molds well. Beat the eggs with the remaining cream, salt and pepper, and let stand for 15 minutes. Pour into molds, filling each about two-thirds full. Poach in a *bain-marie* 15 to 20 minutes in a preheated 250-degree oven. Unmold on toast rounds, and spoon Sauce Velouté over each. (If a single large mold is used, the cooking time should be extended; this will vary somewhat with the size and shape of the mold.) Serves 4.

▪ *EGGS À LA REINE MARGOT*

Louis Bignon, the famous proprietor of Paris' Café Riche, created this dish; not in honor of the Queen of Navarre, but for his friend Alexandre Dumas, whose play of that name opened on the evening the dish was first brought forth.

> *3 tablespoons blanched, slivered almonds*
> *5 eggs*
> *5 tablespoons heavy cream*
> *Dash salt*
> *Dash pepper*
> *Pinch nutmeg*
> *4 tartshells*
> *¾ cup Béchamel Sauce (page 280)*

In a lightly greased skillet, sauté the almonds until they are crisp and brown. Beat the eggs, cream, salt, pepper and nutmeg. Soft-scramble the eggs in the pan with the almonds. Fill the tartshells, divide the sauce among them and place them under the broiler to glaze for a minute before serving. Serves 4.

▪ *ROMAN SCRAMBLED EGGS*

> *5 eggs*
> *3 tablespoons milk*
> *1 cup chopped cooked spinach*
> *Dash salt*
> *Dash pepper*
> *1 teaspoon butter*
> *2 tablespoons Sauce Vinaigrette (page 287)*

Beat the eggs, milk, spinach and seasonings. Scramble in the butter until firm. Sprinkle the portions with Sauce Vinaigrette before serving. Serves 4.

■ *SHARECROPPER EGGS*

From the hog-and-hominy days of a vanished style of Southern cooking comes this poor farmer's breakfast, for the "hog" of "hog-and-hominy" almost always meant salt pork, the poor man's bacon. Your main difficulty in re-creating this dish will probably be to find a good salt pork, for it is a meat which apparently has vanished. When bacon was a smoked meat, salt pork was an unsmoked bacon, made from sides too fat to be smoked well. Bacon now is made by brushing pork side meat of almost any grade with a chemical concoction, and most of it is inferior to yesterday's salt pork. There is meat sold bearing the name "salt pork," but it is usually jowl fat; good salt pork had a pronounced streak of light-pink, lean meat, and the outer rind was thickly crusted with the salt that had become wedded to the meat during the 3 months it cured; the rind was cut away before cooking. Its flavor was between those of bacon and fresh pork, a crisp, sharp taste duplicated by no other meat.

> 2 *tablespoons cooked hominy*
> 1 *tablespoon flour*
> 2 *tablespoons diced salt pork*
> 5 *eggs*
> *Dash pepper*

Drain the hominy well, put the flour in a paper bag, shake the diced pork well in the bag and put it into a skillet over medium heat. Shake the hominy with the flour and add it to the skillet, which by now will have a quantity of grease rendered from the cooking pork. Cook until the pork is crisp and the hominy crusted brown. Stir frequently. Drain excess fat from the skillet, beat the eggs lightly, add the pepper and pour over the pork and hominy. Stir to mix well as the eggs set. If the salt pork is good, no extra salt will be needed. Serves 4.

■ *SPANISH SCRAMBLED EGGS*

> 2 *firm, ripe, medium-sized tomatoes*
> 2 *teaspoons olive oil*

> 1 *tablespoon chopped or shredded green pepper*
> 1 *tablespoon chopped onion*
> 5 *eggs*
> 2 *tablespoons thin milk or water*
> 2 *teaspoons chopped ripe olives*

Peel and halve the tomatoes, but do not drain; the seeds and juice become part of the dish. Heat the oil and sauté the tomatoes cut sides down until they are soft. Lift the tomatoes with a slotted spoon to allow the juices and seeds to drain back into the pan and place them on a warmed plate. Add the green pepper and onion to the pan juices and cook until tender. Beat the eggs with the milk and pour over the pepper and onion; scramble until firm. Place a sprinkling of chopped olives and a tomato half on each serving. Serves 4.

▪ *TRINIDAD SCRAMBLE*

Not the Trinidad of the Caribbean, but a tiny town on the coast of Northern California, is the home of this dish. Each year, the two hundred residents of this little port entertain three to four thousand visitors at an all-day crab feast, serving the big Dungeness crabs from the local waters. On the morning after the feast, the committee that has arranged the affair meets at breakfast in the firehouse to review the preceding day and eat flaked crab cooked in scrambled eggs.

> 5 *eggs*
> 4 *tablespoons cream*
> 1½ *cups flaked crab meat*
> ½ *cup Madeira*
> *Dash salt*
> *Dash pepper*

Beat the eggs, cream, crab meat, wine and seasonings, and cook until very firm over lowest heat in a lightly buttered skillet. Serves 4.

▪ SHIRRED EGGS

Back now to the oven and *plat*, though in many of these substantial shirred egg dishes the *plat* will be a shallow casserole. Again, recipes may be served with one or two eggs per portion without increasing the quantities given.

▪ *EGGS AGENAISE*

> *2 tablespoons chopped onions*
> *1 tablespoon diced eggplant*
> *1 tablespoon oil or butter*
> *½ clove minced garlic*
> *1 egg*
> *1 teaspoon chopped parsley*

Sauté the onions and eggplant in oil or butter until almost done, adding the garlic about midway during the cooking. Lift out the onions and eggplant and spread them on the shirring dish; slide the egg on top of them. Cook 6 to 10 minutes in a preheated 370-degree oven. Just before serving dust the top of the dish with parsley. (If you insist on following strict tradition, the old recipe for this dish calls for sautéeing the eggplant and onions in goose fat.) Makes 1 portion.

▪ *EGGS ALADDIN* substitutes diced green pepper for eggplant.

▪ *EGGS BELLEVILLOISE* is Eggs Agenaise garnished with a pair of small sausages.

▪ *EGGS ESPAGNOLE* uses sliced rather than minced onion and a spoonful of Tomato Sauce (page 278) instead of the parsley garnish.

▪ *ALABAMA FARM EGGS*

> *1 cup diced salt pork or cracklings*
> *1 hard-cooked egg*
> *3 cups cooked rice*
> *2 eggs*
> *½ cup grated Longhorn or other mild cheese*

Fry the diced salt pork until crisp, or heat the cracklings (which are the crisp fluffs of pork fat or rind left after the fat has been rendered from it) in the skillet; chop the hard-cooked egg coarsely and add the pieces to the skillet to cook for a moment. Mix the rice with the pork and chopped egg in the skillet, after draining off any excess fat; stir until the rice is warm. Cover the bottom of a shallow casserole with the pork–rice–egg mixture—or just spread it smoothly on the bottom of an iron skillet, if you are using one—make an indentation for each egg on the surface and slide in the eggs. Sprinkle the grated cheese over the top and cook 10 to 12 minutes in a pre-heated 350-degree oven, or until the eggs set. Makes 1 portion.

This isn't exactly a company dish, and it's pretty heavy by today's breakfast standards, but it's a quick, easy meal-in-a-dish for busy days.

■ *EGGS ANDALOUSE*

> *Olive oil*
> *½ cup slivered green pepper*
> *½ chopped garlic clove*
> *1 egg*
> *Dash salt*
> *Dash pepper*
> *4 cherry tomatoes*
> *Breadcrumb–Cheese Glaze* (*page* 291)

Grease the shirring dish heavily with oil and spread over it the strips of green pepper mixed with the garlic. Slip the egg on top of the pepper, season and place for 5 minutes in a preheated 375-degree oven. Halve the cherry tomatoes and remove the shirring dish long enough to surround the cooking egg with the tomato halves and to sprinkle with the glaze. Then return to the oven 3 to 5 minutes for the egg to become firm. Makes 1 portion.

■ *ARKANSAS EGGS*

Kin to the Alabama Farm Eggs (page 80), this is another hearty breakfast the hard-working farmer ate before hitting the fields.

> *2 cups Longhorn or other mild cheese*
> *1½ cups hominy grits*
> *2 eggs*
> *Dash salt*
> *Dash pepper*
> *½ cup milk*

Mix half the cheese with the grits and spread in an even layer on the bottom of a shallow casserole. Make an indentation on the surface of the grits for each egg; slide the eggs into these dents. Sprinkle the remainder of the cheese over the top, dust generously with salt and pepper and pour the milk over the cheese, distributing it evenly over the surface of the dish. Cook 20 to 25 minutes in a preheated 350-degree oven. Makes 1 portion.

■ *EGGS BOULANGER* (*Bakers' Eggs*)

If this dish was named for that particular Boulanger who is credited with opening the first true restaurant in Paris in 1797, it was probably served by him as a specialty of the house. If it was named for bakers in general, it was probably cooked along with the bread in the bakeshops which preceded restaurants.

> 2 *large potatoes*
> ¼ *teaspoon salt*
> *Dash nutmeg*
> *Dash pepper*
> 1 *cup cream or rich milk*
> 2 *eggs*
> ½ *cup grated Gruyère cheese*

Slice the potatoes very, very thin, and arrange them to cover the bottom of a well-buttered casserole. Add the salt, nutmeg and pepper. Pour on the cream—just enough to cover the potatoes. Slide the eggs into the casserole on top of the potatoes, spaced well apart. Sprinkle with grated cheese. Bake 20 to 25 minutes in a preheated 350-degree oven. Makes 1 portion.

■ *EGGS BOULANGER* (*Baker's Eggs*)

As with the American recipes calling for salt pork, your problem with this one is going to be finding good salt pork.

> 2 *slices salt pork*
> 1 *egg*
> 1½ *tablespoons Maître d'Hôtel Butter* (*page 288*)

Fry the salt pork until very crisp. Place the egg on a greased shirring dish and cook 3 to 4 minutes in a preheated 350-degree oven; the bottom should be set, but the top very soft and runny. Lay the salt pork on the soft egg, and pour over it the Maître d'Hôtel Butter which has been heated to bubbling in a separate pan. The boiling butter completes the cooking, and the eggs are served. For some tastes, this leaves the eggs too soft; if you like them firmer, leave them in the oven an extra minute or so, but they should not be firm when the pork is added and the butter poured on. Makes 1 portion.

▪ *EGGS CARMEN*

> 1 *slice lightly sautéed ham*
> 1 *thick toast round*
> 2 *tablespoons very thick tomato purée*
> 1 *egg*
> *Dash salt*
> *Dash pepper*

Trim the sautéed ham to fit the toast round and place on top of the toast on a well-buttered shirring dish. Make a ring of the tomato purée around the toast round, its walls high enough to contain the egg. Break the egg onto the ham and dust with salt and pepper. Cook 6 to 10 minutes in a preheated 375-degree oven. Makes 1 portion.

▪ *EGGS À LA CHARCUTIERE* (*Pork Butcher's Eggs*)

This is the French equivalent to the British fish-and-chips, or the United States' hot dogs and baked beans; it is usually served even in those small bars and inns that do not call themselves cafés, and that may offer only this one dish.

> 2 *or* 3 *small, link-type pork sausages*
> 1 *egg*
> 3 *or* 4 *cherry tomatoes*
> *Dash salt*
> *Dash pepper*

Parboil (or sauté or grill) the sausages, leaving them underdone. Slide the egg onto a buttered shirring dish, lay the sausages around it and cook 6 to 10 minutes in a preheated 375-degree oven. Add the cherry tomatoes during the last minute or so of cooking so that they are warmed through, but not cooked. Makes 1 portion.

▪ *EGGS BERCY* is a *plat charcutiere* served with tomato sauce or catsup.

▪ *EGGS CHEVREUSE*

These next three dishes belong to the same family of which two members have already been introduced: Eggs Esau (page 42), and Breton Eggs (page 65). They are very close kin.

> *½ cup thick purée of green beans*
> *1 egg*
> *1 tablespoon grated Gruyère cheese*
> *Dash salt*
> *Dash pepper*

Lay a wide circle of the purée on a buttered shirring dish and slip the egg into it. Cover with the grated cheese and seasonings. Cook 6 to 10 minutes in a preheated 375-degree oven. Makes 1 portion.

▪ EGGS CONDÉ

> *½ cup thick purée of red beans*
> *1 slice very lightly sautéed bacon*
> *1 egg*
> *Dash salt*
> *Dash pepper*

Lay a circle or well of the bean purée on a buttered shirring dish, and trim the bacon to fit inside it. Slide the egg on top of the bacon, season and cook 6 to 10 minutes in a preheated 375-degree oven. Makes 1 portion.

▪ *EGGS CONTI* substitutes puréed white beans for red, thus completing the family.

▪ FLORENTINE EGGS

Children tired of the sterile service of spinach with a hard-cooked sliced egg often have their appetites perked up by this change. So do many adults who feel obligated to eat spinach.

> *¾ cup cooked, chopped spinach*
> *1 tablespoon grated Parmesan cheese*
> *1 teaspoon cream or milk*
> *1 egg*
> *Dash salt*
> *Dash pepper*
> *Breadcrumb–Cheese Glaze (page 291)*

Mix the spinach, cheese and milk. Put a generously thick layer of the mixture on a buttered shirring dish, with an indentation to hold the egg. Put the egg in the dent, dust with salt and pepper and sprinkle with a coating of the glaze mix. Cook 12 to 15 minutes in a preheated 350-degree oven. (A poached or sautéed egg may be used and the shirring step omitted; just warm under the broiler.) Makes 1 portion.

▪ *EGGS JACQUELINE*

Not the former First Lady; this dish was born before she was. It came from the old Ritz in Paris in the days between world wars.

> *¾ cup mashed potatoes*
> *1 teaspoon blanched, chopped almonds*
> *½ teaspoon chopped pimiento*
> *1 teaspoon cream*
> *Dash salt*
> *Dash pepper*
> *Dash nutmeg*
> *Milk*
> *½ teaspoon butter*
> *1 egg*

Beat the mashed potatoes, almonds, pimiento, cream and seasonings together; form into a cuplet. Brush with milk and bake on a buttered cookie sheet 4 to 6 minutes in a preheated 350-degree oven. Drop ½ teaspoon butter into the cup, slide the egg atop the butter and dust with more salt and pepper. Return to the oven 6 to 10 minutes, until the egg is firm. Makes 1 portion.

▪ *EGGS OMAR PASHA*

Every schoolchild—or those who have attended schools that still teach history—knows Napoleon's remark as he stood with his African invasion force before the pyramids: "Soldiers, forty centuries are looking down on you." What is overlooked is that the French invasion of Africa created a boom in African-sounding dishes in the homeland. Many a "Provençale" or "Italienne" recipe calling for eggplant, tomatoes, green pepper, onions, olive oil and other Mediterranean-type ingredients suddenly became "Africaine." This is one of them.

> *1 teaspoon olive oil*
> *1 slice eggplant*
> *¼ green pepper, sliced across*

> 1 *egg*
> 2 *anchovy fillets*
> 1 *teaspoon grated Parmesan cheese*
> *Dash cayenne*

In the olive oil, lightly sauté the eggplant slice; it should be slightly underdone. Transfer the eggplant and remaining oil to the shirring dish. Use the section of green pepper to form a collar all around the eggplant, tall enough to contain the egg, which will be put on the eggplant slice after the anchovy fillets are laid crisscross on it. Slide the egg on top of the anchovy-garnished eggplant, sprinkle the Parmesan on top and dust with cayenne. Cook 12 to 15 minutes in a preheated 350-degree oven. Makes 1 portion.

▪ *EGGS PARMENTIER*

Many potato dishes in French cuisine honor the horticultural advisor of Louis XVI, who introduced the Irish potato into France. Legend gives M. Parmentier credit for being as shrewd a psychologist as a horticulturist; it relates how he caused potatoes to be planted in the royal gardens and closely guarded as though the plants were very precious and rare. When the tubers had matured, the guards were withdrawn, and the hungry peasants rushed to steal the potatoes. A short time later, the king publicly announced that he had "graciously consented to share" the potato with his people, and thus the white potato became established as one of the saving mainstays of the national diet.

> 1 *small baked potato*
> 2 *teaspoons rich milk*
> *Dash salt*
> *Dash pepper*
> *Dash nutmeg*
> 1 *egg*
> 1 *teaspoon cream*

Slice the top from the potato and scoop out the pulp, leaving a shell about ½ inch thick. Beat the pulp into a smooth paste with the milk and seasonings, and drop small, irregularly shaped bits of the pulp back into the potato until it is about two-thirds full. Add the egg, fill the shell with cream and replace the top slice. There will be a quantity of the pulp left over; use it to form a base that will hold the filled potato upright on a greased cookie sheet while it cooks 25 minutes in a 350-degree oven. When done, the potato's skin and shell of untouched pulp should be crisply crunchy, the egg white mingled with the bits of beaten filling and the egg yolk soft. Makes 1 portion.

▪ *PORTUGUESE EGGS*

> 1 *small, firm, ripe tomato*
> 1 *teaspoon olive oil*
> 1 *egg*
> *Dash salt*
> *Dash cayenne*
> 1 *teaspoon grated Parmesan cheese*
> ½ *teaspoon chopped parsley*

Peel and chop the tomato, allowing most of its juice to drain away. Sauté it lightly in the oil over medium heat, until it is tender but not soft. Arrange it on a shirring dish so that its center can support the egg, and slide the egg on top. Dust the egg with salt and cayenne, then sprinkle with the grated cheese and parsley. Cook 6 to 10 minutes in a preheated 375-degree oven. Makes 1 portion.

▪ *EGGS RENO*

> 1 *firm, well-shaped green pepper*
> *Generous dash Tabasco sauce*
> ½ *cup Tomato Sauce (page 278), or tomato paste*
>   *thinned with water*
> *Pinch salt*
> 1 *egg*
> ½ *teaspoon butter*

Peel the pepper by plunging it into boiling water for 15 or 20 seconds, then plunging it into cold water; the skin will peel back easily. Remove the top, seeds and pith. Mix the Tabasco sauce into the Tomato Sauce; add a pinch of salt. Fill the pepper shell, allowing room for the egg; add the egg and top with butter. Cook 15 to 20 minutes in a preheated 350-degree oven, the pepper standing upright on a greased cookie sheet. Makes 1 portion.

▪ SAUTÉED OR FRIED EGGS

Most of the dishes based on sautéed eggs are hearty indeed, leaning heavily on such auxiliary ingredients as potatoes, eggplant, tomatoes and meats.

▪ *EGGS BORDELAISE*

> 1 *sautéed egg*
> 1 *tablespoon olive oil*
> ½ *firm, ripe tomato*
> 1½ *tablespoons coarse breadcrumbs*
> 1 *finely chopped clove garlic*
> 1 *teaspoon chopped mushrooms*
> ½ *teaspoon minced shallots*

Sauté the egg in oil; put it aside to drain. Press the excess juice and seeds from the tomato half and sauté it lightly in oil, starting cut side down and turning it a few moments before taking it from the pan. When it is turned, sprinkle the tomato with the breadcrumbs, which have been mixed with the garlic; press the mixture into the cavities. Remove to a warm plate. In the remaining oil, sauté the mushrooms, sprinkling in the shallots and mixing them as they cook. Place the egg on the tomato half, and cover with the mushroom–shallot mixture. If necessary, warm for a moment under the broiler before serving. Makes 1 portion.

▪ *EGGS ESPAGNOLE* replaces the shallot–onion mixture with a thick slice of onion gently sautéed in the oil.

▪ *HARVESTER'S EGGS*

Not from the Midwestern United States, but from the farming areas of Belgium, comes this platter-served dish for hungry men.

> 4 *slices bacon, ¼ inch thick*
> 4 *eggs*
> 3 *cups cooked green peas*
> 3 *cups boiled, diced potatoes*
> 1 *medium head lettuce*
> *Dash salt*
> *Dash pepper*

Blanch the bacon by plunging it into boiling water for about 2 minutes, drain and sauté in a skillet that can be tightly closed. Drain off the excess grease and sauté the eggs as the bacon cooks. Remove the eggs and bacon to a warm platter, arranging them around the edge of the dish. Pour the drained peas and the potatoes into the skillet and sauté 1 or 2 minutes. Cut the lettuce into strips and lay it over the peas and potatoes; close the skillet for 4 to 5 minutes, shaking it occasionally. Uncover, stir and fill the center of the platter containing the eggs and bacon with the pea–potato–lettuce mixture. Serves 4.

▪ *HUEVOS RANCHEROS* (*Ranch Eggs*)

Mexico has contributed three great egg dishes to international gastronomy, and this is one of them. Its fame has spread far beyond the Texas–Mexican border where chili con carne originated about 1830.

> 1 *egg*
> ¾ *cup chili con carne*

Sauté the egg, place it on a warm platter and cover it generously with the chili con carne. If you are using a canned product, choose the kind that does not contain beans. Makes 1 portion.

▪ *MILANESE EGGS*

> 1 *egg*
> 1 *tablespoon butter*
> 1 *tablespoon cream*
> ¾ *cup cooked macaroni*
> 1 *teaspoon grated Parmesan cheese*

Sauté the egg and set it aside on a warmed plate. Melt the 1 tablespoon butter in a skillet and add the cream. Toss the macaroni—which should be firm, not overdone—in the warm butter and cream, sprinkling it with the Parmesan. Pour the macaroni over the sautéed egg. Makes 1 portion.

▪ *SAUTÉED PORTUGUESE EGGS*

Even though it calls for the eggs to be sautéed, this one bears a strong family resemblance to other egg recipes from Portugal.

> 1 *egg*
> 1 *teaspoon olive oil*
> 1 ½ *tablespoons boiled rice*
> 1 *anchovy fillet*
> *Dash salt*

> *Dash pepper*
> *½ large, firm, ripe tomato*
> *1 teaspoon chopped parsley*

Sauté the egg in olive oil and set it aside to drain. Over very low heat, sauté the rice in the remaining oil, mixing in the anchovy fillet, chopped fine, and the salt and pepper. Do not allow the rice to brown. Drain the juice and seeds from the tomato half, stuff it with the rice–anchovy mixture and top with the egg. Stand the tomato in a shallow casserole, cover and steam 10 to 12 minutes in a preheated 300-degree oven. Sprinkle with chopped parsley just before serving. Makes 1 portion.

■ EGGS PROVENÇALE

Eggplant and tomato mark the egg dishes from the Mediterranean coast, whether French, Spanish or Italian. This family is no exception.

> *1 egg*
> *1 thick slice eggplant*
> *1 thick slice tomato*
> *Olive oil*
> *Dash salt*
> *Dash pepper*

Sauté the egg, eggplant and tomato slice in the oil, in that order, making sure not to overcook the tomato, and seasoning each sliced ingredient as it cooks. Place the eggplant slice on a warm plate, then the tomato slice, then the egg. Makes 1 portion.

■ *CATALAN EGGS* calls for sprinkling each slice with minced garlic and parsley.

■ *LANGUEDOC EGGS* introduces flakes of steamed mackerel between the slices and adds a garnish of Tomato Sauce (page 278) over all.

■ EGGS À LA REINE

> *1 egg*
> *½ cup mashed potatoes*
> *Flour for dredging*

1 *tablespoon chopped cooked breast of chicken*
1 *teaspoon Sauce Périgueux* (*page* 277)

Sauté the egg in butter, and remove it to a warm service plate. Form the mashed potatoes into a patty, dip in the flour and sauté in the butter remaining in the pan over medium-high heat until brown and crusty. Place the egg on the potato patty and cover it with the chopped chicken breast. Spoon Sauce Périgueux over the meat. Makes 1 portion.

If serving on a platter for a group, put the meat in a mound in the center of the egg-topped patties and serve the warm sauce in its own dish.

▪ *ROMAN EGGS*

1 *egg*
Cooking oil
¾ *cup chopped raw spinach*
1 *chopped anchovy fillet*
Dash salt
Dash pepper

Sauté the egg in the oil, and remove to a warm plate. Mix the spinach, chopped anchovy, seasoning and a few drops of water together. Drain most of the oil from the skillet; add the spinach mixture. Cover the skillet tightly and keep over medium heat 4 to 5 minutes. Arrange the spinach in a neat patty; top with the egg. Makes 1 portion.

▪ EGGS *EN COCOTTE*

As always, one or two eggs will go with any of these recipes; remember that if two eggs are used, half the solid ingredients should go on the bottom of the *cocotte* unless otherwise stated, then one egg, then the rest of the solids, then the second egg.

▪ *EGGS BACHAUMONT*

1½ *tablespoons puréed celeriac* (*celery root*)
1 *egg*
Dash salt
Dash cayenne
1 *teaspoon cream*

Put the purée, egg, seasonings and cream in the *cocotte;* seal it and poach it in a *bain-marie* 10 to 12 minutes in a 350-degree oven, or 6 to 10 minutes in simmering water on top of the stove. Makes 1 portion.

■ *EGGS BALMORAL*

> 1½ *tablespoons diced carrots, potatoes, peas*
> 1 *egg*
> *Dash salt*
> *Dash pepper*
> 1 *teaspoon cream*

Put the vegetables in the *cocotte;* add the egg, seasonings and cream. After sealing the *cocotte,* cook in a *bain-marie* 10 to 12 minutes in a 350-degree oven, or 6 to 10 minutes in simmering water on top of the stove. Makes 1 portion.

■ *EGGS BÉRANGÈRE*

> 2 *tablespoons ground cooked chicken meat*
> 1½ *tablespoons Sauce Suprême (page 282)*
> 1 *egg*

Bind the meat into a loose paste with part of the sauce and line the *cocotte* with it. Add the egg and remaining sauce, seal the *cocotte* and poach in a *bain-marie* 12 to 15 minutes in a 350-degree oven, or half that time in simmering water on top of the stove. Makes 1 portion.

■ *CALIFORNIA RANCH EGGS*

Since these eggs were laid in California, they are given the name of that state to distinguish them from the better-known Ranch Eggs from Mexico. It would, of course, be easy to tell the difference, not only from the style of cooking, but because no self-respecting Mexican cook ever puts tomatoes into chili con carne.

> 1 *egg*
> 2 *tablespoons tomato purée or thinned tomato paste*
> 1 *teaspoon finely minced onion*
> *Dash salt*

Dash pepper
Generous pinch oregano
1½ teaspoons grated mild cheese
2 chopped ripe olives

Separate the egg; reserve the yolk. Mix the tomato purée, onion, seasonings and cheese, and combine them with the egg white. Do not beat, but stir them together. Place the mixture in the *cocotte*, and lower the yolk in. Sprinkle with the chopped black olives. Seal; poach in a *bain-marie* 8 to 12 minutes in a preheated 350-degree oven, or 6 to 10 minutes in simmering water on top of the stove. Makes 1 portion.

▪ EGGS CARIGNAN

2 tablespoons ground or finely minced shrimp
1 tablespoon butter
1 egg
1 toast round
1 small cooked shrimp
1 teaspoon Sauce Espagnole (page 275)

Combine the ground or minced shrimp with the butter and line a well-buttered *cocotte* with it. Add the egg, seal and poach in a *bain-marie* 10 to 12 minutes in a preheated 350-degree oven, or half that time in an open waterbath on top of the stove. Unmold the *cocotte* on the toast round, put the small shrimp on top, spoon the sauce over it and glaze for a moment under the broiler before serving. Makes 1 portion.

▪ EGGS CHARTRES

2 tablespoons veal gravy or thickened stock
2 or 3 fresh tarragon leaves
1 egg

If veal gravy is used, simply put the tarragon leaves in it, place it in a *cocotte* and slip in the egg, poaching in a *bain-marie* 10 to 12 minutes in a preheated 350-degree oven, or 6 to 10 minutes in simmering water on top of the stove. Makes 1 portion.

If you must use veal broth or stock—chicken broth or stock is equally good—thicken and reduce it by simmering until it is reduced one-half, adding bit by bit tiny pieces of a *beurre manié*. Then go on as directed above.

Eggs a l'Estragon and *Tarragon Eggs* are other names often given this dish.

▪ *EGGS COLETTE*

In the happy days right after the First World War, when Colette's books were exciting all of Europe, the chef at Monte Carlo's Grand Hôtel created this egg dish for the novelist.

> 1 *tablespoon heavy cream*
> 1 *egg*
> *Dash salt*
> *Dash pepper*
> 2 *tablespoons finely chopped turkey meat*
> *Pinch paprika*

Put the cream into a buttered *cocotte;* add the egg, the salt and pepper and the turkey meat. Top with paprika, seal and cook in a *bain-marie* 10 to 12 minutes in a preheated 350-degree oven, or half that time in simmering water on top of the stove. Makes 1 portion.

▪ *EGGS LORRAINE*

A close cousin to the famous *quiche*, this has the heavy richness to be expected from France's dairyland.

> 3 *thin rounds Gruyère cheese*
> 2 *tablespoons crisp fried bacon pieces*
> 1 *egg*
> *Dash salt*
> *Dash pepper*
> 2 *teaspoons cream*

Preheat the *cocotte*. Trim the cheese rounds to fit neatly inside and put one on the bottom of the buttered *cocotte;* sprinkle over it half the bacon, then another slice of cheese. Put in the egg and seasonings, sprinkle with the remaining bacon, top with the final cheese round and add the cream. Seal and poach in a *bain-marie* 12 to 16 minutes in a preheated 350-degree oven, or half that time in simmering water on top of the stove. Makes 1 portion.

▪ *EGGS HOLLANDAISE* is the name given to this recipe when made with Edam cheese and ham.

▪ *EGGS MONGOLE* (*Eggs with Split Peas*)

> *Pinch curry powder*
> 1 *teaspoon minced chicken or ham*
> 2 *tablespoons split pea soup*
> 1 *egg*

Mix the curry powder and meat with the soup, and place it in a buttered *cocotte*. Add the egg and poach in a *bain-marie* 10 to 12 minutes in a 350-degree oven, or half that time in water simmering on top of stove. Makes 1 portion.

▪ HARD-COOKED EGGS

Few of the recipes in this next group are based on individual service; they are family-sized dishes. Most of them can be prepared, at least partially, in advance, ready to pop into the oven for a final few minutes, or warmed on top of the stove for a short while. Here, too, are the big families of creamed and stuffed (or deviled) eggs, along with a few less usual ones.

▪ *EGGS CÉLESTINE*

There is an unlimited number of combinations possible with hard-cooked eggs in a creamed sauce with one or more additional ingredients; to detail all of them would take several hundred pages and even then the list would be incomplete. This recipe is given to remind you of basic procedures, and following it are a few ideas for additional creamed egg dishes.

> 4 *hard-cooked eggs*
> 2 *cups Sauce Velouté* (*page 279*)
> 1 *cup milk*
> 1 *cup finely chopped onion*
> 1½ *cups cooked green peas*
> *Dash salt*
> *Dash pepper*
> *Dash nutmeg*
> 4 *thick bread rounds*
> 2 *tablespoons grated mild cheese*

Quarter or halve the hard-cooked eggs and arrange the sections in the bottom of a well-buttered casserole. In a double boiler, thin the Sauce Velouté with the milk. Sauté the onions very lightly and add them, together with the peas and seasonings, to the warming sauce. Pour the sauce containing the onions and peas into the casserole over the eggs. Toast the bread rounds and butter them thickly, then press both sides of each round into the grated cheese. Float the toast on top of the casserole. Cook 10 to 15 minutes in a preheated 250-degree oven, until the sauce is bubbling well and the cheese is melted. Serves 4.

▪ CREAMED EGGS

The preceding recipe is only one of the dozens of ways of dressing up a dish of hard-cooked eggs in a cream sauce. It might as easily have been served in individual ramekins with a quartered egg in each and the cheese-covered toast used as sort of a lid; in a tartshell or *timbale,* so that the pleasure of eating the container might be enjoyed; or with the cheese-covered toast placed on a serving plate, topped with the halved or quartered eggs, and with the sauce poured over.

Although the Eggs Célestine recipe called for Sauce Velouté (page 279), any of the white sauces in Chapter 11 might have been substituted; most of them should be thinned with milk before using them as a vehicle to carry hard-cooked eggs.

Creamed eggs can be served in a casserole, tartshell or *timbale,* as suggested a few lines earlier, or they can be used to fill the center of a ring mold of spinach, noodles, macaroni, rice, potatoes or any of the farinaceous foods. The filled center can be dusted with paprika, cayenne, grated Parmesan, or Breadcrumb–Cheese Glaze (page 291) and placed under the broiler for a moment before going to the table. It all depends on what your taste and the needs of the meal suggest.

Here are a few of the ingredients that can be used to dress up and extend a dish of creamed eggs:

Asparagus, coarsely chopped
Cauliflower, in small pieces
Chicken, diced
Chipped beef, shredded
Crab meat, flaked
Green beans, coarsely cut
Green peas
Green peppers, diced

Ham, diced or chopped
Kidneys, diced and sautéed
Lobster, coarsely chopped
Mixed vegetables, diced
Pimientos, coarsely chopped
Sardines, chopped
Shrimp, coarsely chopped
Sweetbreads, sautéed

Even this small and incomplete list should be enough to start you thinking about other favorite foods that can be added to creamed eggs and served as a quick and substantial dish.

▪ *KANSAS EGG CASSEROLE*

> 1 *sliced medium potato*
> 1½ *teaspoons flour*
> 1 *sliced medium onion*
> 4 *hard-cooked eggs*
> ½ *teaspoon salt*
> *Dash pepper*
> 2 *cups milk or light cream*

In a buttered casserole arrange a layer of potatoes and dust with flour; then a layer of onions, and dust them with flour; then a layer of sliced egg. Continue in alternate layers until all ingredients are used. Sprinkle salt and pepper over the top layer, and pour in milk. Bake 25 to 30 minutes in a 325-degree oven; during the final few minutes of baking, sprinkle a thin dusting of flour over the top to insure a rich, brown crust. Serves 4.

▪ *EGGS À LA KING*

Chicken à la King has been a standby for years; bearing in mind the chicken to egg to chicken cycle, this recipe offers a logical substitution.

> 2 *cups Cream Sauce* (*page* 281)
> 1½ *cups milk*
> 2 *tablespoons chopped green pepper*
> 1½ *tablespoons butter*
> 2½ *tablespoons chopped mushrooms*
> 1½ *tablespoons chopped pimientos*
> 2 *tablespoons sherry*
> ⅛ *teaspoon nutmeg*
> ½ *teaspoon salt*
> *Large pinch pepper*
> 4 *hard-cooked eggs*

Thin the Cream Sauce with the milk in a double boiler. Sauté the green pepper in the butter until tender, sauté the mushrooms (if uncooked) until tender, and add with the pimientos to the sauce. Stir in the sherry and seasonings. Quarter or chop coarsely the hard-cooked eggs and let them simmer in the sauce. Serve in tartshells or *timbales*, filled very generously. Or serve in a casserole with large *croustades* floating on top, or from a chafing dish, spooning over toast rounds. Serves 4.

▪ EGGS LUCANIAN

> 2½ *cups cooked macaroni*
> 4 *finely chopped anchovy fillets*
> 4 *hard-cooked eggs*
> 1 *cup rich cream*
> 2 *tablespoons butter*
> 2 *tablespoons grated Parmesan cheese*
> *Breadcrumb–Cheese Glaze* (*page* 291)

Place a thick layer of macaroni in a well-buttered casserole and spread the anchovy fillets over its surface. Quarter or slice the eggs and lay them on top; cover with the remaining macaroni. Warm the cream and blend it with the butter, stir in the grated cheese and pour it into the casserole. Spread a thick coating of the glaze mix over the surface and bake 10 to 15 minutes in a 250-degree oven; use the broiler to finish the glaze if necessary. Serves 4.

▪ NEW ENGLAND EGG CHOWDER

For years the argument has gone on over the relative virtues of the creamy New England chowders and the tomato-spicy New York version. Both can be prepared with eggs instead of seafood, and you can choose your own favorite.

> 4 *hard-cooked eggs*
> 1 *cup cracker crumbs*
> 1 *cup diced green pepper*
> 1 *cup diced salt pork or mild bacon*
> 1 *cup chopped onions*
> 2 *cups grated mild cheese*
> ½ *teaspoon salt*
> ¼ *teaspoon pepper*
> 2½ *cups cream*

Slice the eggs. Spread a layer of coarse cracker crumbs on the bottom of a buttered casserole, then a layer of egg slices. Cover with a layer of green pepper, salt pork, onion and cheese; dust with salt and pepper. Add alternate layers of cracker crumbs, eggs, and the cheese–onion–pork–green pepper mix; dust each layer with salt and pepper. Top with a final layer of cracker crumbs and pour the cream into the casserole; it should just cover the top layer of cracker crumbs. Bake 20 to 30 minutes in a preheated 325-degree oven. Serves 4.

▪ *NEW YORK EGG CHOWDER*

> 1 *cup white wine*
> 2½ *cups tomato purée*
> 2 *cups chopped onions*
> Bouquet garni *made of:* 1 *bay leaf,* 2 *whole cloves,*
> *sprig fresh dill (or pinch powdered dill),* 1 *clove*
> *garlic*
> ½ *teaspoon salt*
> *Large pinch pepper*
> 1 *tablespoon butter*
> 4 *hard-cooked eggs*
> 4 *slices toast*

In a saucepan over lowest heat or in a double boiler, simmer the wine, tomato purée, onions, *bouquet garni* (which should be in its own cheesecloth bag), salt and pepper. Simmer 10 minutes to give the flavors time to marry. Remove from the heat, take out the *bouquet garni* and stir the butter in briskly. Halve or quarter the hard-cooked eggs and arrange them in the bottom of a buttered casserole. Pour the sauce over the eggs, and cook 15 to 20 minutes in a preheated 300-degree oven. Trim the toast into triangles and float on top just before the casserole is served. Serves 4.

▪ *SOUTHERN SHORTCAKE*

> 4 *hard-cooked eggs*
> 4 *large biscuits or* 8 croustades
> 2 *cups Cream Sauce (page* 281)
> ½ *cup milk*
> 2 *tablespoons grated mild cheese*

Slice the eggs very thick, and arrange them on the bottoms of split biscuits or *croustades.* Cover with the tops of the biscuits or *croustades.* Thin the Cream Sauce with milk while heating over lowest heat or in a double boiler. Sprinkle the tops of the biscuits or *crous-*

tades with grated cheese and pour the hot sauce over them. This dish is best served in individual bowls, like soup bowls, with the sauce added just before it is eaten. Serves 4.

▪ *EGGS À LA MODE DE TRIPE*

Many people do not really care for tripe, unless it is spiced up, Caen-style or Mexican fashion. The classic accompaniments for tripe are onions or leeks; if tripe is on your don't-serve list, use eggs in its place, as in this peasant-style dish.

> *2 cups coarsely chopped onions*
> *1½ tablespoons bacon drippings*
> *4 hard-cooked eggs*
> *¾ cup Sauce Espagnole (page 275)*
> *2 tablespoons beef stock or broth*
> *4 cracked peppercorns*

Sauté the onions in the bacon drippings, and quarter the eggs. Thin the sauce with the beef stock, adding the cracked peppercorns only during the last minute the mixture is on the heat. Spread the onions over a platter, arrange the egg quarters on top of them and pour the sauce over.

▪ *TYROLESE EGG PIE*

> *4 hard-cooked eggs*
> *2 large tomatoes*
> *1 cup breadcrumbs*
> *1 tablespoon chopped chives*
> *1 tablespoon chopped parsley*
> *1 tablespoon butter*
> *2 eggs*
> *3 cups milk*
> *¼ teaspoon salt*
> *Generous pinch pepper*

Slice the hard-cooked eggs and tomatoes very thick. Sprinkle a layer of breadcrumbs on the bottom of a buttered casserole, place a layer of tomato and egg slices on it and sprinkle with breadcrumbs, chopped chives and parsley. Dot with butter. Add succeeding layers of egg and tomato slices, sprinkling each with breadcrumbs, chives and parsley and dotting with butter. Beat the whole eggs into the milk with the salt and pepper, and pour them over the slices in the casserole. Spread a layer of breadcrumbs over the top and dot with butter. Bake 15 to 20 minutes in a preheated 350-degree oven, finishing under the broiler for a browned top if necessary. Serves 4.

▪ STUFFED OR DEVILED EGGS

Like the creamed egg family (page 96), the stuffed or deviled egg clan is large and can be treated as a group. Properly speaking, a deviled egg is one that has had its yolk mashed with mustard and cayenne and stuffed back into its white hard-cooked casing, but to many the cold stuffed egg is and always will be a deviled egg, regardless of its filling. The stuffed eggs in which we are interested in this section are the cold eggs taken on picnics or served as hors d'oeuvres. In later recipes we will encounter many dishes in which hard-cooked eggs are stuffed and recooked, but here only the cold stuffed egg is contemplated.

One recipe, Eggs Galtz (page 101), is given to suggest what can be done with a cold stuffed egg if you want to take the pains. For the rest, the following list is offered to set you to thinking about the ingredients that can be mashed with the yolk of a hard-cooked egg.

Anchovy fillets
Bacon in crisp crumbles
Capers
Chicken, ground fine
Crab meat, flaked
Foie gras in tiny bits
Lobster, minced very fine
Olives: ripe, green or stuffed
Pickles, minced kosher dill

Roquefort or Blue cheese
Sardines, mashed with lemon
    juice
Sauerkraut, minced with paprika
Sesame seed, sautéed with
    paprika
Sour cream with a pinch of
    cayenne

Most of these mixtures will need to be smoothed out with butter or flavored with a touch of mustard or Mayonnaise (pages 285-286); your own taste will guide you. A slice of stuffed olive, a dab of Mayonnaise, a single caper or sprig of pimiento added as garnish to the stuffed egg half will increase its attractiveness.

▪ *EGGS GALTZ*

As promised, here is an example of how a stuffed egg may be transformed if you want to take the trouble.

> 8 *stuffed olives*
> 2 *teaspoons finely minced cooked ham*
> 4 *hard-cooked eggs*
> 1 *tablespoon Mayonnaise (pages 285-286)*
> ½ *cup vinegar*
> 1 *tablespoon sugar*
> ¾ *teaspoon dry mustard*
> 1 *uncooked egg yolk*
> 1½ *tablespoons light cream*
> 1 *teaspoon butter*

Mince 6 of the stuffed olives, reserving 2 for garnish. Mix the olives, ham, hard-cooked egg yolks and Mayonnaise and stuff them into the egg-white cases, rounding them generously. In a double boiler, warm the vinegar and add the sugar, mustard and uncooked egg yolk, stirring well until the mixture is smooth and creamy; then stir in the cream, remove from the heat and finish by stirring in the butter. Spoon a little of this sauce over each stuffed egg half and garnish each with half a stuffed olive. Serves 4.

▪ EGG CROQUETTES AND PATTIES

Another family begins here, where the hard-cooked egg is used instead of meat, or to extend meat, in croquettes or patties. Four eggs are called for in all recipes in this family, but the resulting dishes will provide service for at least 6.

Usually croquettes and patties are sauced with a white sauce and a sprig of parsley, so be different. Use a Sauce Choron (page 283), a Mornay (page 281) or a Bordelaise (page 276). If you really want to break new ground, try Avgolemono Sauce (page 189).

▪ *EGG CROQUETTES*

> 4 *hard-cooked eggs*
> ½ *cup chopped mushrooms*
> ½ *cup chopped onions*
> 1 *uncooked egg*
> ¾ *cup Béchamel Sauce (page 280)*
> 1 *tablespoon flour*
> 1 *cup fine breadcrumbs*
> *Fat for deep frying*

Chop the hard-cooked eggs very fine; the mushrooms and onions should also be finely chopped. Beat the uncooked egg into the Béchamel Sauce, then beat in the flour a little at a time. Add this to the eggs, mushrooms and onions until a stiff paste is formed, stiff enough to be shaped into croquettes. Roll the croquettes in breadcrumbs and place in a frying basket. Fry 3 to 5 minutes in bubbling fat, or until the outsides of the croquettes turn brown. Serves 6.

■ *EGG CROQUETTES WITH MEAT*

> *1 uncooked egg*
> *¾ cup Béchamel Sauce* (page 280)
> *¾ cup minced meat: ham, veal, beef, turkey or*
>   *chicken*
> *4 minced hard-cooked eggs*
> *¼ cup fine breadcrumbs*
> *1 tablespoon flour*
> *Fat for deep frying*

Beat the uncooked egg into the Béchamel Sauce, and use this to bind the meat, hard-cooked eggs and breadcrumbs into a paste to shape into croquettes. Roll in the flour and fry in deep fat. Serves 6.

Kromeskies is a name often applied to egg croquettes in Europe.

■ *EGG PATTIES*

A separate but equal branch of the family of egg croquettes is the egg patty group, of which three examples are given.

> *½ cup milk*
> *1 bay leaf*
> *1 clove garlic*
> *2 sprigs parsley*
> *1 tablespoon chopped, green celery leaves or ½ tea-*
>   *spoon celery salt*
> *Dash salt*
> *Dash pepper*
> *Dash nutmeg*
> *½ cup minced onions*
> *4 hard-cooked eggs*
> *1½ cups soft breadcrumbs*
> *¼ cup chopped almonds*
> *1 cup very fine breadcrumbs*
> *1 tablespoon butter*

Scald the milk in a saucepan with the bay leaf, garlic, parsley and celery leaves; simmer, then strain and stir in the salt, pepper and nutmeg. Simmer the onions in the milk for a moment until they begin to get tender. Remove from the heat; add the finely chopped eggs, soft breadcrumbs and almonds, and mix into a smooth paste. Spread the mixture on a platter or cookie sheet and chill in the refrigerator at least 15 minutes. Cut it into patties with a cookie cutter, roll them in the fine breadcrumbs and sauté them in butter until crusty brown. Serves 6.

▪ EGG PATTIES WITH RICE OR MEAT

> 1 *uncooked egg*
> 4 *finely chopped hard-cooked eggs*
> 1 *cup boiled rice or finely chopped cooked meat:*
>   *ham, beef, veal or chicken*
> *Dash salt*
> *Dash pepper*
> 1 *tablespoon flour*
> 2 *tablespoons butter*

Beat the uncooked egg lightly, and use it to bind the hard-cooked eggs and the rice or meat into patties; season them as they are mixed. Dip them in flour and sauté them in butter over medium heat. Turn the patties with care, as they will be very tender. Serves 6.

▪ EGG FOO YUNG

This great Chinese egg dish is not really classifiable; perhaps it comes closest to the patties.

> ¾ *cup minced onion*
> ½ *cup minced green pepper*
> 1 *tablespoon peanut oil*
> ½ *cup minced cooked ham*
> 1 *cup chopped bean sprouts*
> ¾ *cup minced water chestnuts*
> 4 *eggs*
> ½ *teaspoon salt*

Sauté the onion and green pepper in ½ tablespoon peanut oil until they are tender; add the ham, bean sprouts and water chestnuts to the pan. Remove the mixture from the heat and stir it well; transfer it to a plate spread with an absorbent cloth or paper towel and let it drain. Beat the eggs lightly with the salt, and add the mixed onion, green pepper, ham and bean sprouts. Mix thoroughly. Over medium-high heat, put the remaining peanut oil in the skillet and drop in a spoonful of the mixture at a time to form patties about 2 inches in diameter. When they are lightly browned on the bottom, turn them and complete cooking. Makes 10 to 12 patties.

▪ *Sauce:* Egg Foo Yung is usually served sauced with a light gravy made by mixing together ½ cup chicken broth, 1 tablespoon soy sauce and 1 teaspoon cornstarch dissolved in 1 teaspoon cold water; the mixture is stirred rapidly for a moment over high heat and poured over the egg patties.

Chinese cooks naturally prepare the dish in a *wok*, that hemispherical frying–braising–sautéeing utensil that is the main cooking method of the three Chinese cuisines. Unless you have had the apprenticeship undergone by the Chinese chef in *wok* cookery, stick to the skillet; the master of the *wok* does not bother with mixing the patties in a bowl, but tosses the onion and green pepper into the *wok's* deepest bottom until they are right, then pulls them up to the rim of the vessel to drain. With his round slotted turner he will flick the right quantity of the cooked ingredients into the bottom, toss on the sprouts and water chestnuts and dash a bit of the egg mixture on top of them. It is a fascinating thing to watch, and you might profit by asking the proprietor of a Chinese restaurant to let you observe his kitchen crew at work.

▪ RISSOLES

Dear to the heart of the British cook is the rissole, that half-moon-shaped fried pastry, very similar to the fried fruit pies common to the Southern United States. The rissole is usually filled with a meat or fish mixture; it works equally well filled with eggs. Use any of the croquette or patty mixtures (pages 102-104). Prepare a batch of Pastry Dough (page 291) and roll it thin; cut it into circles with a large cookie cutter. Lay a spoonful of the croquette or patty mixture in each circle, and fold the dough over, sealing its edges with a water-moistened finger. Fry it in deep fat or sauté it in a skillet; drain well. Though usually eaten out of hand, these may be sauced and served as a fork food.

▪ UNCLASSIFIED EGG DISHES

Some recipes fail to fall neatly into a category; they may combine poaching and shirring, or shirring and scrambling, or they may use a very special sauce.

▪ *DIJON EGGS*

Combining poaching and shirring, this casserole dish can come to the table either bland or sharp, as your whim dictates. If blandness is desired, simply omit the mustard. But do be sure to use a *good* bread, not squish-loaves from the big commercial bakeries, or it won't turn out.

> *4 slices bread, 3/4 inch thick*
> *1/4 cup milk*
> *1/2 pint sour cream*
> *2 tablespoons Dijon mustard*
> *4 eggs*
> *1/4 teaspoon salt*
> *Generous pinch pepper*
> *Generous pinch nutmeg*
> *1/2 pint heavy cream*

If the bread used is very fresh, it should be sliced and cut, then placed in a warm oven to dry—but it should not be toasted. Using a large cookie cutter, cut each bread slice into a round, and with a smaller cutter take out its center; the ring should be 1 1/4 to 1 1/2 inches wide. Mix the milk, sour cream and mustard (omit the mustard if a bland dish is wanted) and spread the mixture in a baking dish large enough to hold all the bread circles. Place the circles in the sour cream mixture until they have absorbed all they can hold; they should be turned once to help this part of the process, which will take 15 to 20 minutes. When the bread circles will hold no more, slip an uncooked egg into the hole of each. Mix the salt, pepper and nutmeg and dust over the tops of the circles. Cook 20 minutes in a preheated 325-degree oven. Whip the heavy cream until it is medium-stiff. Remove the baking dish from the oven, spread each circle with whipped cream and return to the oven for 5 minutes' further cooking. Serves 4.

▪ *LOUISIANA EGGS*

> 1½ *cups tomato soup* (*if canned soup is used, dilute*
> *with equal parts of water*)
> 1¼ *cups crisp breadcrumbs*
> 1 *cup diced mixed vegetables: carrots, peas, potatoes,*
> *green beans, etc.*
> 4 *small green onions or shallots, chopped*
> ½ *teaspoon salt*
> *Generous pinch pepper*
> 4 *eggs*
> 1 *cup grated mild cheese*

Combine the soup, breadcrumbs, vegetables, onions and seasoning; the result should be thick enough to retain the impression made on it when pressed by the bowl of a cooking spoon. If it is too watery, add more crumbs. Pour the mixture into a buttered casserole, make indentations on top to hold the eggs and slide an egg into each one. Cover with grated cheese and bake 25 to 30 minutes in a preheated 325-degree oven. Serves 4.

▪ *MAINE EGG CHOWDER*

This second Down East chowder wasn't included in the group given earlier (pages 97-99) because it is not based on hard-cooked eggs but on uncooked ones. It's also an entirely different approach to the chowder.

> 1 *cup diced salt pork or mild bacon*
> 1 *diced medium potato*
> 1 *diced medium onion*
> 2 *tablespoons dark rum*
> ¼ *teaspoon pepper*
> *Pinch thyme*
> *Pinch marjoram*
> 1½ *cups unsalted cracker crumbs*
> 4 *eggs*

Sauté the salt pork until it starts to brown; add the potatoes, then the onions. It's time to stop cooking when the pork is crisp, the potatoes start to get soft and the onions become transparent. Transfer all the ingredients, including the fat rendered from the pork, to a buttered casserole. Mix the rum, pepper and spices with ½ cup hot water and pour it over the mixture; it should almost but not quite cover it. A little more water may be necessary. Spread the cracker crumbs in a thick layer over the surface, and space the 4 eggs on top of them. Cook 15 to 20 minutes in a preheated 350-degree oven, until the eggs are set and the cracker crumbs are browned. Serves 4.

Two cautions: If bacon is used instead of salt pork, more salt will be necessary. None is given in the recipe because with salt pork the residue in the meat itself generally is enough. And don't try to use light, Cuban-type rum; its flavor does not have what the dish needs. Use a Jamaica, Barbados or Hudson Bay rum, dark with molasses. Serves 4.

■ EGGS PHILLIPSBURG

This is another of the fanciful creations of Dumas *père;* unfortunately, his *Grand Dictionnaire de Cuisine* does not reveal the occasion on which it was conceived.

> 2 *cups poached salmon*
> 2 *tablespoons slivered, blanched almonds*
> ¼ *teaspoon salt*
> *Large pinch pepper*
> 2 *tablespoons onion juice or* 1 *teaspoon onion salt*
> 4 *eggs*
> 2 *tablespoons grated Parmesan cheese*

Flake the salmon and mix it with the almonds, salt, pepper and onion juice. (If canned salmon is used, drain it well to eliminate excess oil.) Spread the mixture in a shallow, buttered casserole, make indentations with a cup or cooking spoon to receive the eggs and slide the eggs into them. Bake 10 to 15 minutes in a preheated 350-degree oven, until the eggs are set. Sprinkle with the Parmesan and glaze a moment under the broiler. Serves 4.

■ PIPÉRADE

When you are faced with the problem of extending 3 eggs to serve 6 people, this mock omelet can be your salvation.

> 4 *large, ripe tomatoes or equivalent canned tomatoes*
> 2 *sweet peppers*
> *Salt*

Pepper
3 eggs
¼ cup milk
Breadcrumb–Cheese Glaze (page 291)

Peel the tomatoes; peel the sweet peppers and remove the seeds and pith. Chop the tomatoes coarsely and simmer them in their juice. Chop the peppers fine and simmer them with the tomatoes; when the peppers are tender, mash the tomatoes into a coarse purée. Season to taste with salt and pepper. (If canned tomatoes are used it will be necessary only to heat them; the pepper may be parboiled separately.)

Beat the eggs very lightly, just enough to mix the whites and yolks, and add the milk. Remove the tomato–pepper mixture from the heat and beat the eggs into it a little at a time, mixing vigorously. Pour the mixture into a warm, lightly buttered casserole and sprinkle the glazing mix over the top. Cook 15 minutes in a preheated 300-degree oven, until the eggs are set. If necessary, brown the top under the broiler before serving. Serves 6.

■ *EGG POTPIE*

This deceptively simple dish could well be called eggs with noodles, eggs with dumplings, egg shortcake or egg cobbler. While it can be made with any pie or biscuit dough, even those from mixes, use of the short biscuit dough given is highly recommended.

> *1½ cups flour*
> *2 teaspoons baking powder*
> *1 teaspoon salt*
> *3 tablespoons oil or shortening*
> *1 cup milk*
> *Large pinch salt*
> *Large dash pepper*
> *4 eggs*

To prepare the dough, sift the flour, baking powder and 1 teaspoon salt together; work the shortening into the flour and add the milk gradually, blending into a smooth dough. Roll it on a lightly floured board until it is ¾ inch thick, and cut the dough into strips 1½ inches wide.

Into a casserole or deep pie pan put 1½ cups boiling water, a large pinch of salt and one of pepper. Break 2 eggs into a cup or saucer and slide them into the water; lay strips of dough over the eggs in a lattice with open spaces about 1 inch square. Add the other 2 eggs and cover them with more strips of dough laid lattice-fashion. Bake 20 to 25 minutes in a preheated 350-degree oven, until the water is gone and the top crust browned. Serves 4.

Cut into pielike slices or squares as you would cut a cobbler; serve with a large pat of butter on each portion, or with your favorite sauce or gravy. It is especially good with chicken or turkey gravy.

■ *QUICHE LORRAINE*

Lost in antiquity is the birthdate of the *quiche;* it is known to have originated in the dairy-rich Moselle–Meuse area of France, where it is also called a *féouse*. Though traditionally made with bacon, the *quiche* can be prepared with ham or the smoked pork tenderloin usually called Canadian bacon. Usually served hot, the *quiche* is equally good cold, sliced in thin triangles and washed down with a glass of good white wine. When served cold (but not, please, icy from the refrigerator!) as an hors d'oeuvre, it is a party-stopper.

> *4 slices ham or bacon*
> *Pastry Dough (page 291)*
> *4 eggs*
> *2 cups heavy cream*
> *Dash salt*
> *Dash pepper*
> *Pinch nutmeg*
> *4 slices Gruyère cheese*

If a precooked ham is used it need not be cooked again, but if you are using bacon, sauté it very lightly, to the stage of transparency, and drain it well. Line a pie tin or casserole with the crust, bringing it over the edges so that the pan may be sealed. Beat the eggs until they are frothy, add the cream and beat well together for a few moments as you add the salt, pepper and nutmeg. Pour enough of the egg mixture into the crust to form a thin layer on its bottom; lay the ham or bacon slices on top, pour over them more of the egg mixture and put in the cheese slices and the remaining egg mixture. Put the top crust on, sealing the edges well; use a few drops of water on the fingertips if needed. Bake 30 to 35 minutes in a preheated 325-degree oven. The addition of a top crust is a matter of taste. Many prefer to omit the pastry covering and let the eggs and cheese form their own brown bubble-dotted crust as the *quiche* cooks. If the topping of pastry is left off, the dish will cook a bit faster. Serves 4.

■ EGG SANDWICHES

There are as many versions of the egg sandwich as there are busy bachelors and harried housewives. Some are made with farm-scrambled eggs on buttered bread, some with sliced hard-cooked eggs, others with the eggs fried or sautéed. The latter is the classic egg sandwich of the home kitchen, while the egg salad sandwich takes first position at the quick-lunch counter. Five samples should be enough to stimulate your creativity—two from abroad, three of native identification.

■ *CLASSIC EGG SANDWICH*

> *1 egg*
> *Butter*
> *Dash salt*
> *Dash pepper*
> *2 slices bread*

Sauté the egg in butter until it is firmly set on the bottom, but still very liquid on top. Sprinkle with salt and pepper, and turn. With a very flexible spatula or turner press gently on the yolk until it breaks; it will then run evenly into the pan under the egg. Continue cooking until it is firm. Transfer the egg to a buttered bread slice, and cover it with a second slice spread with butter, mustard or Mayonnaise (pages 285-286) according to taste. Makes 1 sandwich.

■ *DANISH OPEN EGG SANDWICH*

Though Denmark gets the credit, this version of the egg sandwich will be found throughout Scandinavia.

> *Butter*
> *1 slice rye bread*
> *1 soft-scrambled egg*
> *1½ tablespoons tiny cooked shrimp*

Butter the bread thickly, heap the egg in a high, flat mound and arrange the tiny shrimp on top. The trick is to make the bread hold more than seems possible. Makes 1 sandwich.

▪ *DENVER OR WESTERN SANDWICH*

In the Eastern United States, this is usually called the "Western" sandwich; closer to its point of origin, it is known by the name of its hometown.

> 1½ *teaspoons diced green pepper*
> 1½ *teaspoons diced cooked ham*
> *Butter*
> 1 *egg*
> *Dash salt*
> *Dash pepper*
> 2 *slices bread*

Sauté the green pepper and ham together in butter until the pepper is tender. Break the egg over them, season and scramble with a fork or spatula until it is set. The egg may or may not be turned. Transfer it to a slice of buttered bread, and top with a second slice. Makes 1 sandwich.

▪ *EGG SALAD SANDWICH*

Because the egg salad is only useful as a spread for sandwiches, it will not be found elsewhere in this book. Each cook has a different version; some use onions, some do not; some mix with Mayonnaise (pages 285-286), some with mustard, some with boiled dressing. An imaginative cook might try blending the egg with Sauce Béarnaise (page 282) or Sauce Chasseur (page 276), or with one of the compound butters (page 288). This might remove some of the pallid aura surrounding this sandwich.

> 1 *hard-cooked egg*
> 1 *teaspoon Mayonnaise (pages* 285-286)
> *Dash salt*
> *Dash pepper*
> 2 *slices bread or toast*

Chop the egg; blend it with the Mayonnaise (or mustard), salt and pepper. Spread it on bread or toast and top with a second slice of bread. Makes 1 sandwich.

▪ *EGG TACO*

Until its homeland was invaded by the Yanqui hamburger, the Taco was the Mexican national sandwich, the native meal-on-the-run, offered on streets by itinerant vendors who set up their charcoal stoves made of flattened oil drums wherever they could find customers. Mexican bread is, of course, the thin, flat tortilla made of cornmeal; it is wrapped around anything to form a Taco, but the Egg Taco is most commonly served flat, as given in this recipe.

1 *egg*
1 *tortilla*
2 *tablespoons oil or lard*
1 *tablespoon ground meat*
1 *teaspoon minced onion*
Generous pinch chili powder
Dash salt
1½ *tablespoons grated mild cheese*
Shredded lettuce

Sauté the egg until firm. Fry the tortilla in the oil until crisp, and set it to drain. Fry the meat and onion together, crumbling them as they cook and sprinkling them with the chili powder and salt. When the meat is brown, add the cheese and use it to bind the onion and meat into a thin patty large enough to cover the tortilla. Transfer the meat–cheese–onion mixture to the tortilla, put the egg on top and sprinkle it with shredded lettuce. Makes 1 sandwich.

Usually this dish is sprinkled with a few drops of a hot chili sauce. Use your own discretion here.

6 ∎∎

Special Egg Dishes

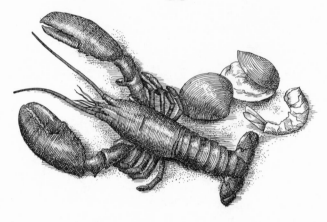

IT IS REGRETTABLE that the busy housewife seldom thinks of eggs when a company dinner is being planned. As an additional entree, eggs can be served with much less trouble in the kitchen than can fish, for example, and there is a long list of dress-up ways to serve eggs that are new to appetites jaded with the roast beef–steak–chicken–vegetables routine. And for the buffet, there is an array of offbeat, eye-catching, appetite-pleasing eggs molded in aspic; this type of dish once held a prominent position in any buffet service, and is now being seen more and more often.

Egg dishes are like all others; to be special they require special ingredients. Those most commonly associated with eggs in company dress are the mushroom, the truffle, and the hauntingly bland *foie gras*. All are expensive, but in egg dishes they are used in such small quantities that their cost is not too great.

One of the big virtues of egg dishes when guests are dining is that many of the recipes require no attention from the cook until immediately before serving, freeing her to concentrate on other aspects of the dinner. They can for the most part be prepared well in advance, the eggs added at the last moment, the broiler fired up for a final glazing, and the company served. Most of the recipes in this chapter respond bravely to this kind of intermittent preparation.

■ POACHED EGGS

As always, the poached egg dishes are given in portions designed for 1 individual serving. Either 1 or 2 eggs may be used without increasing the quantities called for.

■ *EGGS À L'AFRICAINE*

> 1 *teaspoon olive oil*
> 1½ *tablespoons diced green pepper*
> 2 *tablespoons diced eggplant*
> ½ *cup steamed semolina (or boiled rice)*
> *Pinch saffron*
> 1 *poached egg*

Heat the oil and gently sauté the green pepper, adding the eggplant when the pepper begins to become tender. Add the semolina or rice to the pan and stir in the saffron; form the mixture into a patty while it is still in the pan and allow it to brown on the bottom. Transfer the patty to a serving plate or platter, and slide the egg on top of the patty. Makes 1 portion.

■ *EGGS CHENIER* omits the eggplant and garnishes the dish with a spoonful of Tomato Sauce (page 278).

■ *EGGS ORIENTALE* crisps chopped pistachio nuts with the eggplant instead of pepper and garnishes the egg with a pair of crossed strips of pimiento.

■ *EGGS AMBASSADRICE*

> 1 *tablespoon puréed* foie gras *(pages* 292-293)
> 1 *tablespoon puréed truffle*
> 1 croustade
> 1 *poached egg*
> 3 *or* 4 *cooked asparagus tips*
> 1 *tablespoon Sauce Périgueux (page* 277)

Blend the two purées well and spread the *croustade* with them; add the poached egg, garnish with asparagus tips and spoon on the sauce. Makes 1 portion.

■ *EGGS AUBER*

> ⅔ *cup ground, cooked chicken meat*
> 1 *teaspoon Mayonnaise* (*pages 285-286*) (*if served cold*)
> 1 *teaspoon Sauce Espagnole* (*page 275*) (*if served hot*)
> ½ *firm, ripe tomato, drained and seeded*
> 1 *poached egg or egg* mollet

Blend the chicken meat with the Mayonnaise if the dish is to be served cold; with the Sauce Espagnole if it is to be served hot. Stuff the tomato with the mixture and place an egg on top. Garnish the tomato with Mayonnaise if the dish is to be served cold; brush it with Sauce Espagnole and glaze it under the broiler if it is to be served hot. Makes 1 portion.

Incidentally, "cold" does not mean just out of the refrigerator, but a few degrees below room temperature. The only foods that should be allowed to go from the refrigerator directly to the table are ice creams and frozen puddings.

■ *AUVERGNE EGGS*

> 1½ *cups meat stock*
> ¾ *cup coarsely shredded cabbage*
> 4 *thinly sliced rounds hard sausage*
> 1 *teaspoon butter*
> 1 *poached egg or egg* mollet
> *Coarsely ground black pepper*

Bring the meat stock to a boil, and plunge in the cabbage for 2 to 3 minutes. Drain, arrange in patty-form on a serving plate. Lightly sauté the sausage rounds in butter and arrange them around the patty of cabbage. Top with the egg and sprinkle with coarsely ground black pepper. (In place of pepper, the dish is often served with Sauce Vinaigrette, page 287.) Makes 1 portion.

■ *EGGS BELLE-HÉLÈNE*

> ⅔ *cup ground cooked breast of chicken*
> 1 *uncooked egg yolk*
> 1 *teaspoon milk*
> 1 *tablespoon butter*

> 1 *poached egg or egg* mollet
> 2 *tablespoons Sauce Velouté* (*page* 279)

Blend the chicken with the uncooked egg yolk, which has been lightly beaten; form into patties. Dip the patties in milk and sauté them in butter until crusty brown. Top with the poached egg or egg *mollet,* and spoon on the sauce. Makes 1 portion.

▪ *EGGS AU BEURRE NOIR* (*Eggs with Black Butter*)

This is another great classic egg dish, enjoyable out of all proportion to the simplicity of its ingredients and ease of preparation. Two cautions: First, only butter should be used in making the sauce, for many margarines now contain foam-retarding chemicals that keep them from marrying with vinegar. Second, serve the eggs very quickly once the sauce is poured on, and have ample bread or toast at hand.

> ⅓ *pound butter*
> 1 *egg*
> *Dash salt*
> *Dash pepper*
> 1 *tablespoon white* (*grain*) *vinegar*

Melt the butter over very lowest heat; when it is liquid, add the egg. Season the egg, and cover the skillet to allow the egg to poach; poach no longer than 3 minutes. Transfer the egg to a warm plate, and bring the heat very high until the butter begins to brown and foam. Dash the vinegar in at once and swirl the pan or stir to mix. As soon as the spitting and hissing stop, the sauce is done. Pour it over the egg and serve. Makes 1 portion.

A shirred version is given on page 137.

▪ *EGGS BOHÉMIENNE*

> 1 *thin slice ham*
> 2 *tablespoons Madeira Sauce* (*page* 277)
> 1 croustade
> 1 *tablespoon* foie gras *purée* (*pages* 292-293)
> 1 *poached egg or egg* mollet

Slice the ham in julienne (very thin strips) and simmer it in the sauce. Coat the *croustade* with the purée, slip the egg onto it and pour the sauce and ham strips over the top. Makes 1 portion.

▪ *EGGS BOIELDIEU*

As you encounter dishes bearing the names of composers, you will be struck by a peculiarity common to most of them: the use of truffles, *foie gras,* mushrooms and rich cream. Whether the composers in question actually relished the dishes named for them is a very open question; what most probably happened is that restaurateurs anxious to cash in on a good thing attached a currently popular name to an expensive dish already on their menu, much as an American drugstore will name its fountain special after a movie star. At any rate, the music of such composers as Boieldieu has not been forgotten, and the menu names live on.

> *2 tablespoons minced cooked breast of chicken*
> *¼ teaspoon minced truffles*
> *½ teaspoon minced* foie gras *(pages 292-293)*
> *2 tablespoons Sauce Velouté (page 279)*
> *1 tartshell*
> *1 poached egg or egg* mollet

Bind the chicken, truffles and *foie gras* with a little of the sauce; line the tartshell with this mixture and top with the egg. Spoon on the remaining sauce, and glaze under the broiler before serving. Makes 1 portion.

▪ *POACHED EGGS CARÊME*

Each chef who lived after the great master and originator must have given Carême's name to at least one dish. You will find several egg recipes bearing his name in this book.

> *1 large or 3 small artichoke hearts*
> *2 tablespoons butter*
> *½ kidney, cleaned and chopped*
> *1 tablespoon minced mushrooms*
> *¼ teaspoon minced truffle*
> *1 thin slice pickled tongue*
> *1 poached egg or egg* mollet
> *2 tablespoons Madeira Sauce (page 277)*

Sauté the artichoke hearts in the butter, and remove to a warm plate. Sauté the kidneys and mushrooms, adding the truffle. Trim the tongue to cover the artichoke hearts and lay it on top. Put the egg on top of the tongue, cover it with the kidney–mushroom–truffle mixture and spoon the sauce over the dish. Makes 1 portion.

▪ *EGGS À LA CHEVALIÈRE* (*Cavalier's Eggs*) is the original dish from which Eggs Carême elaborated; it is prepared without tongue or artichoke hearts and is served in a tartshell with Sauce Velouté (page 279).

▪ *EGGS CHATEAUBRIAND*

> 1 *large or* 3 *small artichoke hearts*
> 1 *teaspoon butter*
> 1 *egg*
> 1½ *cups veal stock*
> 2 *tablespoons Chateaubriand Sauce* (*page 277*)
> 4 *cooked asparagus tips*

Sauté the artichoke hearts in butter, drain and place on a warm plate. Poach the egg in the veal stock. Coat the artichoke hearts with half the sauce, drain the egg and place on top. Strain the veal stock and reduce one-half over quick heat; stir in the remaining sauce and blend well, adding a flake or two of butter if needed to smooth it. Spoon the sauce over the egg, and garnish with the asparagus tips. Makes 1 portion.

▪ *EGGS CHÂTELAINE* (*Housekeeper's Eggs*)

> 1 *tartshell*
> ½ *cup chestnut purée*
> 1 *poached egg or egg* mollet
> 2 *tablespoons Sauce Suprême* (*page 282*)

Fill the tartshell with the warm purée, top it with the egg, spoon on the sauce and glaze under the broiler for a moment. Makes 1 portion.

▪ *EGGS CLARENCE*

> 2 *thin slices mushroom*
> 1 *teaspoon butter*
> 1 *thin slice cooked tongue*
> 1 *tartshell*
> 1 *poached egg or egg* mollet
> 2 *tablespoons Sauce Poivrade* (*page 278*)

Sauté the mushroom slices in the butter; just before they are done add the slice of tongue, cut in julienne. Line the tartshell with the tongue; put the mushroom slices on top, then the egg. Spoon on the warmed sauce. Makes 1 portion.

▪ *EGGS COMMODORE*

This dish was given the name by which it is known in the United States by a quick-witted maître d'hôtel at the original Waldorf, when crusty old Commodore Vanderbilt asked what he suggested for a good breakfast.

> 1 *thick toast round*
> 1 *tablespoon butter*
> 1 *tablespoon* pâté de foie gras
> 1 *poached egg*
> 2 *tablespoons Béchamel Sauce* (*page* 280)

Sauté the toast round in butter until it is brown; spread it with the *pâté*. Top with the egg, spoon the sauce over it and glaze under the broiler before serving. Makes 1 portion.

Eggs à la Strasbourgeoise is the better-known name of this classic.

▪ *EGGS COMTE POTOCKI*

Its marked paprika accent identifies the origin of this recipe; it actually came from the famous kitchens of the second Count Potocki, Stanislaus Katsha, in Warsaw, and dates from about 1815.

> 1 *toast round*
> 2 *tablespoons Hungarian Sauce* (*page* 277)
> 1 *thick slice firm, fresh tomato*
> 1 *poached egg or egg* mollet
> 1 *tablespoon grated Gruyère cheese*
> *Large pinch paprika*

Soak the toast round in the sauce until it has absorbed all it will hold without becoming soggy. Place the tomato slice on the toast, then the egg on the tomato; sprinkle with grated cheese and dust heavily with paprika. Place under the broiler until the cheese melts. Makes 1 portion.

■ *EGGS À LA COMTESSE*

> ⅛ *teaspoon minced truffle*
> 2 *tablespoons asparagus purée*
> 1 *tartshell*
> 1 *poached egg or egg* mollet
> 2 *tablespoons Sauce Allemande* (*page* 279)

Mix the truffle (or a few drops of Truffle Essence) with the purée; fill the tartshell with the mixture. Add the egg, then the sauce. If truffle is used, reserve a few grains to sprinkle over the top. Makes 1 portion.

Serve this dish hot or cold. If cold, allow it to stand long enough for the truffle flavor to permeate the asparagus purée. If served hot, glaze it under the broiler.

■ *EGGS DAUDET*

> 1 *teaspoon truffle purée*
> 3 *tablespoons finely chopped chicken meat*
> 1 *tartshell*
> 1 *poached egg or egg* mollet
> 2 *tablespoons Sauce Velouté* (*page* 279)

Blend the truffle purée and chicken meat; arrange them around the tartshell's edges to leave a place for the egg. Spoon on the sauce, and glaze under the broiler. Makes 1 portion.

■ *EGGS DINO* uses mushroom purée instead of truffles; the two dishes are otherwise identical.

■ *EGGS DELMONICO*

Restaurants of New York in the Gilded Age were famed more for sturdy fare than fancy, as witness this house specialty of the 1890s.

> 2 *parboiled lamb sweetbreads*
> 2 *tablespoons butter*
> 1 *tablespoon chopped mushrooms*
> 2 *tablespoons Madeira Sauce* (*page* 277)
> 1 *thick toast round*
> 1 *poached egg*

Split the sweetbreads and sauté them lightly in butter, adding the mushrooms during the final minute of cooking. Spoon a little sauce over the toast round, and place the egg on top; cover with the mushrooms. Arrange the pieces of sweetbread around the toast on the warm plate, and cover with the remaining sauce. Makes 1 portion.

▪ EGGS EDWARD VII

> 1 *tablespoon butter*
> 2 *slices pickled tongue*
> ⅔ *cup boiled rice*
> 1 *poached egg or egg* mollet
> 2 *tablespoons veal gravy*

Using a little of the butter, warm the tongue, then toss the rice in the pan to warm. Lay the tongue slices on a warm plate, make a mound of the rice and top it with the egg. Pour warm veal gravy, enriched by the remaining butter, over the egg. Makes 1 portion.

▪ EGGS FAVART

> 1 *boiled veal sweetbread*
> 1 *teaspoon butter*
> 1 *tartshell*
> 1 *poached egg or egg* mollet
> 1 *tablespoon chopped mushrooms*
> *Grated truffle or few drops Truffle Essence*
> 2 *tablespoons Sauce Béarnaise* (*page 282*)

Slice the sweetbread thin, sauté it lightly in butter, remove it and put it in the bottom of a tartshell; put the egg on top. Sauté the mushrooms very lightly, spread them on top of the egg and strew the truffle gratings on the mushrooms. Cover with sauce and place under the broiler for 2 to 3 minutes to warm thoroughly and marry the flavors. Makes 1 portion.

▪ EGGS FRISSAC

> ½ *small head lettuce*
> ½ *teaspoon vinegar*
> 1 *poached egg or egg* mollet
> 2 *tablespoons Sauce Velouté* (*page 279*)
> *Breadcrumb–Cheese Glaze* (*page 291*)

Place the lettuce in a saucepan that can be tightly covered, adding a thin film of water on the bottom of the pan. Sprinkle the lettuce with vinegar, close the pan and keep over medium heat 2 to 3 minutes. Lift the lettuce to a warmed serving plate, top with the egg and cover with warmed sauce. Sprinkle with the glazing mix and place it under the broiler for a moment. Makes 1 portion.

▪ *EGGS MASSÉNA*

Though history tells more about the battles of Napoleon's famous general than it does about the meals he enjoyed, his name has become attached to several dishes, including this one, in which beef marrow plays a prominent part.

> 1 *large or 3 small artichoke hearts*
> 2 *tablespoons butter*
> 1 *poached egg or egg* mollet
> 1 *large round beef marrow*
> *Coarsely ground black pepper*
> 2 *tablespoons Sauce Choron (page 283)*

Sauté the artichoke hearts in butter, drain, place on a warm plate and cover with the egg. Slice the marrow thick, press the slices into black pepper sprinkled thickly on waxed paper and sauté them very gently in butter at low heat. Lay the marrow slices on the egg and cover with sauce. Makes 1 portion.

▪ *EGGS MONSELET*

> 1 *poached egg*
> ¾ *cup veal stock*
> 1 *tablespoon Sauce Velouté (page 279)*
> 1 *teaspoon milk*
> 1 *egg white*
> ½ *cup mashed potatoes*
> 1 *tablespoon flour*
> *Salt to taste*
> *Fat for deep frying*
> 1 *large or 3 small artichoke hearts, sautéed*

Poach the egg in the veal stock; put it aside to drain. Strain the remaining veal stock, stir into it the sauce (or 1 tablespoon very heavy cream) and simmer it in a double boiler 10 minutes. Beat the milk with the egg white, and blend with the mashed potatoes, adjusting for seasoning with salt as required. Form into thumb-sized croquettes, roll in flour, and fry in deep fat until richly brown. Arrange the egg on the artichoke hearts, space the croquettes around the egg, and pour the enriched veal stock over the dish. Makes 1 portion.

■ *EGGS NORMANDE*

Any dish from France bearing the Norman coast's name will contain the seafoods from which the area draws its fame, and probably the special sauce as well. To prepare Sauce Normande properly is not very difficult, and since it comes from the ingredients used in this recipe, it is given here as part of the dish.

> 1 *tablespoon chopped raw mussels*
> 1 *tablespoon raw shrimp*
> 1 *teaspoon raw mushrooms*
> 2 *tablespoons Sauce Velouté* (*page 279*)
> 2 *tablespoons light cream*
> *Salt*
> *Pepper*
> *Cayenne*
> 1 *teaspoon butter*
> 1 *tartshell*
> 1 *poached egg or egg* mollet
> 1 *raw oyster*

Place the mussels and shrimp in 1½ cups cold water and cook them for 5 minutes. Remove the shrimp, shell and devein them, chop coarsely and return them to the water. Add the mushrooms and boil them 2 minutes. Strain the liquid into a separate saucepan and reduce one-half by boiling. Allow to cool to a simmer, stir in the Sauce Velouté and cream, and adjust the seasoning. Simmer another 3 to 4 minutes; remove from the heat and stir in the butter.

On the bottom of the tartshell put half the mixture of shrimp, mussels and mushrooms, then the egg, and top with the remaining seafood–mushroom mix. Cover level with the warm Sauce Normande; place the raw oyster in the center of the tartshell on top of the sauce just before serving. Makes 1 portion.

■ *EGGS MOLLET À LA REINE*

> 1 *cup ground breast of chicken*
> 1½ *teaspoons Mayonnaise* (*pages 285-286*)

> *Truffle gratings*
> 1 *small Brioche* (*page* 290)
> 1 *egg* mollet
> *Truffle or pimiento decoration*

Bind the chicken with the Mayonnaise into a paste, adding the truffle gratings (or a few drops of Truffle Essence). Slice the top from the Brioche, and scoop out the crumbs to form a case. Line this with the meat mixture and place the egg on end in the cavity, then lightly pack with the remaining meat mixture until the top is level. Garnish with a thin coating of Mayonnaise, and a truffle or pimiento decoration. Makes 1 portion.

This dish is usually served cold, but do not prepare so far in advance that the Brioche will become soggy. On the other hand, do prepare far enough in advance so that the aroma and flavor of the truffle will permeate the meat mixture.

▪ POACHED EGGS ROSSINI

Dishes dedicated to composers always call for the richest, most expensive ingredients, as has already been mentioned. Here's more proof.

> 1 *large thin slice* foie gras
> 1 *tartshell*
> *Grated truffle or Truffle Essence*
> 1 *poached egg or egg* mollet
> 2 *tablespoons Sauce Périgueux* (*page* 277)

Lay the *foie gras* on the bottom of the tartshell, sprinkle with truffle gratings, put the egg on top, then the remaining truffle gratings. Cover with sauce, and glaze under the broiler; let it stand a few minutes so that the flavors marry before the dish is served. Makes 1 portion.

Poached Eggs Bohémienne is a name often attached to this dish; *Poached Eggs Périgourdine* was its name before it was changed in honor of Rossini.

▪ EGGS ROTONDE

A specialty of the house from Paris' famous restaurant is marked by rich simplicity.

> 1 *teaspoon chopped shallots*
> 1 *teaspoon butter*
> 1½ *tablespoons heavy cream*
> 1 *tablespoon sherry*
> *Dash salt*
> *Dash pepper*
> 1 *poached egg*
> ¾ *cup milk*
> 1 *toast round*

Over very low heat, sauté the finely chopped shallots in the butter; when they begin to become tender, add the cream, sherry, salt and pepper. Poach the egg in the milk, and place it on the toast round. Cover with the sauce. Makes 1 portion.

■ *EGGS ROYALE*

> ½ *cup cooked breast of chicken*
> ½ *cup cooked shrimp*
> 1 *tablespoon Mayonnaise (pages 285-286)*
> *Dash salt*
> *Dash pepper*
> 1 *tablespoon mushroom purée*
> 1 *egg* mollet
> 1 *shallow tartshell*
> *Truffle or pimiento garnish*

Grind the chicken and shrimp together, using the finest blade of a foodmill. Bind into a paste with Mayonnaise and blend in the purée, seasoning with salt and pepper to taste. Stand the egg on end in the tartshell and pack the meat around it lightly, but firmly enough to hold the egg upright; its top should stand above the level of the filled tartshell. Garnish the top with a dab of Mayonnaise, or with a truffle or pimiento decoration. Serve cold. Makes 1 portion.

■ *EGGS VICTORIA*

> 1 *egg*
> ¾ *cup light cream or rich milk*
> *Dash salt*
> *Dash pepper*
> 1 *tablespoon chopped cooked lobster*
> ⅛ *teaspoon minced truffles*

1 *thick toast round*
2 *tablespoons Sauce Mornay* (*page* 281)

Poach the egg in the cream, seasoning with salt and pepper. Remove the egg to drain, and strain the cream. In the cream, simmer the lobster and truffles. Strain them from the cream, allowing some to cling, and cover the toast round with the mixture. Place the egg on top, and cover with sauce. Glaze under the broiler for a moment before serving. Makes 1 portion.

▪ SCRAMBLED EGGS

Proof that scrambled eggs need not be served in a naked state on an ungarnished plate will be found in almost all the recipes that follow. Any of them would make you proud at a bridge luncheon.

▪ *SCRAMBLED EGGS À L'ANCIENNE*

2 *tablespoons diced mushrooms*
4 *tablespoons diced parboiled kidneys*
1 *tablespoon butter*
Grated truffle or Truffle Essence
5 *eggs*
5 *tablespoons light cream*
Salt to taste
4 *tartshells*
1 *cup Sauce Velouté* (*page* 279)
2 *tablespoons sherry*

Sauté the mushrooms and kidneys in the butter, adding the truffle gratings. Beat the eggs with the cream and salt, and soft-scramble them with the mushrooms and kidneys. Fill the tartshells. Simmer the Sauce Velouté, stirring in the sherry; divide the sauce among the tartshells. Serves 4.

▪ *EGGS BUCKINGHAM*

Though credited to George Villiers, the first Duke of Buckingham and court favorite of England's James I, his unknown chef must really be responsible. At some time during his visit to Italy in 1630, Buckingham must have been served Uova alla Cacciatora (page 153) and attempted to have it re-created in Britain; the family resemblance cannot be mistaken.

8 *slices bacon*
4 *chicken livers*
5 *eggs*
4 *teaspoons tomato paste thinned with 1 teaspoon*
 water
Dash salt
Dash pepper
4 *slices toast*
4 *teaspoons tomato catsup*

Cook the bacon very crisp and drain it; sauté the chicken livers in the bacon fat and drain them. Pour all but the thinnest film of fat from the pan; place it on very lowest heat. Mix the eggs with the thinned tomato paste, salt and pepper, and soft-scramble them. Serve the eggs over toast triangles, making a small cavity on top of each serving in which a teaspoon of catsup is placed with a chicken liver; 2 slices of bacon are then laid over the portion. Serves 4.

■ *SCRAMBLED EGGS CRÉOLE*

Olive oil
2 *tablespoons minced onions*
2 *tablespoons diced, drained tomatoes*
2 *tablespoons minced mushrooms*
5 *eggs*
3 *tablespoons tomato juice*
1 *teaspoon capers*

In enough olive oil to cover the skillet's bottom, sauté the onions, tomatoes and mushrooms. When these are just underdone, add the eggs, which have been beaten lightly with the tomato juice and capers. Soft-scramble. Though no salt is called for here, the oil and capers providing the flavor, your taste may require the use of a dash of salt. Serves 4.

■ *EGGS GALLI-MARIE*

5 *eggs*
5 *tablespoons light cream*
Dash salt
Dash pepper
1 *tablespoon minced pimiento*

> *2 tablespoons butter*
> *4 large artichoke hearts*
> *1 cup boiled rice*
> *¾ cup Béchamel Sauce (page 280)*

Beat the eggs with the cream, salt, pepper and pimientos; soft-scramble them in half the butter. Fill molds with the eggs and poach in a *bain-marie* 6 to 10 minutes in a preheated 275-degree oven. Poach the artichoke hearts in lightly salted water, and drain well. Sauté the rice in the remaining butter until it is crisp but not tough; test by biting a grain between the front teeth. Form the rice into patties over and around the artichoke hearts, unmold the eggs on top of these patties and spoon the sauce over them. Serves 4.

▪ *EGGS LAFITTE*

Along about 1956, shrimpers testing new waters in the Gulf of Mexico discovered a variety of large, golden shrimp that has become a regional delicacy around New Orleans and Galveston, out of which ports Jean Lafitte sailed on his piratical cruises. Though this recipe was created for this new shrimp, it works with any of the more common varieties of large shrimp.

> *8 large shrimp or prawns, parboiled*
> *5 eggs*
> *5 tablespoons milk or light cream*
> *Salt to taste*
> *Pepper to taste*
> *2 tablespoons butter*
> *4 tartshells or timbales*
> *½ teaspoon capers*
> *1 cup heavy cream*
> *Large pinch nutmeg*

Cut each shrimp into 3 pieces of approximately equal length. Chop the thickest section very fine; the yield should be about 3 tablespoons of meat. Add this to the eggs as they are beaten with the milk, a dash of salt and a dash of pepper; the eggs are then soft-scrambled with 1 tablespoon butter and while still very soft are placed in the tartshells or timbales. Cook them 6 to 10 minutes on a buttered cookie sheet in a preheated 250-degree oven. Pound and sieve the middle portions of the shrimp with the capers and blend this in a double boiler with the cup of cream, 1 tablespoon butter, a dash of salt and a dash of nutmeg. (Or pass the shrimp sections through a blender with a little of the cream for 5 or 10 seconds at high speed and add this to the remaining cream and the butter in the double boiler.) Cook very gently for 15 minutes, stirring frequently. Put the tart-shells or timbales containing the eggs on warm plates, pour over each a portion of the sauce and garnish with the shrimp tails. Serves 4.

▪ *EGGS MARTIN*

> *2 slices crumbled crisp bacon*
> *1 tablespoon shredded green pepper*
> *5 eggs*
> *3 tablespoons milk or light cream*
> *Dash salt*
> *Dash pepper*
> *½ cup chopped cooked spinach*
> *1 tablespoon shredded red sweet pepper*

Cook the bacon and remove it from the pan; in a very light film of bacon fat sauté the pepper shreds until they are tender. Beat the eggs with the milk, salt and pepper, and mix into them the spinach and bacon. Soft-scramble the eggs in the pan with the pepper over very low heat. Scramble until the eggs are firm. Serves 4.

▪ *EGGS MILANAISE*

> *4 slices bread*
> *2 tablespoons olive oil*
> *4 tablespoons grated Parmesan cheese*
> *1 tablespoon chopped shallots*
> *1 tablespoon chopped chives*
> *5 eggs*
> *3 tablespoons white wine*
> *Dash salt*
> *Dash pepper*

Sauté the bread on both sides, very lightly, in oil; press one side of each slice onto 2 tablespoons grated cheese spread on waxed paper, and place on a cookie sheet in a warming oven to become crisp. Sprinkle the remaining 2 tablespoons cheese on the hot oil in the skillet, and add the shallots and chives. Beat the eggs lightly with the wine, salt and pepper; scramble them with the shallots and chives until they are firm. Serve on the crisp cheese-covered toast. Serves 4.

■ *EGGS MORTEMART*

>*4 truffle slices*
>*5 eggs*
>*1 tablespoon light cream*
>*Salt to taste*
>*Pepper to taste*
>*4 toast rounds*
>*¾ cup mushroom purée*

Butter small molds and place a truffle slice in the bottom of each. Soft-scramble the eggs (do not overcook), with the cream and seasonings, and place them in the molds. Poach the eggs 10 minutes in a *bain-marie* in a preheated 300-degree oven. Turn the molds out on the toast rounds and cover the sides with a coating of mushroom purée. Serves 4.

■ *EGGS ORLOFF*

>*5 eggs*
>*4 tablespoons heavy cream*
>*2 teaspoons caviar*
>*2 tablespoons butter*
>*4 tartshells*
>*8 small cooked shrimp*
>*4 thin truffle slices*
>*Dash cayenne*

Beat the eggs with the cream, adding the caviar; soft-scramble the eggs, using a little of the butter. Place a layer of eggs in the tartshells, put two shrimp on top of each and fill the shells with the remaining eggs. Put a truffle slice on top of each; blend the remaining butter with the cayenne and spread the tops generously. Place in a preheated 250-degree oven 10 minutes to allow the butter to penetrate through the eggs. (There should be no need for salt; the salt in the caviar will do the trick.) Serves 4.

■ *EGGS PRINCESS MARY*

Auguste Escoffier's name is recognized even by those who are not familiar with culinary matters. This dish was created by the great chef during his long tenure at London's Savoy Hotel, for the then-Princess Mary, wife of George V; it dates from around 1900.

> 5 *eggs*
> 2 *tablespoons cream*
> 2 *tablespoons Sauce Espagnole* (*page 275*)
> 2 *teaspoons grated Parmesan cheese*
> *Grated truffle or Truffle Essence*
> 1 *tablespoon butter*
> 4 *tartshells, dough to cover*
> 4 *mushroom buttons*

Beat the eggs with the cream, Sauce Espagnole, Parmesan and truffle; soft-scramble them in the butter over lowest heat. Fill the tartshells with the eggs and seal the tops, pressing a mushroom button into the center of each. Bake 10 minutes in a preheated 325-degree oven on a buttered cookie sheet, or until the tops are browned. Brush with butter or a little Sauce Espagnole before serving. Serves 4.

▪ *EGGS PRINTANIER* (*Springtime Eggs*)

> 1 *tablespoon each of the following, all parboiled:*
> *diced carrots, diced potatoes, diced celery, green*
> *peas*
> 5 *eggs plus 1 egg white*
> 4 *tablespoons milk or light cream*
> *Salt to taste*
> *Pepper to taste*
> 4 *toast rounds*
> 2 *tablespoons Printanier Butter* (*page 288*)
> ¾ *cup Sauce Velouté* (*page 279*)
> 1 *teaspoon chopped parsley*

Butter shallow molds and line them with the mixed vegetables. Beat the 5 eggs and the extra white with the milk, salt and pepper. Fill the molds three-quarters full. Poach in a *bain-marie*, in water well up along the sides of the molds, for 20 to 25 minutes in a preheated 275-degree oven. Butter the toast rounds with the Printanier Butter, turn out the molds on the rounds, cover with warm sauce and sprinkle with chopped parsley. Serves 4.

▪ *EGGS RACHEL*

> 5 *eggs*
> 4 *tablespoons milk or light cream*
> 2 *tablespoons minced cooked asparagus*

> *Grated truffle or Truffle Essence*
> *Dash salt*
> *Dash pepper*
> *4 tartshells*
> *12 small cooked asparagus tips*
> *¾ cup Sauce Allemande (page 279)*
> *Paprika*

Beat the eggs with the milk, minced asparagus, truffle, salt and pepper; soft-scramble the eggs and fill the tartshells. Arrange the asparagus tips on top of the eggs. Cover with sauce, dust with paprika and glaze under the broiler a few minutes before serving. Serves 4.

▪ *EGGS ROSSINI*

> *5 eggs*
> *2 tablespoons light cream*
> *1 cup Sauce Périgueux (page 277)*
> *Grated truffle or Truffle Essence*
> *3 tablespoons minced* foie gras
> *1 teaspoon butter*
> *4 tartshells*

Beat the eggs with the cream, 2 tablespoons Sauce Périgueux, the truffle and the *foie gras,* and soft-scramble them in butter. Fill the tartshells, cover with the remaining sauce and glaze for a moment under the broiler. Serves 4.

Eggs Perigourdine was the original name of this dish.

▪ *EGGS ROTHSCHILD*

> *5 eggs*
> *3 tablespoons light cream*
> *1 tablespoon Madeira*
> *Grated truffle or Truffle Essence*
> *Dash salt*
> *Dash pepper*
> *1 trout, poached in white wine*
> *4 tartshells*
> *2 tablespoons heavy cream*

Beat the eggs with the light cream, Madeira, truffle, salt and pepper. Skin and bone the trout, and flake its flesh; there should be ¾ cup fish. Scramble the eggs over very low heat in a buttered pan, adding the trout. Fill the tartshells; place them in a preheated 325-degree oven on a buttered cookie sheet, and cook 10 minutes. Remove the eggs; place ½ tablespoon heavy cream on top of each portion and return to the oven for 5 minutes. Serves 4.

▪ *EGGS SAGAN*

Not the charming young lady novelist of the twentieth century, but the sagacious Talleyrand, Count Sagan, who said to his master, Louis XVIII of France, "My casseroles are more important, sire, than your instructions," is recalled by this dish. It was probably originated either by Bouché or Carême, both of whom served Count Sagan as head chef.

> *2 cups brains*
> *1½ cups white wine*
> *1 bayleaf*
> *2 cracked peppercorns*
> *Pinch thyme*
> *Pinch nutmeg*
> *Pinch salt*
> *5 eggs*
> *¾ cup grated Gruyère cheese*
> *4 tartshells or timbales*
> *¾ cup Chateaubriand Sauce (page 277)*

Wash, clean and drain the brains well; poach them in the wine to which the bayleaf, peppercorns, thyme, nutmeg and salt have been added. With the wine just simmering, poach 4 to 6 minutes. Lift out the firmed brains with a slotted spoon, allowing all liquid to drain back into the saucepan. Set aside on a warm plate. Strain the poaching liquid, beating 4 tablespoons into the eggs. Scramble the eggs in a lightly buttered skillet, adding the grated cheese as the eggs cook. Spoon equal portions of the eggs and brains into the tartshells or timbales. Cover with sauce and glaze under the broiler for a moment or two before serving. Serves 4.

▪ *SAN FRANCISCO SCRAMBLED EGGS*

In this city of good food, there is at least one Italian restaurant on every block, three to the block in the North Beach section. Each restaurant features the variation on Roman Scrambled Eggs (page 77) which this recipe gives, and the proprietor of each restaurant will with solemn face assure you that he, himself, is the originator of the dish, which by now has attained the status of a regional recipe.

> *Olive oil*
> 1 *cup raw ground beef*
> 1 *cup chopped raw spinach*
> 5 *eggs*
> 2 *tablespoons white wine*
> 2 *tablespoons grated Parmesan cheese*
> *Dash salt*
> *Dash pepper*

In enough oil to cover the skillet's bottom, sauté the ground beef, crumbling it into small bits as it cooks. As it begins to brown, add the chopped spinach; cover the skillet for 3 to 4 minutes. Beat the eggs with the wine, cheese, salt and pepper, reduce the flame under the skillet to lowest heat and pour the eggs over the meat and spinach. Stir several times to mix the ingredients as the eggs set firm. Serves 4.

■ *TRUFFLED EGGS*

> 5 *eggs*
> 4 *tablespoons cream*
> *Generous quantity of grated truffle, truffle shavings or Truffle Essence*
> *Dash salt*
> *Dash pepper*
> 1 *teaspoon butter*

Beat the eggs with the cream, truffle, salt and pepper; soft-scramble them in the butter over lowest heat. Serves 4.

■ *EGGS À LA PIÉMONTAISE* is the name applied to this classic dish when a Piedmont truffle is used for flavoring.

■ SHIRRED EGGS

One of the easiest ways you will find to escape hard labor in the kitchen when entertaining is to serve shirred egg dishes. Many of them can be more easily prepared for a group than they can for a couple.

▪ *EGGS ALSACIENNE*

> 1 *slice ham*
> 1 *teaspoon butter*
> 2 *tablespoons drained sauerkraut*
> 1 *egg*
> *Salt to taste*
> *Pepper to taste*

Lightly sauté the ham in butter, and transfer it to a warm shirring dish. Over a very low flame, braise the sauerkraut in a tightly covered skillet for 2 or 3 minutes. Arrange the sauerkraut on the ham slice with a nest to receive the egg; add the egg and dust with salt and pepper. Cook 6 to 10 minutes in a preheated 375-degree oven. Makes 1 portion.

▪ *EGGS AUGIER*

> ¾ *cup parboiled, minced sweetbreads*
> 1 *tablespoon butter*
> 1 *egg*
> 3 *tablespoons heavy cream*
> *Dash salt*
> *Dash pepper*

Sauté the sweetbreads lightly in butter and cover the shirring dish with them, leaving a small depression in the center for the egg. Slide in the egg, pour the cream over it and dust with salt and pepper. Cook 6 to 10 minutes in a preheated 375-degree oven. Makes 1 portion.

▪ *EGGS BABINSKI*

> ¾ *cup ground chicken meat*
> 1 *egg white*
> *Dash salt*
> *Dash pepper*
> *Pinch nutmeg*
> *Fat for deep frying*
> 2 *tablespoons minced, lightly sautéed mushrooms*
> 1 *egg*
> 2 *tablespoons Sauce Velouté (page 279)*

Bind the chicken meat with the egg white and form into thumb-sized croquettes. Season with salt, pepper and nutmeg, and fry in deep fat until crisp. Arrange the mushrooms as a lining to the shirring dish, put the egg on them, dust with more salt and pepper and cook 6 to 10 minutes in a preheated 375-degree oven. Remove the egg and surround it with the tiny croquettes; spoon the sauce over it. Makes 1 portion.

▪ *SHIRRED EGGS AU BEURRE NOIR*
 (*Shirred Eggs with Black Butter*)

This is the companion to the poached egg dish (page 117), the egg offering a firmer texture due to the different cooking process.

> *2 tablespoons butter*
> *1 egg*
> *Dash salt*
> *Dash pepper*
> *1 teaspoon vinegar*

Using ½ tablespoon butter, shirr the egg 6 to 10 minutes in a preheated 375-degree oven, dusting with salt and pepper before it begins cooking. In a saucepan, melt the remaining butter over highest heat; when it turns brown and foams, dash in the vinegar and swirl the pan or stir until the hissing stops. Pour the butter over the eggs. Remember, butter must be used, due to the introduction of chemicals into many margarines that prevent the marriage of the fat with the vinegar. Makes 1 portion.

▪ *SHIRRED EGGS BOHÉMIENNE*

> *2 very thin slices cooked ham*
> *1 teaspoon butter*
> *1 egg*
> *Dash salt*
> *Dash pepper*
> *2 tablespoons Sauce Périgueux (page 277)*

Sauté the ham very lightly in the butter. Empty the melted butter into a shirring dish, lay one slice of the ham on the dish, slide the egg on top of it and dust with salt and pepper. Cut the second slice of ham into julienne and crisscross the strips over the egg. Cook 6 to 10 minutes in a preheated 375-degree oven. Spoon on the sauce just before serving. Makes 1 portion.

▪ *EGGS AU CHASSEUR* (*Hunter's Eggs*)

Italy has given us several classic egg dishes, but this is very probably
the best known; it has traveled around the world, taking a new name
here and there: Buckingham in England, au Chasseur in France,
Isolene in Scandinavia. In some lands it undergoes a slight alteration
in its components, but by and large it remains recognizable wherever
it's encountered. You will find other versions on pages 153 and 201.

> 1 *tablespoon olive oil*
> ½ *clove minced garlic*
> 2 *chicken livers*
> 1 *slice firm, ripe tomato*
> 1 *egg*
> *Dash salt*
> *Dash pepper*
> ½ *tablespoon chopped parsley*

Heat the oil with the garlic in a skillet. (If you object to too much
garlic, simply omit the raw garlic and season the dish with garlic
salt.) Sauté the chicken livers 3 to 4 minutes over low heat, leaving
them slightly underdone. Pour the oil from the skillet into a chafing
dish, place the slice of tomato in it, slide the egg on top of the tomato
and lay a chicken liver on each side of it. Dust with salt and pepper
and cook 8 to 12 minutes in a preheated 350-degree oven. Sprinkle
generously with chopped parsley just before serving. Makes 1 portion.

This dish is called *Uova alla Cacciatora* in Italy, and *Eggs Isolene*
in Scandinavia.

▪ *DANISH SHIRRED EGGS*

> ¾ *cup flaked smoked salmon*
> 1 *egg*
> *Dash pepper*
> 1 *tablespoon heavy cream*

Spread the salmon on a buttered shirring dish, making a dent to
hold the egg. Add the egg and dust with pepper. (If smoked salmon
is used no salt will be necessary; for any other type of salmon it
must be added.) Pour the cream over the egg, and cook in a preheated 350-degree oven 8 to 12 minutes. Makes 1 portion.

▪ *JOCKEY CLUB EGGS*

France's Jockey Club was much more than a sports-loving organization; it was the social center of the titled and wealthy group that ran the nation until a pair of wars disrupted the land. This was one of the specialties of the house.

> 1 *tablespoon butter*
> 3 *or* 4 *toast crescents*
> 1 *egg*
> 1 *tablespoon* foie gras *purée*
> ½ *kidney, parboiled lightly in salted water*
> *Dash salt*
> *Dash pepper*
> 2 *tablespoons Sauce Espagnole* (*page* 275)

Butter a shirring dish heavily, and arrange the toast crescents around its rim so that the egg may be slid into the center. Spread the toast with the puréed *foie gras*. Cover the toast and egg with the kidney, chopped into small dice; dust with salt and pepper. Brush over all a heavy coating of Sauce Espagnole. Cook 10 to 12 minutes in a preheated 350-degree oven. (A European chef would not parboil the kidney, as the custom there is to serve kidney quite rare; American taste demands meats of this type to be cooked more thoroughly.) Makes 1 portion.

▪ *EGGS LAS VEGAS*

Nevada's gambling capital leans toward hearty rather than delicate fare, and its round-the-clock operation favors dishes that will be edible even if held in a warming-oven for instant service. This egg dish meets those specifications.

> 1 *sweet red pepper*
> ½ *cup creamed tomato soup thinned with* 1 *table-spoon cold water*
> ½ *teaspoon capers*
> 2 *tablespoons grated Cheddar cheese*
> 1 *egg*
> *Dash salt*
> *Dash pepper*
> *Breadcrumb–Cheese Glaze* (*page* 291)

Skin the pepper by plunging it into boiling water, then cold water; the skin will then slip off. Cut off the top and remove the pith and seeds. Mix the soup, capers and cheese; a thick paste will result. Fill the pepper with this, break an egg on top, dust with salt and pepper and cover with the glazing mix. Cook 15 to 20 minutes in a pre-heated 325-degree oven; finish glazing under the broiler if necessary. Makes 1 portion.

■ *EGGS LULLY*

Both the French Baroque music of this composer and the dish named in his honor survive; Lully seems to have avoided being linked with rich food, however.

> ½ *cup cooked macaroni*
> 1 *tablespoon chopped prosciutto or capocollo*
> 1½ *tablespoons chopped firm, ripe tomato*
> *Pinch pounded basil*
> 1 *egg*
> 2 *tablespoons light cream*
> *Large pinch parsley*

Mix the macaroni, ham, tomato and basil; line a shirring dish with it, leaving a nest for the egg. Add the egg, pour the cream over it and dust with parsley. Cook 10 to 12 minutes in a preheated 350-degree oven. Makes 1 portion.

■ *EGGS MEYERBEER*

> 1 *parboiled small kidney*
> 1 *tablespoon butter*
> 2 *tablespoons Sauce Périgueux* (*page 277*)
> 1 *egg*
> *Dash salt*
> *Dash pepper*

Slice the kidney thin and brush it with butter; line a shirring dish with butter and place the kidney slices on the bottom. Spoon on half the sauce. Slide on the egg, dust with salt and pepper and cook 8 to 10 minutes in a preheated 375-degree oven. Add the remaining sauce over the egg before serving. Makes 1 portion.

▪ *EGGS MIRABEAU*

> 1 *tablespoon butter*
> 3 *or* 4 *blanched tarragon leaves*
> 3 *or* 4 *anchovy fillets*
> 1 *egg*

Use all the butter to grease a shirring dish. Lay the tarragon leaves on the bottom of the dish, and arrange the anchovy fillets in a circle to contain the egg. Slide in the egg, and cook 6 to 10 minutes in a preheated 375-degree oven. Makes 1 portion.

▪ *EGGS À L'OPÉRA*

> *Butter*
> 3 *or* 4 *cooked stalks asparagus*
> 1 *egg*
> *Dash salt*
> *Dash pepper*
> 2 *chicken livers*
> 2 *tablespoons veal gravy*

Butter the shirring dish well; trim the asparagus to cover the bottom. Slide on the egg, and dust with salt and pepper. Undercook the chicken livers in a small amount of butter; lay one on each side of the egg. Cook 8 to 12 minutes in a preheated 350-degree oven; spoon on warm veal gravy before serving. Makes 1 portion.

▪ *EGGS À LA PARISIENNE*

> 2 *tablespoons cooked ground chicken meat*
> 2 *tablespoons cooked ground tongue*
> 2 *tablespoons sautéed ground mushrooms*
> *Butter*
> 1 *egg*
> 2 *tablespoons Sauce Espagnole (page 275)*
> *Truffle grating or Truffle Essence*

Blend the chicken, tongue and mushrooms into a loose paste and line a buttered shirring dish with it, leaving a dent to accommodate the egg. Spread over the meat half the sauce into which has been stirred the truffle. Add the egg; cook 8 to 12 minutes in a preheated 350-

degree oven. Spoon on the remaining sauce before serving. Makes 1 portion.

■ *ROTHOMAGO EGGS*

> *Butter*
> 2 *thin slices ham*
> 3 *or* 4 *lightly parboiled small link sausages*
> 1 *egg*
> 3 *tablespoons Tomato Sauce* (*page* 278)
> *Breadcrumb–Cheese Glaze* (*page* 291)

Line the buttered shirring dish with ham, trimming to fit. Arrange the link sausages in a circle or square to contain the egg. Break the egg into the dish, cover it with Tomato Sauce and sprinkle with the glazing mix. Cook 8 to 12 minutes in a preheated 350-degree oven. Finish glazing under the broiler if necessary. Makes 1 portion.

■ *EGGS TETRAZZINI*

Like most opera stars who flourished before the recording age, Luisa Tetrazzini is mostly legend, her voice preserved only on a few dim, scratchy disks. The chicken dish and egg dish named for her are still very much with us, though.

> 2 *tablespoons minced* foie gras
> 1 *tablespoon chopped green olives*
> 1 *tablespoon minced artichoke heart*
> 1 *teaspoon minced chives*
> 2 *teaspoons blanched, slivered almonds*
> *Butter*
> 4 *tablespoons Sauce Velouté* (*page* 279)
> 1 *egg*

Mix the *foie gras*, olives, artichoke, chives and half the almonds together into a loose paste. Line the bottom of a buttered shirring dish with this paste; spread half the sauce over it. Slide on the egg, and cook 8 to 12 minutes in a preheated 350-degree oven. Remove from the oven, pour on the remaining sauce and sprinkle with the remaining almonds. Put under the broiler a minute to allow the sauce to glaze and the almonds to crisp. Makes 1 portion.

▪ SAUTÉED OR FRIED EGG DISHES

Serve a plain old fried egg at a special dinner? Why not, if it's offered in one of the special styles you will find in this section?

▪ *EGGS BAMBOCHE*

> 3 *tablespoons Cream Sauce* (*page* 281)
> ½ *cup cooked, flaked codfish*
> 2 *tablespoons mixed vegetables: carrots, potatoes,*
>   *peas*
> 1 *egg*

Using a spoonful of the sauce, bind the codfish and vegetables and mix them into a patty; serve the egg on top of the patty. Makes 1 portion.

▪ *CARACAS EGGS*

> 1 *teaspoon oil or butter*
> ½ *minced garlic clove*
> ½ *cup boiled rice*
> 1 *tablespoon tomato paste*
> 1 *tablespoon sour cream*
> 1 *teaspoon minced onion*
> ½ *teaspoon minced parsley*
> ½ *teaspoon minced chives*
> *Dash salt*
> 1 *egg*
> 1 *teaspoon grated Parmesan cheese*
> *Large pinch paprika*
> *Small pinch cayenne*

Heat the oil in a skillet with the garlic. Over lowest heat, stir in the rice, tomato paste, sour cream, onion, parsley, chives and salt. Form into a mound on a warm plate, and top with the egg. Mix together the Parmesan, paprika and cayenne, and sprinkle them thinly over the egg. Heat under the broiler to be sure the dish is warm before serving. Makes 1 portion.

■ *EGGS LORENZO*

> 1 *toast round* or croustade
> 1 *teaspoon Anchovy Butter* (*page* 288)
> 2 *tablespoons flaked crab meat*
> 2 *tablespoons Sauce Mornay* (*page* 281)
> 1 *sautéed egg*

Spread the toast round with Anchovy Butter; place it in a warming oven until crisp. Bind the crab meat with a little of the Sauce Mornay and cover the toast with it. Top with the egg and spoon over it the remaining sauce. Glaze before serving. Makes 1 portion.

■ *EGGS LUCULLUS*

> 1 *parboiled lamb sweetbread*
> 2 *tablespoons butter* (*no substitutions*)
> 1 *large or* 3 *small artichoke hearts*
> 1 *sautéed egg*
> ½ *teaspoon lemon juice*

Slice the sweetbread thinly and sauté it in butter; sauté the artichoke hearts. Reserve the butter. Arrange the artichokes on a warm plate, cover with the slices of sweetbread and top with the egg. Add the lemon juice to the butter remaining in the pan, swirl briskly a moment and pour over the egg. Makes 1 portion.

■ *EGGS MÉNAGÈRE* (*Thrifty Wife's Eggs*)

> 1 *small potato*
> 1 *small carrot*
> 1 *small turnip*
> 2 *cups veal broth*
> *Dash salt*
> *Dash pepper*
> 1 *sautéed egg*
> 2 *tablespoons Tomato Sauce* (*page* 278)

Parboil the peeled vegetables in the veal broth to which salt and pepper have been added. Slice the vegetables thin, and sauté them a moment in a lightly oiled skillet. Arrange the slices on a warm plate, top with the egg and spoon Tomato Sauce over it. (In a thrifty farm kitchen, these would probably be vegetables left in the stockpot.) Makes 1 portion.

▪ EGGS *EN COCOTTE*

Ranging from delicate to robust, this small special-occasion selection may lead you to new ones of your own devising. Remember, 1 or 2 eggs may be used with no alteration of quantities.

▪ *EGGS BIZET*

> 1 *large, thin slice cooked tongue*
> 2 *teaspoons minced cooked artichoke*
> *Truffle grating or Truffle Essence*
> 1 *egg*
> *Truffle grating or Truffle Essence*
> 2 *tablespoons Sauce Périgueux* (*page 277*)

Butter the *cocotte* well. Trim the slice of tongue so that it will line the sides of the *cocotte;* reserve the trimmings. Mince the trimmings and mix with the minced artichoke and the truffle; place a layer of this mixture in the bottom of the *cocotte*. Put in the egg, add the remaining minced mixture, seal the *cocotte* and poach in a *bain-marie* 10 to 12 minutes in a preheated 350-degree oven, or half that time in simmering water on top of the stove. Unmold on the artichoke heart; spoon on the sauce. Makes 1 portion.

▪ *EGGS CARÊME* EN COCOTTE are identical with this dish except that Sauce Velouté (page 279) is used rather than Périgueux.

▪ *EGGS À LA MARAÎCHÈRE* (*Eggs with Pot Herbs*)

> 2 *tablespoons chopped raw spinach*
> 2 *tablespoons chopped lettuce*
> 1 *tablespoon chopped sorrel*
> *Dash salt*
> *Dash pepper*
> *Butter*
> 1 *egg*
> 1 *teaspoon milk*

Toss the vegetables well together with a little salt and pepper, and put them into a well-buttered *cocotte;* add the egg and milk. Poach in a *bain-marie* 8 to 10 minutes in a preheated 350-degree oven, or half that time in water simmering on top of the stove. Makes 1 portion.

▪ *EGGS* EN COCOTTE *WITH MUSHROOMS*

Too much has already been said about the affinity of the egg and the mushroom for any amplification to be necessary. But you will do well to experiment with timing before offering this dish to guests, if fresh mushrooms are used, since what may be too little cooking for some of the more delicate fungi may be too much for others.

> ½ *teaspoon butter* (*more if you wish*)
> 1 *tablespoon heavy cream*
> *Dash salt*
> *Dash pepper*
> *Dash nutmeg*
> 2 *tablespoons chopped mushrooms*
> 1 *egg*

Put the butter in the bottom of the *cocotte;* add the cream, seasonings, mushrooms and egg. Seal the *cocotte* and poach in a *bain-marie* 6 to 10 minutes in a preheated 350-degree oven, or half that time in a top-of-stove waterbath. Makes 1 portion.

▪ HARD-COOKED EGGS

If you've thought of the hard-cooked egg as a special dish only when stuffed or deviled in buffet service, or as a source of grated egg yolk to be served with caviar, be prepared for pleasant surprises. And for very special occasions, remember the aspic-molded eggs that occupy their own section at the end of this chapter, starting on page 159.

▪ *EGGS BÉCHAMEL*

There's little doubt that the Marquis Louis de Béchamiel did not even have a finger in the saucepot from which came the creamy sauce bearing his name; most probably some unsung chef of the royal household, in search of job security, dedicated the sauce to the Marquis during the years around 1650, when Béchamiel was the royal steward, and thus was in charge of the palace's busy kitchens. There's no doubt at all that the egg dish here is a creation of another chef trying to butter up the boss.

> 6 *hard-cooked eggs*
> 1 ½ *tablespoons* pâté de foie gras

2 teaspoons finely minced truffle
2 tablespoons butter
¼ teaspoon powdered tarragon
¼ teaspoon powdered chervil
Pinch salt
Pinch thyme
½ cup Béchamel Sauce (page 280)
Breadcrumb–Cheese Glaze (page 291)

Split the eggs lengthwise; remove the yolks and reserve the egg-white cases. Mash the yolks with the *pâté*, truffle, butter, tarragon, chervil, salt and thyme. Mix well; stuff the cavities in the whites until level. Press the halves together and hold with a toothpick if necessary. Place in a shallow buttered casserole, cover with the sauce and sprinkle thickly with the glazing mix. Cook 5 to 10 minutes in a preheated 350-degree oven; serve very hot. (Any stuffing left over—and there should be quite a bit—makes an interesting spread for very thin toast or for cocktail canapés.) Makes 6 portions.

▪ *HARD-COOKED EGGS CARÊME*

1 hard-cooked egg
1 poached artichoke heart
3 small cooked shrimp
1 tablespoon heavy cream
Pinch nutmeg
Grated truffle or Truffle Essence
½ cup Béchamel Sauce (page 280)
1 tartshell

Chop and mix well the egg and artichoke. Cut the shrimp in the middle, reserving the tails. Pound the bodies with a little cream, nutmeg and the truffle into a smooth paste, or put them through a blender. Mix this purée with the remaining cream and sauce in a double boiler. Put the egg–artichoke mixture into the tartshell and pour the sauce over it. Glaze under the broiler and at the last minute add the shrimp tails to the top for garnish. Makes 1 portion.

▪ *EGGS CELIA*

1 hard-cooked egg
½ cup Sauce Mornay (page 281)
1 teaspoon chopped green pepper

> 1 *teaspoon chopped pimiento*
> 1 *tablespoon grated mild cheese*
> *Dash salt*
> *Dash pepper*
> 1 *batch Pastry Dough* (*page* 291)
> *Butter*

Slice the egg thickly, and place it in a shallow buttered ramekin (an individual small soufflé dish does as well, or group service may be prepared in a casserole). Heat the sauce, add the green pepper and pimiento, stir in the cheese and seasonings and blend smoothly. Pour the sauce over the egg, seal the top with Pastry Dough and bake 10 minutes in a preheated 350-degree oven, or until the top browns. Brush the top with butter before serving. Makes 1 portion.

▪ *EGGS CHIMAY*

Another very old dish whose origins are lost, although it did come from the little Belgian marble-quarrying town whose name it bears.

> 1 *hard-cooked egg*
> ¼ *teaspoon chopped sautéed mushrooms*
> 2 *teaspoons heavy cream*
> ¼ *teaspoon Sauce Espagnole* (*page* 275)
> *Dash salt*
> *Dash pepper*
> ½ *teaspoon grated Parmesan cheese*

Split the egg lengthwise, remove the yolk and reserve the white cases. Mix the yolk with the mushrooms and 1 teaspoon cream, into which has been stirred the Sauce Espagnole, and the salt and pepper. Stuff the white cases, rounding off generously. Place them on a buttered cookie sheet, brush with a little cream and sprinkle with the cheese. Place under the broiler long enough to set the cheese into a glaze; by then the egg will be warm. Makes 1 portion.

▪ *DANISH EGGS*

> 6 *hard-cooked eggs*
> 4 *tablespoons butter*
> 6 *medium-sized raw mushrooms* (*about* ⅓ *pound*)
> 2 *teaspoons minced parsley*

>½ *teaspoon salt*
>¼ *teaspoon pepper*
>2 *tablespoons flour*
>¾ *cup milk*
>1 *cup Samsoe or other mild Danish cheese*
>2 *tablespoons white wine*

Cut the eggs in half lengthwise, remove the yolks, and reserve the egg-white cases. Mash the yolks with 2 tablespoons butter; blend with the mushrooms, parsley, salt and pepper. Return this mixture to the white casings, rounding off the tops to resemble whole eggs. Place in a well-buttered casserole. Melt 1 tablespoon butter in a saucepan, stir in the flour to make a smooth white *roux* and slowly add the milk while stirring smoothly. When the milk is hot, add the grated cheese, stirring regularly. Smooth this sauce by adding the wine and stirring for about 2 minutes off the heat. Pour over the eggs, and bake 20 to 25 minutes in a preheated 350-degree oven. Makes 6 portions.

▪ *EGGS ELIZABETH*

>1 *hard-cooked egg*
>1 *teaspoon artichoke purée*
>*Dash salt*
>*Dash pepper*
>1 *artichoke heart, parboiled in salted water*
>1½ *tablespoons Sauce Mornay (page 281)*
>½ *teaspoon grated Parmesan cheese*

Trim the egg at the top and bottom with a sharp knife so it resembles a small barrel. In the bottom, cut out a round of the white and remove the yolk without breaking the sides of the case. Mash the yolk with the artichoke purée, salt and pepper. Return the mixture to the white case; avoid overstuffing. Stand the egg with the open end down on the artichoke heart, cover with sauce, sprinkle with Parmesan and place under the broiler for a minute until the cheese browns. Makes 1 portion.

▪ *EGGS FARCI (Stuffed Eggs)*

This is the ancestor recipe for all stuffed egg dishes; no one knows anything about its origin, but it is the pattern, the traditional reheated stuffed egg.

> 6 *hard-cooked eggs*
> 4 *sautéed chicken livers*
> 1 *tablespoon sour cream*
> *Dash salt*
> *Dash pepper*
> 3 *tablespoons finely grated Gruyère or other mild*
>   *cheese*

Split the eggs lengthwise, remove the yolks and reserve the egg-white cases. Mash the chicken livers, or pass them through a blender. Combine them with the egg yolks, sour cream, salt and pepper; work them until smooth. Stuff the egg-white cases, rounding off the tops. Put a generous layer of grated cheese on top of each stuffed half, and bake 10 to 12 minutes in a preheated 300-degree oven, until the cheese melts. Makes 6 portions.

■ *FRITTATA MILANESE* (*Recooked Milan Eggs*)

In Italy these are sometimes substituted for meatballs in pasta, especially in the pasta dishes cooked *al magro*.

> 6 *hard-cooked eggs*
> 1 *cup flaked boiled fish*
> ½ *teaspoon pounded basil*
> 1 *finely minced garlic clove*
> 1 *uncooked egg white*
> 1 *tablespoon milk*
> *Dash salt*
> 2 *tablespoons flour*
> *Fat for deep frying*

Halve the eggs lengthwise, remove the yolks and reserve the egg-white cases. Mash the yolks, and blend with the fish, basil and garlic; beat the uncooked egg white and milk together with a dash of salt, and blend this with the mixture of mashed yolks until smooth. Stuff this into the egg-white cases, rounding them off to resemble whole eggs. Roll in flour and fry in deep fat until crisply brown, 3 to 6 minutes. If they are not served with a sauced pasta, serve them with a tomato sauce. Makes 6 portions.

■ *HARD-COOKED EGGS JEANNETTE*

> 6 *hard-cooked eggs*
> 4 *slices firm bread* (*French or Italian type*)

> ¾ *cup milk*
> 2 *tablespoons finely chopped parsley*
> 1 *clove finely minced garlic*
> *Dash salt*
> *Dash pepper*
> 3 *tablespoons butter*
> ½ *cup Sauce Vinaigrette* (*page* 287)

Slice the eggs in half lengthwise, remove the yolks and reserve the egg-white cases. Soak the bread in the milk; when soft, mash it with the yolks, parsley, garlic, salt and pepper. Stuff the egg-white cases with this mixture, rounding the tops to resemble whole eggs. Sauté the eggs in the butter over low heat, turning them so that they brown evenly. Sprinkle with Sauce Vinaigrette before serving. Makes 6 portions.

▪ *EGGS MONTFERMIEL*

> 6 *hard-cooked eggs*
> 3 *tablespoons butter*
> ¾ *cup ground raw onions*
> 1 *cup ground fresh mushrooms*
> 1 *tablespoon flour*
> 2 *tablespoons heavy cream*
> 1 *tablespoon sherry*
> *Dash pepper*
> *Dash nutmeg*
> 1 *uncooked egg*
> 1 *cup very fine breadcrumbs*
> *Fat for deep frying*

Halve the eggs lengthwise, remove the yolks and reserve the egg-white cases. (Set aside the yolks; you will not need them for this dish.) Melt 1 tablespoon butter in a saucepan or skillet; sauté the onions for 2 minutes, then add the mushrooms and cook an additional minute. Remove to an absorbent cloth or paper towel to drain. Add the remaining 2 tablespoons butter to the saucepan; when it melts, begin sprinkling in the flour, stirring to form a *roux*. When this is smooth, stir in the cream, then the sherry, adding pepper and nutmeg while blending. Add the mushrooms and onions to this sauce; it should form a stiff paste. If not, add a little more flour. Set it aside to cool, then stuff the egg-white cases, rounding to resemble whole eggs. Beat the raw egg, dip the stuffed cases in it, then roll in breadcrumbs. Fry in deep fat until crusty, about 3 or 4 minutes. Makes 6 portions.

You are now left with six perfectly good hard-cooked egg yolks. What do you plan to do with them? This is a challenge to your ingenuity as a creative cook.

▪ *EGGS VERDI*

> 6 *hard-cooked eggs*
> 1 *cup cooked ground ham*
> ½ *teaspoon minced chervil*
> ½ *teaspoon minced parsley*
> ½ *teaspoon minced shallots*
> *Dash salt*
> *Dash cayenne*
> 3 *tablespoons heavy cream*
> 1 *tablespoon flour*
> *Fat for deep frying*
> 3 *tablespoons Sauce Suprême* (*page* 282)
> 1 *tablespoon chopped parsley*

Halve the eggs lengthwise, remove the yolks and reserve the egg-white cases. Blend the yolks with the ham, chervil, parsley, shallots, salt and cayenne; use the cream to bind them into a paste, adding a little flour if needed. Stuff the egg-white cases, roll them in flour and fry in deep fat 3 to 4 minutes, until brown. Spoon the sauce over the eggs and sprinkle them with a little chopped parsley before serving. Makes 6 portions.

▪ *EGGS VERDIER*

A creation of the great Parisian restaurateur whose name it bears, and a specialty of the house at his Maison d'Or when it was the headquarters for good eating during the 1870s.

> 6 *hard-cooked eggs*
> 1 *tablespoon minced* foie gras
> 6 *thick slices sweet onion*
> 2 *tablespoons butter*
> 3 *tablespoons Béchamel Sauce* (*page* 280)
> 1 *teaspoon curry powder*
> 2 *tablespoons grated Parmesan cheese*

Split the eggs lengthwise, remove the yolks and reserve the egg-white cases. Mash the yolks, blend with the *foie gras* and stuff the cases, rounding them off to use all the stuffing. Sauté the onion slices very lightly in butter, handling them carefully so they will stay together. Return the slices to a warm plate, put two egg halves on each and cover with the Béchamel Sauce into which has been stirred the curry powder. Sprinkle with Parmesan and glaze under the broiler until the cheese browns. Makes 6 portions.

■ EGG CASSEROLES

Here are casseroles using eggs in almost every fashion: whole, hard-cooked, poached and scrambled. They come from the United States, France, Italy and South America.

■ *UOVA ALLA CACCIATORA* (*Eggs au Chasseur,* *Hunter's Eggs*)

This version seems to be the favored one in the land where this worldwide egg dish originated; there it is usually prepared as a casserole. In France, it is usually served in individual ramekins. Take your choice.

> ½ *cup olive oil*
> ½ *cup minced onions*
> 8 *chicken livers*
> ½ *teaspoon powdered basil*
> 1 *teaspoon minced parsley*
> 2 *tablespoons chopped shallots*
> ½ *teaspoon salt*
> ¼ *teaspoon pepper*
> 3 *skinned ripe tomatoes*
> 1 *clove minced garlic*
> 1 *cup dry white wine*
> 1 *cup chopped mushrooms*
> 4 *eggs*
> ¾ *cup grated Parmesan cheese*

With oil in a skillet over low heat, sauté the onions until they begin to become transparent. Add the chicken livers and sauté them, then add the basil, parsley, shallots, salt and pepper. Chop the peeled tomatoes coarsely, and put them along with their juices into the pan; add the garlic, then pour in the wine. Stir occasionally, mashing the tomatoes a little with the spoon. Take out the chicken livers and set them aside; add the mushrooms. Cook the sauce 15 to 20 minutes, until one-third of the liquid has cooked away, then transfer it to a buttered casserole. Slide the eggs onto the surface of the sauce; by now it should be thick enough to support them. Lay a chicken liver beside each egg, and sprinkle the surface with grated Parmesan. Cook 20 to 25 minutes in a preheated 350-degree oven; the sauce should be thick, the eggs firmly set and the top nicely browned when served. Serves 4.

Other versions of the same dish will be found on pages 138 and 201. Chasseur Sauce, which is often poured on scrambled eggs when they are served with chicken livers, will be found on page 276.

■ FLORIDA EGGS

> 4 hard-cooked eggs
> ½ cup light cream
> 1 bayleaf
> 2 whole cloves
> 2½ cups tomato juice or thinned tomato paste
> 1 clove minced garlic
> 1½ cups coarsely chopped onion
> 2 tablespoons chopped mushrooms
> 1 tablespoon chopped green pepper
> 1 tablespoon chopped celeriac or celery heart
> 1 teaspoon salt
> ½ teaspoon pepper
> Breadcrumb–Cheese Glaze (page 291)

Remove the yolks from the hard-cooked eggs and chop the whites coarsely. Scald the cream with the bayleaf and cloves; strain the liquid. Mash the egg yolks with the cream, and blend with the tomato juice. Add the garlic, onion, mushrooms, green pepper, celeriac, salt and pepper; blend by stirring frequently as the mixture simmers 10 minutes in a saucepan on low heat. Transfer to a buttered casserole or individual ramekins. Sprinkle the top thickly with the glazing mix, and bake 10 minutes in a preheated 300-degree oven. Finish under the broiler if necessary to brown the top. Serves 4.

■ EGG FONDUE

Half the fun of a fondue is in the dunking, but if you'll settle for less fun and a fondue served with a spoon, here it is.

> 1½ *pounds aged Emmenthaler or Gruyère cheese*
> ½ *cup flour*
> 3 *cups dry white wine*
> ¼ *cup Kirsch or cognac* (*dry gin can also be used*)
> 4 *eggs*
> ½ *teaspoon cornstarch*
> 2 *cups very dry, very coarse breadcrumbs*
> *Paprika*

Cut the cheese into ½-inch dice; dredge it in the flour, covering all surfaces of the cheese. Over very low heat bring the wine to a simmer in the pan you will use, either the fondue *caquelon* or a casserole. When the wine begins to bubble, add the cheese, stirring while it melts. Put in half the Kirsch and stir until smooth. Beat the eggs lightly. Take the casserole off the heat and stir vigorously while pouring in the eggs in a slow, steady stream. Stir in the cornstarch, then the breadcrumbs. Dust the surface with paprika and cook 15 to 20 minutes in a preheated 250-degree oven. Serves 6.

If you use a wine of light acidity, such as a Rhine wine, it may be necessary to add 1 to 2 tablespoons lemon juice to get a smooth mixture; do this if the cheese begins to string or lump. Remember, you must use an aged, natural cheese. Process cheeses will not work.

▪ *FRENCH EGG PIE*

> 1 *batch Pastry Dough* (*page* 291)
> 1 *cup sliced parboiled mushrooms*
> 8 *parboiled link sausages*
> 4 *eggs*
> ¼ *teaspoon salt*
> *Dash cayenne*
> *Pinch powdered cloves*
> ½ *cup light cream*
> 1 *teaspoon flour*
> 1 *teaspoon butter*
> ½ *teaspoon dry mustard*
> ½ *cup sherry*

Butter a pie plate or shallow casserole, and line it with half the rolled-out dough. Spread the mushroom slices to cover the bottom, and arrange the sausages so that they will form compartments for the eggs; 1 egg and 2 sausages will be taken in every slice of the pie when cut. Slip an egg into each of the compartments; dust the eggs with salt, cayenne and cloves. Place the cream in a saucepan over lowest heat, blend the flour and butter into a *manié* and add a little at a time to the cream as it is stirred; do not allow the cream to boil. Add the mustard. When it begins to thicken, pour this mixture into the pan and cover with the rest of the rolled-out pastry. Make a hole in the center of the top crust and slash it in several places to allow steam to escape. (Slashes marking the location of the sausages will guide you in cutting later.) Bake 10 to 15 minutes in a preheated 325-degree oven, until the crust begins to brown. At this point, using a small funnel, pour the sherry through the hole in the center of the top crust, and return to the oven for 5 minutes. Serve at once. Serves 4.

▪ *HUEVOS EN RABO* (*Egg Casserole*)

Several versions of this dish are to be met with in Mexico and in Central and South America; some use sautéed eggs or poached eggs, and one or two incorporate sliced, hard-cooked eggs simmered in the sauce. In one version the cheese topping is replaced by a coating of heavy cream floated on the surface of the sauce, a procedure that requires a steady hand both in pouring and in placing the casserole in the oven. In its native habitat, the cheese most used is a firm, light, goat's milk cheese; importation of this cheese into the United States is forbidden, as it is made from unpasteurized milk.

> 3 *large mild green chilis* (*poblano chilis are usual, but Bell pepper also is good*)
> 1 *small, finely chopped onion*
> *Oil or fat for frying*
> 3 *peeled ripe tomatoes or* 1½ *cups well-drained canned tomatoes*
> ½ *teaspoon salt*
> ¼ *teaspoon chili molido* (*chili powder*)
> 4 *eggs*
> 6 *slices Monterey Jack or other very mild cheese; they must cover the surface of the casserole used*

Skin the peppers by plunging them into boiling water, then cold water, or by roasting 10 minutes in a preheated 400-degree oven; either way slips the pepper skins. Slice the peppers lengthwise into halves, and remove the stems, seeds and pith. In a heavy skillet slowly sauté the peppers and onions in oil or fat until they are tender, but still firm. Add the tomatoes, salt and chili molido; simmer 10 minutes, until most of the liquid is gone. Space the eggs on the sauce, and cover with slices of cheese. Cover the skillet and cook 15 to 20 minutes in a preheated 350-degree oven. Uncover and cook an additional 5 minutes to allow the cheese to form a light crust. Serves 4.

▪ *EGGS JOSEPHINE*

> *4 poached eggs*
> *2 uncooked egg yolks*
> *1½ cups Béchamel Sauce (page 280)*
> *Dash salt*
> *Pinch nutmeg*
> *1 cup ground cooked ham*
> *2 tablespoons butter*
> *3 tablespoons grated Parmesan cheese*

Drain the poached eggs well. In a double boiler, beat the uncooked egg yolks into the sauce with the salt and nutmeg; when they are blended smoothly, stir in the ham. Pour into a well-buttered casserole or shallow baking dish, and space the eggs on top of the sauce. Sprinkle the top thickly with grated cheese, and dot with flakes of butter. Bake 5 minutes in a preheated 250-degree oven; finish under the broiler if necessary to complete the glaze. Serves 4.

▪ *MATELOTE OF EGGS* (*Egg Stew*)

Strictly speaking, a *matelote* is a stew of tiny onions and new potatoes in white wine; the meat traditionally was fish, but over the years it has come to include such light meats as veal and chicken. This *matelote* with eggs is another of Alexandre Dumas' originals.

> *2 large sweet onions*
> *4 cups white wine*
> *1 teaspoon salt*
> *¼ teaspoon pepper*
> Bouquet garni *in cloth bag of bayleaf, 2 cloves, clove*
> *garlic, sprig chervil*
> *4 poached or lightly sautéed eggs*
> *3 cups tiny pearl onions*
> *3 cups tiny new potatoes (or rounds cut with ball*
> *cutter from large potato)*

Slice the large onions into a skillet, cover them with wine, sprinkle with salt and pepper and add the *bouquet garni*. Bring the wine quickly to a boil, reduce the heat and simmer gently 10 minutes.

Place the eggs in the bottom of a buttered casserole; strew them with the pearl onions and tiny potatoes. Strain the liquid from the skillet into the casserole; if it does not cover the contents, add a little wine. (Discard the sliced onion and spices.) Place in a preheated 375-degree oven for 10 to 15 minutes, or until the potatoes are tender to the fork. (Serve, Dumas admonishes, with good, crusty bread to dip in the sauce.) Serves 4.

If you would make a traditional *matelote*, choose boneless fillets of any fish, and poach them on top of the onion slices as the wine simmers during the first cooking step; then lay them atop the eggs in the casserole before completing the cooking.

▪ *EGGS MIRELLE*

> 1 *uncooked egg*
> 3 *cups boiled rice*
> ¼ *teaspoon saffron*
> ½ *teaspoon salt*
> ¼ *teaspoon pepper*
> 2 *medium-sized firm, ripe tomatoes*
> 3 *tablespoons butter*
> 2 *tablespoons sour cream*
> 4 *poached or lightly sautéed eggs*

Beat the uncooked egg lightly, adding the rice, saffron, salt and pepper. Poach in a *bain-marie* in a ring mold for 15 minutes in a preheated 350-degree oven, and turn out on a round chop plate or platter. Peel the tomatoes and chop them coarsely; sauté them in butter for 5 minutes at lowest heat. Stir in the sour cream just before removing from heat. Fill the center of the ring mold with the tomatoes, and lay the poached or sautéed eggs on top. Serves 4.

▪ *PARISIAN EGG RING*

> 4 *eggs*
> 4 *tablespoons milk or light cream*
> *Dash salt*
> *Dash pepper*
> 1 *egg white*
> 1½ *cups Sauce Soubise (page 281)*
> 2 *cups chopped precooked meat: veal, chicken, ham, tongue or pork*

Beat the 4 eggs with the milk, salt and pepper. Scramble them very,

very soft in a lightly greased skillet. Whip the egg white until it forms soft peaks, and fold it into the scrambled eggs; place the eggs in a well-buttered ring mold, and poach in a *bain-marie* 15 to 20 minutes in a preheated 300-degree oven. Bring the sauce to a simmer in a double boiler; mix in the chopped meat. Turn the ring mold out on a platter and fill its center with the sauced meat. (Or vary the sauce according to the meat: Suprême for veal or chicken, Béarnaise for beef, Mornay or Chivry for fish, and so on for an endless number of combinations.) Serves 4.

▪ SARDINIAN EGGS

> 6 *large, thinly sliced mushrooms*
> 2 *tablespoons olive oil*
> ½ *cup chopped artichoke hearts*
> ½ *cup tomato juice or thinned tomato paste*
> ½ *cup white wine*
> 1 *tablespoon chopped shallots or chives*
> *Dash salt*
> *Dash pepper*
> 4 *eggs*
> 1 *tablespoon grated Parmesan cheese*
> 4 *strips crisp bacon*

Sauté the mushrooms in the oil for 2 minutes, then remove to an oiled casserole, spreading them to cover its bottom. Sauté the artichoke for 2 or 3 minutes, and while it is in the oil add to it the tomato juice, wine, shallots, salt and pepper. Simmer 5 minutes over medium heat. Pour this sauce into the casserole, slide the eggs on top and bake 15 to 20 minutes in a preheated 350-degree oven. Remove from the oven, sprinkle the grated cheese over the top, crumble the bacon slices and spread them evenly over the cheese; return the dish to the oven for 5 minutes. Serves 4.

▪ ASPIC-MOLDED EGGS (*Eggs en Gelee*)

Eggs in aspic, whether hard-cooked, *mollet* or poached, form an appealing display, which may be as simple or as elaborate as your patience allows. It takes time, for this presentation was evolved in the deluxe hotels and restaurants and the great château kitchens when help was plentiful and cheap. It is a type of service that once was featured at all buffet affairs, and is once more swinging back into popularity. There is more patience and imagination involved in preparing molded eggs than there is expense, and the combinations of garnishes are unlimited.

A molded egg may be a simple poached egg on a *croustade*, coated with aspic and with a cross of pimiento strips on its top. It may be half a hard-cooked egg encased in a shallow mold and turned out on an artichoke heart, or a whole egg *mollet* set on end in a deep aspic-filled mold which has previously been lined with the garnish. The aspic itself may be flavored with wine or a thinned sauce, and usually the egg is coated with a white Chaud-Froid Sauce that enhances its appearance before the aspic glaze is applied. Chaud-Froid Sauce adheres better to aspic than to egg white, so a thin coating of aspic is generally brushed on the egg before saucing; the garnish is then stuck on, and a final thicker coating of aspic added. These eggs should be served on a *croustade*, which has less tendency to become soggy than does toast.

A sampling of the traditional services of aspic-molded eggs follows the recipes for Chaud-Froid Sauce and Aspic, but be uninhibited in creating your own.

■ *Chaud-Froid Sauce:* Simmer ½ cup chicken broth or mushroom broth, add 1½ cups Sauce Velouté (page 279), 1½ cups chicken or veal jelly (use canned consommé madrilène) and ¾ cup cream. Simmer until it is reduced one-third, and chill. Test its coating qualities by dipping a cool metal spoon in the cooled sauce; it should cling in a thin, even layer. If it does not, reduce further by simmering over very low heat. Chaud-Froid Sauce will set when cold, but it can be heated over very low heat to restore it to a liquid condition. It keeps well under refrigeration in a tightly closed container.

■ *Aspic:* Dissolve 1½ tablespoons plain gelatin in ¼ cup cool water; add it to 1½ cups simmering chicken or veal broth. Stir in ¼ cup sherry after removing from heat, and allow it to cool.

■ *Aspic-Molded Eggs:* Have the eggs chilled and the aspic liquid; coat with a thin layer of aspic and chill until it sets. Apply a coating of Chaud-Froid Sauce and stick the garnishes on it; chill, then apply a final coating of aspic. The eggs are refrigerated until a quarter-hour before they are served.

■ *EGGS ALEXANDRA*

Place a poached egg on a shallow tartlet shell; lay a thin cross of black caviar across the top and add a ring of caviar between the edge of the trimmed egg and the tartlet shell. Makes 1 portion.

▪ *ASPIC-MOLDED EGGS À L'ANCIENNE*

Place an egg *mollet* on an oval *croustade;* modify the aspic by adding Madeira. Makes 1 portion.

▪ *ANDALUSIAN EGGS*

Place a poached egg on a large *croustade;* the aspic is modified by the addition of Tomato Sauce (page 278); thin pimiento strips are arranged to crisscross the egg under its aspic glaze. Makes 1 portion.

▪ *ASPIC-MOLDED EGGS ARGENTEUIL*

Stand an egg *mollet* or hard-cooked egg on end on a slice of boiled potato with a depression scooped out for the egg. The Chaud-Froid Sauce is modified by the addition of puréed asparagus, the egg tiny stars or crescents cut from thin truffle slices (or black olives) put on it before the final aspic glaze is applied. Makes 1 portion.

▪ *ASPIC-MOLDED EGGS AUBER*

Slice a hard-cooked egg in half crosswise, and stand it on a chicken-stuffed tomato half the same diameter as the egg; the egg and tomato are bound by a coating of aspic on their cut surfaces. Place the tomato on a *croustade*, decorate the top of the egg with truffle or black olive shapes and coat with aspic, or simply with a curl of Mayonnaise (pages 285-286) on top of the final glaze. Makes 1 portion.

▪ *EGGS EN BELLE VUE*

Stand an egg *mollet* on end on a slice of tomato that is on a round *croustade;* modify the aspic with Tomato Sauce (page 278) and press a spiral of pimiento strips into the Chaud-Froid Sauce before the final glazing. Makes 1 portion.

▪ *ASPIC-MOLDED EGGS BERNIS*

Place a poached egg on a patty of ground chicken meat atop a round *croustade;* bind the chicken meat with Mayonnaise (pages 285-286) and a little aspic; coat the egg with Chaud-Froid Sauce and center a ripe olive circle in its yolk before applying the final aspic glaze. Makes 1 portion.

▪ EGGS CAPUCINE

Place a poached egg on a patty of codfish or tuna atop a round *croustade*. Coat the egg with Chaud-Froid Sauce, then cover half of it with puréed truffle; apply a final aspic glaze. (The round patties called for in this type of service may be prepared most easily by rolling out the meat, usually mixed with Mayonnaise [pages 285-286] or a sauce and a little aspic, into a thin layer, and cutting the rounds with a cookie cutter of the proper size.) Makes 1 portion.

▪ ASPIC-MOLDED EGGS CARÊME

Cook a shirred egg until it is firm, trim it into an oval shape and wipe it free of any cooking fat; lay it atop a patty of pounded lobster meat that has been bound with Mayonnaise (pages 285-286) and a little aspic. Use only a clear aspic glaze with truffle or black olive decorative shapes pressed into it under the final coating. Place the patty and egg on an oval *croustade*. Makes 1 portion.

▪ ASPIC-MOLDED EGGS CHARTRES

Dip an egg *mollet* in beaten egg white and roll it in tender fresh tarragon leaves that have been finely minced. Place the egg on a *croustade* that has been spread thickly with Mayonnaise (pages 285-286), and coat it with aspic.

For another traditional service, slice a hard-cooked egg lengthwise and place it on an oval *croustade* thickly coated with Mayonnaise (pages 285-286). Press a single tender tarragon leaf, which has been blanched in white wine, along the egg's length. Cover the egg with Chaud-Froid Sauce and apply a final glaze. Makes 1 portion.

Eggs à l'Estragon and *Tarragon Eggs* are other names for this presentation.

▪ ASPIC-MOLDED EGGS CHÂTELAINE
(*Housekeeper's Eggs*)

Place a poached egg or half a hard-cooked egg that has been cut lengthwise in a shallow tartshell filled with chestnut purée; crisscross thin strips of pickled tongue in a Chaud-Froid coating and glaze. Makes 1 portion.

▪ *EGGS COLBERT*

Coat a poached egg with Chaud-Froid Sauce; cover the sauce with alternate stripes or squares of puréed spinach and puréed *pâte de foie gras* to which a little aspic has been added. Put on a final aspic coating, and place the egg on a *croustade*. If this is the only type of molded eggs offered, the platter on which they are served is filled in its center with a mound of diced mixed vegetables and diced aspic. Makes 1 portion.

▪ *EGGS COLINETTE*

Place an egg *mollet* in a shallow tartshell half-filled with finely diced egg yolk and truffle bound with Chaud-Froid Sauce; the egg is coated with Chaud-Froid Sauce, the truffle decorations are pressed on and the egg is glazed. If it is served on a platter, the center of the dish should contain julienne-cut celery, carrots and cucumbers on diced aspic. Makes 1 portion.

▪ *ASPIC-MOLDED EGGS ESPAGNOLE*

Trim a poached egg so that only a thin rim of white is left; center the egg on a thin, thin slice of sweet onion that has been marinated in salted water and drained. Around the rim of the onion place halves of tiny cherry tomatoes, which have been seeded and marinated in red wine vinegar, pressing them into a coating of aspic; the onion slice should be placed on a large *croustade* and the whole glazed again with plain aspic. Makes 1 portion.

▪ *EGGS FROU-FROU*

Spread a *croustade* with Mayonnaise (pages 285-286); place a poached egg on top, and thickly coat it with Chaud-Froid Sauce blended with the mashed yolk of a hard-cooked egg. Place a black olive ring in the center, and add a final aspic glaze. Makes 1 portion.

▪ *MUSCOVITE EGGS*

Cut the top and bottom from a hard-cooked egg to give the egg the shape of a small barrel; withdraw the yolk from an opening in the bottom, and mash it with caviar sprinkled with lemon juice. Stuff the mixture back into the egg-white case, using any remaining yolk to spread on an artichoke heart. Set the egg on the artichoke and glaze it with aspic; press an anchovy fillet around its base and add a final glaze of aspic. Makes 1 portion.

▪ *NANTUA EGGS*

Trim the top and bottom from a hard-cooked egg to give the egg the shape of a barrel; withdraw the yolk from a cut in the bottom and mash it with an equal amount of pounded shrimp and the trimmings of egg white, minced very fine. Stuff this mixture into the egg-white case and stand the egg on an artichoke heart. Glaze the egg with aspic, and place a tiny curled shrimp on its top before the final glaze is applied. Makes 1 portion.

▪ *EGGS FOR NEW YEAR'S*

Split a hard-cooked egg lengthwise; blend the yolk with Mayonnaise (pages 285-286) to which onion juice has been added. Stuff the egg-white case until it is level, spreading the remainder of the yolk mixture on an oval *croustade*. Place the egg on the *croustade* cut side down, and coat the whole with Chaud-Froid Sauce. Write the date of the New Year in thin strips of pimiento or parboiled green pepper on top of the egg; add a final aspic glaze. Makes 1 portion.

▪ *EGGS POLIGNAC*

Lay a poached egg in a shallow aspic-filled mold so that when unmolded its yolk will be on top; unmold it on a *croustade* and garnish the top with a curl of Mustard Butter (page 288) or Mayonnaise (pages 285-286). Makes 1 portion.

▪ *EGGS RUBENS*

Place an egg *mollet* in a deep mold that has been lined with a thin coating of aspic with tender young parboiled hop shoots pressed into it; put the egg in, fill the mold with aspic and chill it. Turn it out onto a drained aspic-filled tomato slice atop a *croustade*. Makes 1 portion.

▪ *ASPIC-MOLDED EGGS TROUBADOR*

Place an egg *mollet* in a shallow tartshell half-filled with a purée of *pâté de foie gras;* add enough purée to fill the shell level. Coat with aspic, place a small button mushroom on top of the egg and glaze again. Makes 1 portion.

● ●

Surprising Egg Dishes

IN THE RECIPES in this chapter, no holds are barred; indeed, some of them have all the elements of a *savate* or karate attack. Here is the chef's imagination unrestrained; eggs cooked with such unlikely companions as beer, club soda, champagne and tea. This chapter has the egg soups, the fried custards, the eggs cooked on a rotisserie spit. In it you will find that you do not need to wait ten centuries to enjoy a Chinese "thousand-year" egg; you will learn how to make Egg Sausage; and you will meet a surprising number of unlikely combinations that have joined the select list of classic dishes.

Not all the dishes are wild; they are odd, perhaps, but not insane. Though the combinations are those you might not come up with yourself, their results are pleasantly surprising; where the ingredients have small novelty, the unusual is in the presentation of the dishes, or the manner of their preparation. Omelets in the "surprising" category will be found in their own chapter under that listing; here the dishes are divided as in other chapters by the manner in which the eggs are cooked.

▪ POACHED EGGS

These are still based on the individual service or portion, and may include 1 or 2 eggs with little or no change in the quantities of the other ingredients.

▪ *EGGS AIGRE-DOUX* (*Sweet and Sour Eggs*)

If you enjoy the Chinese sweet and sour pork, try transferring the subtleties of its flavor to a base of poached eggs.

> 1 *toast round*
> 1½ *tablespoons Madeira Sauce* (*page 277*)
> 1 *tablespoon currant jelly*
> 1 *poached egg*

Moisten the toast round lightly with the Madeira Sauce. Melt the currant jelly by pouring into it a few drops of very hot water and stirring until it is the consistency of cold honey. Coat the egg with the jelly, and place it on the toast round. Pour over it the remainder of the sauce. Makes 1 portion.

▪ *EGGS COBB*

Irvin S. Cobb, author of so many laugh-provoking stories of the South, was as noted an eater as he was a humorist. It's only fitting that this unorthodox dish bear his name.

> 1 *cup white cornmeal*
> ½ *teaspoon salt*
> ½ *cup fresh corn kernels* (*or canned whole kernel*
>   *corn, well drained*)
> 1 *uncooked egg*
> *Bacon drippings for frying*
> 4 *poached eggs or eggs* mollet

Sift together the cornmeal and salt; add about 1 cup of boiling water slowly while stirring, to produce a heavy batter. It should be almost too stiff to stir. Add the corn and mix well, then beat in the uncooked egg. Form the batter into two large oval pones, at least 1½ inches thick, and fry them in hot bacon drippings deep enough to come halfway up the sides of the pones. When they are brown on the bottom, turn and cook until they are brown on top. Split the pones and scoop out 4 cavities in the soft interiors, each large enough to accommodate 1 egg. Insert the poached eggs. Drain the skillet of all but a thin coating of fat. Crumble the soft cornmeal removed from the pones into very small bits, and brown it in the skillet. Sprinkle the browned crumbs over the egg in the hollowed cornpone. Serves 4.

▪ *EGGS DIANE*

> 1 *extra-thick toast round*
> 2 *tablespoons butter*
> 3 *tablespoons ground meat of any wild game or fowl*
> 1 *teaspoon ground pickle: gherkins are best because*
>   *they are usually crisp*
> 3 *tablespoons concentrated Sauce Espagnole (page*
>   *275), reduced by simmering until very thick*
> 1 *poached egg*

Sauté the toast in the butter until it is crisp; make a high mound of the mixed meat and pickle bound with 1 tablespoon sauce. Make a depression on top of the mound of meat and insert the egg; brush it thickly with the sauce and glaze it for 1 or 2 minutes under the broiler. Makes 1 portion.

▪ *EGGS ST. HUBERT* substitutes Sauce Poivrade (page 278) for the Sauce Espagnole.

▪ *FRIED POACHED EGGS*

> 1 *poached egg*
> 1 *tablespoon flour*
> 1 *uncooked egg white*
> 1½ *tablespoons breadcrumbs*
> *Oil or fat for deep frying*

Roll the poached egg in the flour, dip it in the egg white and roll it in breadcrumbs; fry in a basket in deep fat until the crust is crisply brown. Makes 1 portion.

▪ *HOT POACHED EGGS*

> 2 *cups rich milk or light cream*
> 1 *teaspoon Tabasco sauce*

> *Dash salt*
> *Dash pepper*
> *Dash cayenne*
> *2 egg yolks*
> *2 teaspoons red wine vinegar*
> *1 egg*
> *1½ tablespoons coarse cracker crumbs*

Heat the milk to the scalding point but do not allow it to boil; use a pan that can be tightly covered, preferably one that can also serve as a service dish. Add the Tabasco sauce, salt, pepper and cayenne to the milk. Beat the egg yolks briskly with the wine vinegar and add them to the simmering milk, stirring continually to keep the mixture from curdling. When it is well blended, remove the pan from the heat, slide in the raw egg, cover the pan at once and let it sit 10 minutes. Just before serving, sprinkle the cracker crumbs over the surface. Makes 1 portion.

▪ *EGGS MARIANNE*

> *2 tablespoons butter*
> *½ firm, ripe tomato, peeled and drained*
> *1 thick slice potato*
> *1 poached egg*
> *Dash salt*
> *Dash pepper*

Melt the butter over low heat and gently sauté the tomato half, removing it from the pan while it is still firm. Sauté the potato slice until it is done but neither soft nor crisp. Set the tomato, cut side up, on a warm serving plate, and slip the egg into its cavity, cutting away as much of the tomato's dividing membranes as is necessary to let the egg sit below the rim of the tomato. Set the potato slice on the tomato half; it should be trimmed to cover it neatly and completely. Dust with salt and pepper and serve. Makes 1 portion.

▪ *EGGS MIRETTE* (*Goggle-Eyed Eggs*)

> *2 or 3 egg yolks*
> *2 tablespoons Sauce Velouté* (*page* 279)
> *1 teaspoon Madeira*
> *1 shallow tartshell*
> *1 thick slice cooked breast of chicken*

Poach the egg yolks. Simmer the sauce, adding the Madeira, until it is blended. Brush the inside of the tartshell with the sauce and arrange the poached egg yolks in it. Cover it with the slice of chicken breast trimmed to fit inside the shell, and pour the remainder of the sauce on top. Makes 1 portion.

▪ *EGGS MOSCOW*

> 1 *egg*
> 1 *or 2 teaspoons caviar*
> 1 *tablespoon flour*
> 1 *egg white*
> 2 *tablespoons very fine breadcrumbs*
> *Oil or fat for deep frying*

Poach the egg in only enough water to cover the white; the yolk must be very liquid. Drain well, remove the yolk with a spoon and fill the cavity with caviar. Roll the egg with flour, dip it in the uncooked egg white and roll it in breadcrumbs. (The expression "roll" is used in its cooking sense; it will not be possible to turn the egg yolk side down. It must be covered with the flour, egg white and breadcrumbs while upright.) Place the egg in a basket and fry it in deep oil or fat until the breadcrumbs are crisp. Makes 1 portion.

▪ *EGGS POACHED IN RED WINE*

> 1 *egg*
> ½ *cup dry red wine*
> 1 *buttered toast round*
> *Dash cayenne*

Poach the egg in the wine at very low heat. Transfer it from the saucepan to the toast round without draining it; dust it with cayenne and serve. Salt is an enemy in this recipe; if used it will destroy the flavor. Makes 1 portion.

▪ *EGGS RODRIGUEZ*

> 2 *thin slices sweet onion*
> 2 *thin slices raw apple*
> 1½ *teaspoons bacon drippings*
> *Dash salt*

Dash pepper
1 poached egg
1 tablespoon grated mild cheese

Over medium heat sauté the onion slices and apple slices in the bacon fat. Season with salt and pepper while they cook. Lift the slices to a warmed serving plate and slide the egg on top of them. Cover it with grated cheese; place it under the broiler until the cheese melts. Makes 1 portion.

∎ *EGGS ROMANOV*

In today's Russia, these would probably be called "Eggs Commissar," or "Eggs Party Chairman," but they originated when Russia and Czar were synonymous.

2 tablespoons olive or peanut oil
½ cup tomato juice
Generous dash Tabasco sauce
4 eggs
½ pint beer

Simmer the oil and tomato juice together in a skillet, and stir until they are blended, adding the Tabasco sauce. Poach the eggs in this liquid until they are done, and lift them out with a slotted spoon; place them on a warm serving plate (or on toast slices). Strain the poaching liquid to remove bits of froth and divided egg white, and bring up the heat until it is just below the boiling point. Pour in the beer—which should be at room temperature—and stir the mixture a half-dozen times; pour it over the eggs and serve at once. Serves 4.

∎ *EGGS VILLEROI*

1 poached egg or egg mollet
2 large sprigs very fresh parsley
1 egg white
Oil or fat for deep frying
1 slice toast
1 teaspoon Anchovy Butter (*page* 288)

Prepare and fry the poached egg or egg *mollet* according to the recipe for "Fried Poached Eggs" on page 168. Dip the parsley in the egg white and plunge it into boiling oil until it is crisp and light brown. Spread the hot toast with Anchovy Butter. Arrange the parsley on the toast to form a nest for the egg. Makes 1 portion.

■ SCRAMBLED EGGS

■ *SCRAMBLED EGGS BOHÉMIENNE*

> 5 *eggs*
> 4 *individual Brioches* (*page* 290)
> 2 *tablespoons cooked chopped ham*
> 2 *tablespoons chopped* foie gras (*pages* 292-293)
> *Truffle grating or Truffle Essence*
> 2 *tablespoons Sauce Robert* (*page* 278)

Soft-scramble the eggs. Cut the tops off the Brioches (rolls may be used, of course) and scoop out the centers to form cases. Fill with alternate layers of eggs, ham, eggs and *foie gras*, the truffle being mixed with the meat. Put a spoonful of sauce on top of the final layer of filling, replace the tops of the Brioches and warm for 10 minutes in a preheated 200-degree oven. Brush the outsides and tops of the Brioches generously with the remaining sauce. Serves 4.

In some versions of this recipe, the chopped *foie gras* and ham are mixed with the eggs as they cook; the Brioche cases are toasted before filling, and are brushed with sauce and glazed just before serving.

■ *EGGS SCRAMBLED WITH CLUB SODA*

> 5 *eggs*
> *Dash salt*
> *Dash pepper*
> 1 *cup club soda*
> 2 *slices thin dry toast*

Beat the eggs with the seasonings and club soda, and soft-scramble them in a lightly greased pan; constantly pull the cooked portions from the pan's bottom and sides as the eggs cook. Serve over toast. Serves 4.

■ *SESAME SEED EGGS*

> 1½ *tablespoons sesame seeds*
> 1 *tablespoon butter*
> 5 *eggs*
> 5 *tablespoons milk or light cream*

Dash salt
Dash pepper

Over medium heat, sauté the sesame seeds in butter until they are just turning color. Beat the eggs with the milk and seasonings, reduce the heat very low and soft-scramble the eggs. Serves 4.

Through substitution, this recipe can be adapted to add a new crisp note of interest with several ingredients besides sesame seeds. Try chopped almonds or peanuts, hulled sunflower seeds, chopped cardamon seeds or dill seeds. Or break small sprigs of dry basil into seed-sized bits; your choice is as wide as you allow your imagination to roam.

■ SOUFFLÉ-CAPPED SCRAMBLED EGGS

This is not, to be sure, a true soufflé; it might be most accurately described as a mock soufflé for timid cooks.

5 eggs plus 2 egg whites
3 tablespoons milk or light cream
Dash salt
Dash pepper
*1½ cups mixed precooked vegetables, or 1½ cups
    chopped cooked meat*

Separate 2 of the whole eggs and add their whites to the 2 extra egg whites. Put them aside. Beat the remaining 3 whole eggs and the 2 yolks with the milk and seasonings, and scramble very soft in a lightly greased skillet. Transfer the scrambled eggs to a well-buttered casserole and cover them with the vegetables or meat in an even layer. Beat the four egg whites with a dash of salt until they form soft peaks, and pour them into the casserole on top of the vegetables or meat. Bake 10 to 15 minutes in a preheated 300-degree oven, until the meringue rises and browns. Serves 4.

■ SWEDISH EGGS

5 eggs
4 tablespoons milk or light cream
Dash pepper
1 teaspoon caraway seed
2 teaspoons drained capers

Beat the eggs with the milk and pepper (the capers will provide the salt); let the caraway seeds warm for a few minutes in a lightly greased skillet over low heat to liberate their flavor. Bruise the capers lightly. Add the eggs to the seeds in the skillet; as they are stirred, drop in the capers, a few at a time. Scramble medium-soft for best flavor. Serves 4.

▪ SHIRRED EGGS

As always, the shirred egg dishes can be prepared with either 1 or 2 eggs depending on the size of the appetite of the individual served. No additional ingredients are needed when 2 eggs are used.

▪ *EGGS ANTIBOISE*

On the Bordeaux coast where this dish originated, the fish used in its preparation are the tiny *nonats*, which correspond very closely to the smelt or whitebait or gudgeon of the United States.

> ¾ *cup whitebait, smelt or gudgeon*
> *Fat for deep frying*
> 1 *clove garlic*
> ½ *cup grated Gruyère or other mild cheese*
> 1 *egg*
> *Dash salt*
> *Dash pepper*
> 1 *tablespoon breadcrumbs*

Deep-fry the fish in the fat until it is very crisp (put the clove of garlic in the fat, but remove it before it burns up; it will brown faster than the fish). Drain the fish. Cover a greased shirring dish with the grated cheese and spread the cooked fish on top; slide the egg over it. Cook 8 to 10 minutes in a preheated 350-degree oven. Dust the egg with salt and pepper (use garlic salt if you like the extra flavor). Turn the shirring dish upside down on the serving plate, allowing the egg to remain on the bottom; sprinkle the soft cheese with the breadcrumbs and put the dish under the broiler a moment until they brown. Makes 1 portion.

▪ *EGGS BORDALUE*

> 2 *tablespoons Sauce Espagnole* (*page 275*)
> ½ *teaspoon hot water*

>*½ teaspoon white wine vinegar*
>*2 small sweet gherkins*
>*1 egg*
>*Breadcrumb–Cheese Glaze (page 291)*

In a saucepan blend the sauce, hot water and vinegar. Add the gherkins, chopped very fine. Cover the bottom of the shirring dish with a portion of the sauce, slide the egg into the dish and pour the remaining sauce over it. Sprinkle with the glaze mix. Cook 6 to 10 minutes in a preheated 375-degree oven. Makes 1 portion.

▪ EGGS AU DIABLE

>*2 tablespoons butter*
>*1 egg*
>*2 tablespoons heavy cream*
>*Dash salt*
>*Dash cayenne*
>*½ teaspoon Tabasco sauce*

Melt 1 tablespoon butter in the shirring dish, tilting the dish to spread it evenly, and slide in the egg. Cook 2 to 3 minutes in a preheated 350-degree oven. Warm the cream with the remaining butter and the salt and cayenne. Remove the shirring dish from the oven, and dash the Tabasco sauce over the egg. Pour in the seasoned warm cream and return to oven for 5 to 6 minutes. Makes 1 portion.

▪ REVERSE SHIRRED EGGS

This dish is easy to prepare for a group if you have a muffin tin with large compartments. If only a few are to be served, individual molds are better.

>*1½ tablespoons very fine breadcrumbs*
>*Dash salt*
>*Dash pepper*
>*½ teaspoon melted butter*
>*1 egg*
>*1 toast round*
>*1 sautéed mushroom cap*
>*1½ tablespoons Sauce Mornay (page 281)*

Mix the breadcrumbs with the seasonings, then with the melted butter. Line the well-greased molds with the crumbs. Put the egg into a mold; cook 12 to 15 minutes in a preheated 350-degree oven. Unmold on the toast round, top with the mushroom cap and spoon on the sauce. Makes 1 portion.

To unmold on a platter if a muffin tin is used, put a toast round over each egg, lay the platter face down on the tin, turn it over and lift the tin off.

▪ SAUTÉED OR FRIED EGGS

▪ *BAYONNAISE EGGS*

> 1 *slice pumpkin, ½ inch thick*
> 1 *toast round*
> 1 *tablespoon butter*
> *Salt*
> *Pepper*
> *Pinch nutmeg*
> 1 *sautéed egg*
> 2 *tablespoons Sauce Soubise (page 281)*

Parboil the pumpkin slice lightly; trim it to fit the toast round, drain it well and sauté it lightly in butter. Dust it with salt, pepper and nutmeg, and place it on the toast round. Top with the sautéed egg; spoon over it the warm Sauce Soubise. Makes 1 portion.

Any of the large, firm-fleshed squash, such as Hubbard, may be substituted for the pumpkin.

▪ *SICILIAN EGGS*

Served with chicken oven-cooked in the Italian style, with a sauce of tomatoes simmered with chopped onions and a little white wine, this dish is indeed surprising. It is also good as a light meal all by itself.

> ½ *small zucchini (6 to 7 inches long), cut lengthwise*
> 2 *teaspoons salt*
> 1 *egg*
> 1 *tablespoon olive oil*
> 1½ *teaspoons grated Parmesan cheese*

Score the face of the zucchini with several deep cuts and sprinkle it generously with salt; more than the 2 teaspoons indicated may be required. Let it stand 1 hour while the salt draws out the plant's juices, then scrape off the salt and wipe the squash with a damp cloth.

Sauté the egg in olive oil. It should be cooked very soft and folded in the European style (see page 37). Set the egg aside to drain. Place the zucchini face down in the oil and sauté it over low heat, about 5 minutes. Scoop out the pulp, leaving a thin layer on the skin. Blend the pulp with 1 tablespoon cheese, place the cooked egg in the shell and fill with the pulp. Sprinkle with the remaining cheese, and glaze under the broiler a minute. Makes 1 portion.

Please don't try to find 1 big zucchini, thinking you'll fill it with a half-dozen eggs and serve a crowd. A zucchini is the tenderest of all squashes, but if allowed to grow longer than 8 inches it is only fit to be plowed under. The best are about the size of a very large cucumber; the size used for this recipe should be a bit bigger than that.

▪ EGGS *EN COCOTTE*

Wine and raw beef are the most intriguing ingredients you will find in this small but select assortment.

▪ *EGGS CHAMBERTIN*

> 2 *tablespoons Red Wine Sauce* (*page* 283)
> 1 *egg*

If your sense of traditional obligation is very strong, you will make the Red Wine Sauce using Napoleon's favorite red wine, but the half-dozen of the choice Burgundies entitled to be recognized as Chambertin deserve a better fate than to go into a sauce. Use a good Burgundy, or a Pinot Noir from California, and make your Red Wine Sauce; it is the work of perhaps 15 to 20 minutes. When it is completed, put the necessary quantity into your *cocotte,* slip in an egg and cook in a *bain-marie* in a preheated 350-degree oven for 6 to 10 minutes, or half that time in a waterbath atop the stove. Makes 1 portion.

▪ *EGGS CHARTREUSE*

> 1½ *tablespoons of a mixture of carrots, turnips and*
> *green beans cut thin as toothpicks and short*
> *enough to go into the* cocotte
> 2 *or* 3 *thin slices of sausage* (*salami type*)
> 2 *or* 3 *tender inner cabbage leaves*
> 1 *egg*
> *Dash salt*

Dash pepper
1 *toast round or* croustade

Sliver the mixed vegetables and one slice of the sausage to look like stubby toothpicks, and drop them into boiling salted water for 1 or 2 minutes. Pass the cabbage leaves through the water, remembering that the objective is less to cook than to tenderize. Drain the vegetables well. Trim 1 cabbage leaf to line the buttered *cocotte* and put in the egg with a dash of salt and pepper; gently add the toothpick-like bits of vegetable and sausage. Seal and poach in a *bain-marie* 8 to 12 minutes in a 275-degree oven, or half as long in a waterbath on top of the stove. Trim the remaining cabbage leaves to cover the top of the toast round or *croustade*, placing the thin slices of sausage between them. Unmold the *cocotte* on the garnished *croustade*. If you want to serve this dish with a sauce, choose Mornay (page 281), Soubise (page 281) or Poivrade (page 278). Makes 1 portion.

▪ EGGS TARTARE

In preparing this, keep in mind the story of the young woman who pretended to a knowledge of food far beyond what she really had. She gave herself away by saying to the waiter when she followed the example of her luncheon-mates in ordering Steak Tartare, "Make mine well done." Let a light touch in timing be your guide.

2 *tablespoons Steak Tartare*
1 *egg*
1 *teaspoon light cream*

Line the buttered *cocotte* with the Steak Tartare; add the egg and cream. Cook in a *bain-marie* 4 to 8 minutes in a preheated 350-degree oven; 3 to 5 minutes in a top-of-stove waterbath. Makes 1 portion.

▪ *Steak Tartare:* Steak Tartare is best when it is made by scraping raw beef with a spoon or the edge of a knife. This can be done only if a steak cut such as round is used. Chuck and other less costly cuts can be used if care is taken to remove all fat and white fibers from the meat; it can be put 2 or 3 times through the meat grinder, using the finest blade. Season the ground beef with onion juice or onion salt, freshly ground pepper and a tiny touch of cayenne.

▪ EGGS VAUDOIS

From Switzerland's southern canton of Vaud comes this fondue-like dish of shirred eggs. It is beautifully adapted to service as a hot luncheon dish, since the cooking time is flexible within reasonable limits and its heat holds well out of the oven.

> 1½ *cups whipping cream* (*no substitutes*)
> 8 *eggs, separated*
> 1 *teaspoon salt*
> 2 *cups grated Emmenthaler cheese or the equivalent in thin slices*
> *Paprika*

Whip the cream very thick; it should be at room temperature. Beat the egg whites stiff, adding the salt as they are beaten. Line shirring *plats* with the cheese. Cut the cream gently into the egg whites with a knife or spatula. Divide this meringue among the 4 *plats*; drop 2 egg yolks into each *plat*, allowing them to sink into the meringue. Dust the tops generously with paprika. Cook 10 to 12 minutes (a short overcooking will do no harm) in a preheated 400-degree oven; the cheese should be melted, the tops of the dishes brown, the egg yolks cooked but still liquid. Serves 4.

▪ *EGGS YVONNE*

A house specialty from the old Paris Ritz; the Yvonne who merited its dedication is unknown.

> 1½ *tablespoons dark meat of fowl: turkey, pheasant, guinea-hen, etc.*
> 1 *egg*
> *Dash salt*
> *Dash pepper*
> *Pinch chervil*
> 1 *tablespoon light cream*
> 1 *toast round*
> 1 *tablespoon minced ham*
> 1½ *tablespoons Tomato Sauce* (*page 278*)

Chop the meat coarsely and put half of it in the bottom of a well-buttered *cocotte;* add the egg, salt, pepper and remaining meat. Sprinkle on the chervil; pour in the cream. Poach in a *bain-marie* 8 to 12 minutes in a preheated 350-degree oven, or half that time in a waterbath on top of the stove. Spread the toast round with the minced ham, unmold the *cocotte* onto the toast and spoon on the sauce. Makes 1 portion.

■ HARD-COOKED EGGS

There are still a few things that can be done with a hard-cooked egg. Several of these things will be suggested in the next group of recipes.

■ *EGGS WITH BASIL*

> 4 *hard-cooked eggs*
> 2 *teaspoons finely minced parsley*
> 2 *teaspoons finely minced shallots*
> 2 *teaspoons finely minced sautéed mushrooms*
> 1 *clove finely minced garlic*
> ½ *cup milk*
> 2 *tablespoons toasted coarse breadcrumbs*
> 1 *uncooked egg*
> 2 *tablespoons pounded basil*
> *Breadcrumb–Cheese Glaze (page 291)*

Halve the eggs lengthwise, remove the yolks and reserve the egg-white cases. Mash the yolks with the parsley, shallots, mushrooms and garlic; pour the milk over the toasted breadcrumbs, and blend them with the mashed yolks, binding with the uncooked egg. Stuff the egg-white cases with this mixture, rounding off the tops to give the appearance of whole eggs. Line a shallow baking dish with the remainder of the stuffing mixture and space the eggs on top; mix the basil with the glazing mixture and sprinkle it generously over the top. Cook 10 to 15 minutes in a preheated 300-degree oven. Serves 4.

These may be buttered and eaten out of hand while still hot, or served with your favorite white sauce.

■ *EGG FILLETS*

Any good dry white wine may be used in this recipe, but there is something opulent about preparing the dish at the table in front of guests, as suggested by its originator, Dumas *père*, and pouring the champagne into the chafing dish with a lordly gesture.

> 2 *tablespoons butter*
> ½ *cup chopped onions*
> ½ *cup chopped mushrooms*

Dash salt
Dash pepper
1 cup chicken broth
4 hard-cooked eggs
1 split champagne (about 1¼ cups)
4 slices toast

In a saucepan over low heat, melt the butter, sauté the onions until they become transparent, add the mushrooms and cook until they are soft; season with salt and pepper. Mash the mushrooms with a spoon until they blend into a pulp. Pour in the chicken broth, simmer 3 or 4 minutes, then slice the eggs into fairly thick slices, lengthwise, and slip them gently into the simmering sauce. Allow them to cook 2 or 3 minutes, then pour in the champagne. When the mixture has bubbled again from the heat, not the wine, lift the egg slices out onto the toast, and pour the sauce over them. Serves 4.

When cooking this at the table in a chafing dish, do not use the waterjacket; have all ingredients, including the champagne (or white wine) at room temperature; the broth may even be slightly warmed.

▪ *KEDGEREE*

Another much-traveled egg dish, which migrated from India to England, then moved across the Atlantic. It is—or was—a mainstay of the British buffet breakfast.

2 tablespoons butter
2 cups flaked smoked mackerel
1 cup boiled rice
1 teaspoon curry powder
½ teaspoon cayenne
4 hard-cooked eggs
Toast triangles

Melt the butter in a double boiler, or over lowest heat in a skillet. Add the flaked fish, then the rice and seasonings. Chop the eggs coarsely and stir them into the mixture; stir well. Serve over toast points. Serves 6.

Kedgeree is often made with scrambled eggs, the precooked eggs being mixed into the hot rice–fish combination before serving. There are less pungent versions, in which poached halibut is substituted for the mackerel and the quantities of cayenne and curry powder reduced. Your taste is the best guide to how bland or sharp your own service should be.

▪ *SCOTCH WOODCOCK*

Another British buffet breakfast standby, as can be seen from its bluntly unequivocal flavor.

> 3 *hard-cooked eggs*
> 4 *tablespoons butter*
> 1½ *cups light cream or rich milk*
> 4 *anchovy fillets*
> 4 *slices toast*
> *Dash cayenne*

Chop the eggs coarsely. Melt 2 tablespoons of the butter in a saucepan, add the cream, then the chopped eggs. Simmer but do not boil until the eggs are warmed. Blend the anchovy fillets with the remaining butter, and spread the toast with it. Pour the hot eggs in cream over the toast. Dust cayenne over the top of each portion. Serves 4.

▪ *TEA EGGS*

> 6 *hard-cooked eggs*
> 1½ *tablespoons salt*
> 1 *tablespoon anise extract*
> 3 *tablespoons double-strength black tea (brewed)*

Cool the hard-cooked eggs; crack the shells in several places but do not peel. Add the salt, anise extract and eggs to 1½ pints cold water; bring to a boil. At the boiling point, add the tea. Simmer over lowest heat 1 hour. Remove from the heat and leave the eggs in the water until it is completely cool; place them in the refrigerator, still in the water, for 24 hours. Shell the eggs; serve halved or whole as an hors d'oeuvre. Makes 6 Tea Eggs.

▪ PRESERVED EGGS

▪ *PEI DAN EGGS* (*Thousand-Year Eggs*)

These are the famed and fabled "thousand-year" eggs of China. Their preparation requires 2 to 4 months. If you are not positive you'll like them, put down only 3 or 4, reducing the quantities given in this recipe in the proper ratio.

> 1 *pound lye*
> 1 *pound salt*
> 12 *eggs*

A caution before you begin: Lye is a corrosive substance; do not allow it to spatter on your skin. Do not handle it unless you are wearing rubber gloves. Never add hot water to lye, only cold water. Do not use metal pots or containers, or stir with a metal spoon. And do not use for cooking any pot or pan that has held a lye mixture.

Put the lye in a thick earthenware crock and slowly add 1½ pints of cold water, stirring with a wooden paddle or spoon. Add the salt when the lye has been absorbed and stir until the salt is dissolved. Cut strands of straw about 6 inches long, enough to wrap all the eggs thoroughly, and soak or steep 3 to 4 days in the lye water. A feed store or garden-supply store will have the heavy, coarse straw needed. Wearing rubber gloves, wrap each egg in the lye-soaked straw, covering the shell completely and tying the straw with string at the top and bottom. Then wind each egg in strips of cloth, to bring the straw into firm contact with the eggshells. Place the wrapped eggs in a dry crock, cover but do not seal, and set in a cool place for 2 months.

At the end of the 2 months, wearing rubber gloves, unwrap one of the eggs, rinse its shell, and peel the shell off. The eggs will have been hard-cooked by the action of the lye, and will range in color from a coppery tan to a light green. The longer the eggs remain in contact with the lye-impregnated straw, the more pronounced their flavor and color. When the eggs are done to your taste, remove them from the wrappings and rinse the shells. They will keep without refrigeration.

Serve the eggs sliced very thin on a cracker with a sliver of preserved ginger on each slice, or use the Two-Tone Egg recipe (page 185) for a less pungent canapé for your party 6 months from now.

▪ *SMOKED EGGS*

While this recipe and the next do not result in true preserved eggs, they are closely akin to them.

> 6 *hard-cooked eggs*
> 2 *tablespoons soy sauce*
> 1½ *tablespoons sugar*
> 1 *tablespoon salt*
> 4 *tablespoons liquid smoke*

Have the eggs completely cold, shell them and run a thin skewer through them from top to bottom and side to side. Heat 2 cups water, and add the soy sauce, sugar, salt and 2 tablespoons of the liquid smoke. Bring the mixture to a rolling boil. Put the pierced eggs in a crock or jar, and pour the boiling liquid over them. When they are cooled, place them in the refrigerator for 24 hours. Remove them, add the remaining 2 tablespoons liquid smoke and shake the jar or crock thoroughly. Refrigerate 6 hours longer. Drain and rinse them, and if stored for additional time, keep them in a covered container; the eggs should be wiped dry before serving.

Cut them in half lengthwise and serve a half-egg on toast, or slice them and serve as canapés on unsalted round crackers. Makes 6 Smoked Eggs.

▪ *PICKLED EGGS*

Before refrigeration there were two ways to preserve eggs: fresh eggs were put down in a crock and covered with waterglass; hard-cooked eggs were pickled. Both kinds of preserved eggs have almost vanished, though occasionally one will meet a slice of pickled egg topping a round cracker as a canapé. There's no point in pickling only a few eggs; if you're going to pickle, put down at least a dozen. They keep well in a covered jar in the refrigerator.

> 12 *hard-cooked eggs*
> 1 *teaspoon whole peppercorns*
> 4 *cups white (grain) vinegar*
> 1 *teaspoon whole allspice*
> ½ *teaspoon salt*

The eggs must be freshly hard-cooked, cooled quickly in water, shelled and cooled further either in the refrigerator or in very cold water. Wipe them dry before putting them in the pickle.

Crack the peppercorns in a mortar or with a rolling pin and boil the vinegar with the spices for 15 minutes. Put the eggs in a jar or crock; pour over them the hot pickling liquid. Close the container loosely; do not seal. Allow to stand 4 weeks. Rinse before serving. Makes 12 Pickled Eggs.

To please the children, or simply to be coy, add beet juice to the pickling mixture. Where the eggs touch each other, white spots will remain. These are, predictably, called "Polka Dot Eggs."

Sliced, pickled eggs make a garnish for cold meats or a canapé on a cracker spread with Mayonnaise (pages 285-286); cut into julienne strips, they add the unexpected to a tossed green salad.

▪ *EGG SAUSAGE*

A Lenten delicacy from medieval England, this sausage is another
unusual way of preserving eggs.

> *2 sausage skins 1 inch in diameter and 8 inches long*
> *6 eggs*
> *1 teaspoon salt*
> *½ teaspoon white peppercorns*
> *¼ teaspoon cayenne*
> *1 teaspoon minced chives*
> *1 teaspoon minced onion*
> *1 teaspoon minced green pepper*
> *1 teaspoon minced olives*
> *1 cup heavy cream*

Sausage skins or casings may usually be bought from a butcher or
wholesale meat dealer. Tie one end of each casing very tightly with
string and set it aside.

Beat the eggs until frothy, adding all the remaining ingredients
except the cream; the peppercorns should be cracked, but not ground.
When these ingredients have been added to the eggs, beat in the
cream. Use a large funnel to fill the sausage casings, and tie off the
tops, leaving about 2 inches of the casing unfilled to allow for expan-
sion. Bring a large pot of water to a rolling boil, and drop in the filled
casings. Remove from the heat and let stand 30 to 45 minutes, occasionally stirring with a spoon (which avoids punctures) so that the
filling does not separate. Have a pot of cold water ready, and when
the sausage casings are firm, remove them from the hot water and
drop them into the cold. Let them stand 30 minutes. Store under refrigeration; they keep well. Makes 2 sausages.

These sausages may be treated like any meat sausage: sautéed or
poached, or sliced and eaten cold. Repay yourself for the trouble of
making them with the thought that it's a delicacy that cannot be
bought at the supermarket or delicatessen.

▪ *TWO-TONE EGGS*

> *3 uncooked eggs*
> *1 Pei Dan Egg (page 182)*

Lightly beat the uncooked eggs; chop the Pei Dan Egg and beat it
into them. Pour the eggs into a shallow buttered baking dish or cas-

serole and in a *bain-marie* with the baking dish covered, cook 12 to 18 minutes in a preheated 250-degree oven. Cool, cut the eggs into squares or rounds and place them on crackers or very thin crisp toast. Makes 12 to 15 canapés.

▪ EGG CASSEROLES

Such unlikely ingredients as cider, capers and cottage cheese are the surprising ingredients in these dishes, each of which is ample to serve 4 very heartily, or 6 moderately.

▪ *COURONNE NORMANDE* (*Norman Crown*)

> 6 *eggs*
> 5 *tablespoons flour*
> 1 *teaspoon baking powder*
> 1 *teaspoon salt*
> 1½ *cups sweet cider*
> ½ *cup minced onions*
> ½ *cup chopped mushrooms*
> 1 *tablespoon chopped chives*
> 1 *tablespoon chopped parsley*
> 2 *medium-sized, firm, ripe tomatoes or* 1½ *cups*
>   *drained canned tomatoes*
> 2 *parboiled kidneys or sweetbreads*

Separate the eggs; beat the yolks, sifting in the flour, baking powder and salt. When they are well blended, begin adding the cider, beating all the time, until the mixture is smooth. Beat the egg whites to stiff peaks, and fold in the yolk mixture. Pour into a ring mold; bake 30 to 35 minutes in a preheated 300-degree oven. Test for firmness with a skewer or straw.

Sauté the onions until they become transparent, add the mushrooms, then the chives and parsley. Add the tomatoes, cover the pan and simmer over very low heat 15 minutes, stirring occasionally. Dice the kidney or sweetbread meat and add it during the final 5 minutes of cooking.

Turn out the ring mold on a chop plate or platter. Fill its center with the tomato–meat mixture, and serve. And there is nothing more enjoyable to serve with it than glasses of cool cider. Serves 4.

▪ *EGGS OVER EGGS*

How Dumas found any time away from eating and creating new dishes to get any writing done is one of life's great mysteries. This is another of his culinary originals.

> *8 eggs*
> *½ teaspoon salt*
> *Large dash nutmeg*
> *1 teaspoon capers*
> *1 teaspoon chopped parsley*
> *½ teaspoon chopped chives*
> *⅛ teaspoon pepper*
> *2 anchovy fillets*

Separate 4 of the eggs; beat the whites with a dash of salt until they form stiff peaks. Beat the yolks with a dash of salt and nutmeg; while beating, add the capers, parsley, chives and pepper, and the anchovy fillets which have been chopped very fine. Butter a shallow casserole and in its bottom place the 4 remaining eggs, broken into a saucer one at a time and slid into place so the yolks are intact. Fold the beaten yolks into the whites and pour over the whole eggs in the bottom of the baking dish. Bake 20 to 25 minutes in a preheated 350-degree oven. Serves 4.

▪ *OMELET PIE*

> *4 tablespoons butter*
> *3 tablespoons cream cheese*
> *2 cups flour*
> *1 cup milk*
> *1 cup chopped ham*
> *½ cup grated medium-sharp cheese*
> *½ teaspoon salt*
> *¼ teaspoon pepper*
> *6 eggs, separated*

Prepare the piecrust a day in advance. Blend 3 tablespoons butter, the cream cheese, and 1¾ cups flour, working them together until smooth. Chill overnight; remove the dough from the refrigerator an hour before it is to be used so that it will reach a workable consistency, then line a pie pan with the dough.

Scald the milk; allow it to cool. Stir it vigorously while adding the remaining 1 tablespoon butter and ¼ cup flour, and the ham, cheese, salt and pepper. Beat the egg yolks until they are frothy and add the milk mixture. Beat the whites until they form soft peaks; fold the yolk mixture into the whites and blend well but with a light touch. Fill the piecrust with this mixture and spoon 1 tablespoon very cold water over its surface. Bake 15 minutes in a preheated 450-degree oven; reduce the heat to 325 degrees and bake 20 minutes longer.

When baked without the piecrust, the filling becomes what is popularly known as an "oven omelet." It is not a true omelet, in the strict sense of the word, but it may be used in combination with any of the traditional fillings in the chapter covering omelets to ease the strain of preparing a number of omelets when a group is to be served. When you are not using the crust, reduce the baking time to 10 minutes in a preheated 450-degree oven, which is then lowered to 325 degrees for 12 to 15 minutes. The omelet may then be folded and served. Serves 4.

▪ *SOUTHERN FLEECE*

> 1 *pint cottage cheese*
> ¼ *pound cream cheese*
> ¼ *pint milk or whey from cottage cheese*
> ¼ *pint sour cream*
> ¼ *teaspoon cayenne*
> ½ *teaspoon salt*
> ⅛ *teaspoon pepper*
> 6 *eggs*

Drain the cottage cheese well; break the cream cheese into fingertip-sized bits and stir the two together. Place in an even layer in a well-buttered shallow baking dish or casserole and put in a preheated 250-degree oven for 10 minutes, until the water from the cheese begins to flow and the cheese softens. Remove from the oven, add the milk, sour cream, cayenne, salt and pepper. (If your taste runs to the bland side, use milk; if you like a sharper flavor, use the whey drained off the cottage cheese instead of milk.) Break 4 eggs into the casserole and stir in well; they should almost be beaten into the hot mixture. Replace the casserole in the oven for 20 minutes, remove it and beat in the remaining 2 eggs, beating briskly. Cook 10 minutes longer, and serve at once. Serves 4.

This dish has an unusual, almost unique texture, and repays the trouble of repeated trips to the oven.

▪ EGG SOUPS

China, Greece, Austria and Italy each contribute a famous national dish to our list of hot egg soups.

▪ *EGG THREAD SOUP* (*Spun Egg Soup*)

> 3 *cups clear broth or consommé*
> 1 *egg*
> *Dash salt*
> *Dash pepper*

Bring the broth or consommé to a brisk boil. Beat the egg lightly with the salt and pepper. Hold a colander over the pot of boiling broth and slowly pour the egg through it so that it strains in threads into the soup. Serve as soon as the threads are firm. Serves 2.

▪ *MOUSKARIS AVGOLEMONO* (*Broth with Egg-Lemon Sauce*)

Saltsa Avgolemono, on which this soup is based, is one of the great sauces of the world and a classic in Greek cuisine; it is met with on meats, eggs and vegetables, as well as in this soup.

> 1 *quart broth: veal, chicken, fish, etc.*
> *Saltsa Avgolemono*

Bring the broth to a simmer, and beat in the sauce. Do not allow it to boil. Makes 1 quart soup.

▪ *Saltsa Avgolemono:* Beat 2 eggs lightly, add a pinch of salt and the juice of 1 lemon (3 tablespoons); continue beating until the sauce is smooth.

▪ *SCHNEEKLOSSCHEN* (*Snow Peak Soup*)

The home of this egg soup with white wine is Austria.

> 2 *tablespoons butter*
> 2 *tablespoons flour*
> 1 *teaspoon milk*
> 4 *cups white wine, Rhine or Moselle*

> ¼ *teaspoon cinnamon*
> ½ *finely grated lemon rind*
> 4 *eggs, separated*
> 3 *tablespoons sugar*
> *Dash nutmeg or cinnamon*

Melt the butter over lowest heat; slowly stir in the flour, but do not allow it to brown. Add the milk and stir into a smooth paste (this may require a little more or a little less milk than the recipe calls for; the paste should be thin rather than thick). Stir in the wine, cinnamon and lemon rind; simmer slowly for 5 minutes but do not allow to boil. Beat the egg yolks until creamy and stir them into the simmering wine, beating slightly to produce a smooth mixture. Simmer 10 to 12 minutes. Beat the egg whites, adding the sugar a bit at a time, until they form stiff peaks. Dish up the soup into individual bowls, divide the whites between them and float them on the surface of the soup. Dust the tops with nutmeg or cinnamon before serving. Serves 4.

▪ *ZUPPA BOLOGNESE* (*Bolognese Soup*)

> 4 *eggs*
> 1 *finely grated lemon rind*
> 1 *cup grated Parmesan cheese*
> 4 *cups toasted fine breadcrumbs*
> 1½ *quarts chicken or veal broth*

Beat the eggs until frothy, adding the lemon rind and cheese. Little by little, add the breadcrumbs to the eggs until the mixture is too thick to beat; then add them by hand and mix until the mixture is kneaded into a firm dough. Form into a ball and refrigerate 3 to 4 hours. When you are ready to serve the soup, bring the broth to a rolling boil. Hold the dough over the boiling broth and grate it into the broth, using the coarsest side of a grater; it should come from the grater in strips about ¼ inch wide and 2 or 3 inches long. When the last of the dough is in the broth—and it should be added very quickly —simmer for another minute or two and serve it at once.

▪ UNCLASSIFIABLE DISHES

Several of these mischievous unclassifiables require effort in their preparation, but the effort is worth expending. Most people who have never met the *délicacies* greet them with wide-eyed wonder; the jacketed eggs are fun; and the incredulity induced by eggs cooked on a barbecue spit is something that must be seen.

■ *DÉLICACIES D'EMMENTHALER* (*Swiss Cheese Fritters*)

Please don't cut corners here; get the very best tawny-gold Emmenthaler cheese you can find when you prepare this dish.

> *3 eggs, separated*
> *½ cup finely grated Emmenthaler (Swiss) cheese*
> *¼ cup finely grated Gruyère or Jack cheese*
> *Dash salt*
> *Dash pepper*
> *Dash nutmeg*
> *2 cups heavy cream*
> *1 cup very fine breadcrumbs*
> *Peanut oil to cover bottom of skillet ¼ inch deep*

Beat the egg yolks with the cheeses, which must be grated very fine; add the seasonings. Whip the cream lightly and fold in the beaten yolks. Beat the egg whites until they form soft peaks and fold them into the yolk–cream mixture. Spread it in an inch-thick layer on a cold buttered platter and chill in the refrigerator 30 minutes, or longer if you wish; it should be very firm. Cut into strips 1 inch wide and 2 inches long. Roll each strip in breadcrumbs, and fry in very hot oil; the pan should not be overcrowded. Turn each *délicacie* once, after it is browned on the bottom; as soon as the other side has browned, remove it to an absorbent cloth or paper towel to drain for a moment. Serve hot. Serves 4.

■ *DÉLICACIES ROYALE* (*Royal Fritters*)

A close cousin, in Sunday finery, of the Emmenthaler *délicacies*.

> *6 eggs*
> *3 tablespoons heavy cream*
> *Dash salt*
> *Dash pepper*
> *Dash nutmeg*
> *Pinch thyme*
> *¼ cup flour*
> *1 tablespoon peanut oil*

> 2 *tablespoons warm water*
> 2 *tablespoons sherry*
> ½ *teaspoon garlic salt*
> ½ *teaspoon chopped chives*
> *Dash cayenne*
> 2 *egg whites*
> *Oil or fat for deep frying*

Beat the 6 whole eggs with the cream, salt, pepper, nutmeg and thyme. Pour them in a shallow square baking dish and cook in a *bain-marie* for 20 minutes in a preheated 300-degree oven. (The cooking may be done on top of the stove in a double boiler, if you want to stir it constantly as it cooks; it must then be poured into a shallow square baking dish anyhow.) Chill in the baking dish in the refrigerator for 30 minutes; it should be quite firm.

Sift the flour into the peanut oil while stirring briskly, then add the water and sherry alternately in small dashes while continuing to stir. Add the garlic salt, chives and cayenne, and beat until very smooth. Set aside for at least 30 minutes. Just before cooking the *délicacies*, beat the two egg whites until they form stiff peaks and fold in the oil–water–sherry batter, blending well.

Cut the cooled custard into squares; they should be about 2 inches wide each. Dip into the batter, place in a frying basket and fry in very hot oil until crisply brown on the outside. Serves 4.

▪ DIJON EGG TARTS

These tarts are very like small soufflés served in individual, edible containers. By varying the fillings, you can serve them in infinite variety.

> 3 *tablespoons flour*
> ¼ *teaspoon nutmeg*
> 1½ *cups milk*
> 1 *teaspoon Dijon mustard*
> ½ *cup grated Parmesan cheese*
> 6 *eggs, separated*
> ¼ *teaspoon salt*
> ½ *teaspoon cream of tartar*
> 1 *cup filling, which may be chopped nutmeats, on-*
> *ions, green pepper, whole kernel corn, ham, bacon,*
> *mushrooms or any other ingredient or combination*

of ingredients you fancy. If very characterful foods
are used, such as Roquefort cheese, pimientos or
green olives, use only ¾ cup
6 *deep tartshells*

Combine the flour and nutmeg in a saucepan, add enough milk to moisten and place over very lowest heat. While stirring constantly, add the remainder of the milk, then stir in the mustard. Add the Parmesan and simmer a few minutes longer, stirring until smooth. Remove from the heat. Beat the egg yolks until they are creamy, adding the salt. Stir the yolks into the milk and blend well. Beat the egg whites until they are foamy, add the cream of tartar and beat until they form stiff peaks. Add the cup of filling to the yolks, and stir until well blended; fold the yolks into the beaten whites. Fill the tartshells half-full, place on a buttered baking sheet and cook 20 minutes in a preheated 375-degree oven, or until the mixture puffs over the tops of the tartshells and browns nicely. Makes 6 tarts.

▪ *EGGS IN JACKETS*

1 *batch Pastry Dough* (*page* 291)
4 *eggs* mollet
1 *tablespoon flour*
3 *tablespoons Anchovy Butter* (*page* 288)

Roll the Pastry Dough thin, about ⅛ inch thick. Lightly grease the unshelled eggs and form the dough into jackets over them, using a dab of water to seal any edges. Chill 30 minutes in the refrigerator or 10 minutes in the freezer, until the dough is very firm. Make a circular cut around each egg and slip off the dough jackets, retaining their shape as much as possible. Shell the eggs, roll them in flour, then in melted Anchovy Butter, then in flour again, and put them back into the jackets, again sealing the edges with water. Bake standing on end on a buttered cookie sheet 10 minutes in a preheated 375-degree oven, or until the jacket browns. Brush with Anchovy Butter before serving. Serves 4.

▪ *EGGS MELBA*

Carême reportedly created this dish for Dame Nellie, who had a weight problem, when the soprano was dining frequently with King Edward VII.

2 *egg whites*
Dash Tabasco sauce
1 *round Melba toast*

Beat the egg whites very stiff, adding the Tabasco sauce. Pile on the toast round, and place in a preheated 400-degree oven 3 to 4 minutes, until the meringue sets. Makes 1 portion.

▪ *EGG PIROSHKIS*

Piroshkis are prominent on the Russian appetizer table at parties; usually they are encased in a dough crust. These are not.

6 *eggs*
½ *teaspoon curry powder*
Dash salt
Filling, which may be caviar, flaked crab, lobster, minced ham, chopped onion or diced vegetables, usually bound with a small quantity of stock or gravy

Beat the eggs with the curry powder and salt; strain them and let them stand 15 minutes. Drop a tablespoon at a time into a lightly greased skillet over medium-high heat. Just as the top firms, place a teaspoon of filling in the center, fold half the cake over, and press the edges together to seal. Turn once after sealing to allow both sides to brown evenly and to give the filling time to warm. Makes 1 dozen Piroshkis.

Serve these warm, as a finger food at a buffet or cocktail party, or as a dinner course covered with a suitable sauce.

▪ *ROTISSERIE EGGS*

Challenge an overboastful addict of the outdoor grill (which most people quite inaccurately call a "barbecue") and then win your challenge by demonstrating this creation attributed to Vuillemot, one of the founding fathers of French cuisine, who lived in the pre-kitchen-range days of the sixteenth century.

8 *slices very dry bread*
4 *eggs*
½ *pound butter*

If necessary, dry the bread in a warm oven, but do not toast it. Roll the bread between sheets of waxed paper with a rolling pin to make very fine crumbs. Beat the eggs until they are frothy. With wet hands, form the butter into a ball, roll it in the beaten eggs until it is covered, then roll it in the breadcrumbs until coated. Dip and roll alternately in beaten eggs and breadcrumbs until all the eggs are absorbed. Put it on a spit and roast it over a very low fire, turning the spit constantly, until the ball is crisply browned. Serves 4.

▪ *SCOTCH EGGS*

> *4 hard-cooked eggs*
> *1 uncooked egg*
> *1 tablespoon flour*
> *½ pound bulk sausage*
> *½ teaspoon cracked peppercorns*
> *Dash salt*
> *Oil or fat for deep frying*

Shell the hard-cooked eggs; beat the uncooked egg lightly and dip the hard-cooked eggs in it, then roll them in flour. Roll out the sausage with a well-greased rolling pin, or between two sheets of waxed paper. Cover each egg with a jacket of the sausage. Roll in flour to which has been added the cracked peppercorns and a dash of salt. Fry in a basket in hot fat until the outside is very crusty and crisp. Serves 4.

▪ *VOLCANOES*

Not quite the dieter's delight that Eggs Melba is, this bears a very close kinship.

> *2 egg whites*
> *Dash Tabasco sauce*
> *1 tablespoon grated cheese*
> *1 toast round*
> *1 egg yolk*

Beat the egg whites until they form stiff peaks, adding the Tabasco sauce while beating. Spread the grated cheese on the toast round and put it under the broiler until the cheese softens. Pile the egg whites on the toast round, and make an indentation on top of the mound to hold the egg yolk. Slip in the yolk and place it in a preheated 400-degree oven until the meringue is firm and lightly browned. Makes 1 portion.

Omelets and Soufflés

■ OMELETS

WHERE, HOW AND BY WHOM the first omelet was cooked will probably never be known. It is mentioned in the pre-Christian writings of the Romans, but it reached its greatest flowering in France. Probably the omelet was carried to France by the soldiers of Louis XII, returning from the war in Italy during the years between 1495 and 1500. There is an omelet named after Agnès Sorel, the mistress of Charles VII; it was Charles VII's grandson, Louis XII's predecessor, who ordered the French invasion of the Italian peninsula.

Since the flowering of the French *haute cuisine* began about 1500, the omelet inevitably flowered with it, and multiplied in uncountable varieties. It is impossible even to estimate how many omelet recipes have been created since that time; for each of the hundred given in this chapter, three have been ruled out as being identical in composition with an omelet better known by another name. In some cases there is little to choose between in the names by which identical omelets are known; where this double identity exists, both names are attached to the recipe just to set the record straight. Because there are so many names for some popular omelet families, such as the long list of cheese omelets, these are simply listed under their generic names, such as "Cheese Omelet" or "Omelet with Chicken Livers."

Like Caesar's Gaul, all omelets are divided into three sections: the folded omelet, the flat omelet, and the fluffy omelet. The first is by far the best known and most common; it is the image that flashes into our minds when the very word "omelet" is mentioned. The flat omelet is often called an omelet *paysanne*, or peasant-style omelet; it is turned and cooked on both sides like a pancake and served flat. The puffy omelet may be described as a souffléed omelet or omelet *mousseline;* its preparation will be fully covered in this chapter. An omelet may be oven-cooked; the details for this preparation will be found in the Omelet Pie recipe on page 187. The preparation of such dessert dishes as jelly omelets is discussed in this chapter, but the family of so-called "Surprise Omelets" will be found in the chapter on desserts.

All omelets come from the same processes of mixing and cooking, which are based on beating eggs and cream and cooking the mixture in a hot pan so that it will puff up while a tender skin is formed to enclose it. Filling or character ingredients are added at some point, and it is these which give the omelet its individuality or individual identity. In this chapter, omelets are classified in three groups—simple, substantial and surprising—with ingredients and preparation growing more complicated in each category. Only one basic recipe is given, on page 198; it is used for all omelets unless different instructions appear in an individual recipe.

Far too many cooks throw up their hands in despair when the word "omelet" is mentioned, because for a long time cookbooks and magazines approached the preparation of omelets (and soufflés, too, for that matter) with undue reverence. Pages were written about special pans, special procedures, special skills. This is nonsense, of course. An omelet is easier to make than a cake, if approached with an open mind and no preconditioned fears. There are a few simple, straightforward procedures to be followed, but they are really very easy.

Three eggs is the smallest number that can be used with any real success in an omelet, and a three-egg omelet, with its filling, serves two people admirably. Six eggs is the largest number that should be used in an omelet; use of more requires a large pan, very difficult to handle and to heat properly on most ranges. Four are served by a six-egg omelet; if more are to be served, prepare two small omelets, or three if need be, instead of attempting one gigantic effort. Two six-egg omelets will serve eight, and can be offered simultaneously even without two pans, if the first cooked is removed while still slightly underdone and kept warm in the oven while the second is cooking.

All recipes following are based on a three-egg omelet; quantities of filling called for should be increased one-half for a six-egg omelet, which is the next logical size to cook.

■ *BASIC OMELET*

> 3 *eggs*
> ½ *tablespoon cream (or rich milk) or* ¼ *teaspoon*
>   *water per egg*
> *Dash salt*
> *Dash pepper*
> ½ *teaspoon butter per egg*
> *Oil for cooking*

Beat the eggs, cream and seasonings together until the mixture begins to froth, then begin adding the butter in tiny flakes while continuing to beat. When blended, let the mixture stand 10 minutes. If filling ingredients are to be mixed into the batter, add them after the beaten eggs have rested, by stirring gently just before the mixture is poured into the pan.

Oil is preferred to butter or a solid shortening, and peanut oil is by far the best in which to cook omelets, with olive oil used if its flavor is wanted in the finished dish. The pan is brushed very lightly with oil and brought over high heat to the point where it just begins to smoke. Remove the pan until the smoking stops, then return it to the heat and pour in the egg mixture.

With a narrow spatula, lift the edges of the egg mixture away from the pan as soon as a bottom skin begins to form, at the same time tilting the pan to allow any liquid in its center to trickle along the valleys formed and reach the metal of the pan. Drop the edge at once, and let the liquid marry with the surface already formed.

If the omelet is to be folded, this should be done just as the top surface begins to solidify; if it is to be turned, the top should still be in a semiliquid state. Before turning or folding, give the pan a sharp, quick shake to be sure the omelet is free; if it has stuck, loosen it with a flexible spatula. (Sticking should never be a problem if you use either a heavy iron skillet or the special omelet pan.) Professional chefs and amateurs who cook omelets soon learn the special tossing twist of the wrist, impossible to describe, which folds the omelet as it is sliding from pan to platter; a spatula does the job with equal efficiency, though perhaps with less flourish.

Filling or character ingredients may be added at any point in the cooking stage; each recipe specifies the traditional way in which its omelet is offered. The time to add ingredients to the batter has been given on page 198. If the ingredients are among those that extra cooking might affect badly, they should be spread on the surface of the cooking omelet either immediately after it goes into the pan, or after the top has set, just before folding. In some omelets the filling is poured over the surface as a garnish or sauce instead of being incorporated as the eggs cook. Omelets not glazed or sauced will benefit in appearance if their surface is brushed with butter after being turned onto the warm serving plate. When a glaze is called for, it is, unless otherwise stated, Sauce Espagnole (page 275). Serves 2.

▪ SIMPLE OMELETS

▪ *OMELET AGNÈS SOREL*

We have met the lady before; the mistress of Charles VII, about whom little is known except that an omelet was named for her. Still, what more pleasant way for a royal mistress to be remembered?

> *½ cup chopped sautéed mushrooms*
> *Basic Omelet (page 198)*
> *3 or 4 very thin slices smoked or pickled tongue*
> *2 tablespoons veal gravy*

Spread the mushrooms over the surface of the omelet just before folding. Cover its surface with the sliced tongue after the omelet is on its serving dish; spoon the gravy on top. Serves 2.

▪ *OMELET ALSACIENNE*

> *¾ cup sauerkraut*
> *1 tablespoon goose fat*
> *Basic Omelet (page 198)*
> *Sauce Espagnole (page 275)*

Drain the sauerkraut well and braise it in goose fat in a closed pan. Spread it over the omelet's surface just before folding. Glaze with Sauce Espagnole, and place the omelet under the broiler for a moment. Serves 2.

▪ *ANCHOVY OMELET*

> 6 *well-drained anchovy fillets*
> *Basic Omelet* (*page* 198)

Chop two of the fillets fine and mix them in the batter; space the remaining fillets on the surface of the folded omelet just before serving. Serves 2.

▪ *OMELET ANVERSOISE* (*Hop Shoot Omelet*)

> ¾ *cup chopped tender young hop shoots*
> ½ *cup Cream Sauce* (*page* 281)
> 2 *teaspoons milk*
> *Basic Omelet* (*page* 198)

Plunge the hop shoots into lightly boiling salted water for a minute to blanch them; chop them coarsely and simmer in the Cream Sauce that has been thinned with the milk. Put half the filling on the surface of the omelet just before folding, and pour the remainder over it after it is on the serving plate. Serves 2.

▪ *OMELET ARGENTEUIL*

> ¼ *cup Sauce Velouté* (*page* 279)
> 2 *tablespoons milk*
> 1 *cup tender, cooked asparagus tips*
> *Dash nutmeg*
> *Basic Omelet* (*page* 198)
> 3 *or* 4 *cooked perfect asparagus stalks*

Thin the sauce with the milk in a double boiler; add the asparagus tips and nutmeg. Spoon the tips and a little sauce on the omelet just before folding. Transfer it to a service plate, garnish its top with the asparagus stalks and pour the remaining sauce over it. Serves 2.

▪ *OMELET PRINCESSE* is the same recipe with a pinch of truffle grating or a few drops of Truffle Essence added to the sauce.

▪ *BACON OMELET*

> 2 *slices bacon*
> *Basic Omelet* (*page* 198)

Cook the bacon until it is crisp; reserve the drippings. Crumble the bacon into the cooking omelet just after it has been poured into the pan. Fold it and serve after brushing it with bacon drippings. Garnish with additional slices of bacon if desired. Serves 2.

■ *OMELET PASCALE* adds chopped parsley to the bacon.

■ *OMELET À LA BRUXELLOISE*

> ½ *cup very tiny Brussels sprouts, parboiled*
> 1 *teaspoon butter*
> *Basic Omelet* (*page* 198)

Sauté the sprouts in the butter; chop them if they are too large. Spread them on the surface of the omelet just before folding. Serves 2.

■ *OMELET AU CHASSEUR* (*Hunter's Omelet*)

> 2 *chicken livers*
> 1 *tablespoon butter*
> 2 *tablespoons white wine*
> ½ *cup Sauce Chasseur* (*page* 276)
> *Basic Omelet* (*page* 198)

Sauté the chicken livers in butter; drain and dice them. In the pan where they were cooked, add the white wine to the remaining butter; stir in the Sauce Chasseur and allow it to simmer. Spread the diced chicken livers on the omelet's soft surface and spoon on a little of the sauce. Fold the omelet, transfer it to a serving plate and pour on the remaining sauce. Serves 2.

There are infinite variations. The whole livers may be served on top of or on each side of the cooked omelet; or the diced livers may be returned to the sauce, a tomato slice placed on the cooked omelet and the sauce poured over it. Small half or whole tomatoes are often served as an additional garnish.

■ *OMELET WITH CHICKEN LIVERS* is usually an omelet without the Sauce Chasseur that contains mushrooms bits.

■ *OMELET WITH CHICKEN LIVERS AND MUSHROOMS* is filled with a dice of mixed sautéed mushrooms and livers, usually brushed with butter or Sauce Espagnole (page 275) and glazed.

▪ *OMELET CHÂTELAINE*

> ⅓ cup puréed chestnuts
> Basic Omelet (page 198)
> Butter

Just before folding, spoon the purée over the surface of the omelet. Brush with butter before serving. Serves 2.

▪ *CHEESE OMELET*

All cheese omelets are the same, even though they may be known by the name of the cheese used in preparing them. The use of Sapsago is recommended with any cheese as a flavor amplifier.

> ½ teaspoon finely grated Sapsago cheese
> Basic Omelet (page 198)
> ½ cup grated cheese: Cheddar, Swiss, Gruyère, etc.

Beat the Sapsago into the eggs along with the seasonings. Spread the cheese over the surface of the omelet just after it goes into the pan. Fold and serve it after brushing with butter. Serves 2.

▪ *CHERVIL OMELET*

> ¼ cup fresh chervil leaves
> ½ teaspoon butter
> Basic Omelet (page 198)

Blanch the chervil by plunging it into boiling water, chop it and sauté it lightly in butter over low heat. Spread the leaves and butter over the surface of the omelet just after it has been poured into the pan. Fold and serve. Serves 2.

▪ *OMELET CHOISY*

> ½ cup Sauce Velouté (page 279)
> 2 teaspoons milk
> Dash nutmeg
> ½ small lettuce heart
> Basic Omelet (page 198)

In a double boiler or over lowest heat, thin the sauce with the milk, adding the nutmeg. Shred the lettuce coarsely; when the sauce simmers, add the lettuce and cook no more than 2 minutes. Spread the lettuce over the omelet just before folding, and cover the folded omelet with the remaining sauce after transferring it to a plate. Serves 2.

▪ *CLAM OMELET*

> 1 *tablespoon diced boiled potatoes*
> 1 *tablespoon butter*
> ¼ *cup minced steamed clams*
> 1½ *tablespoons heavy cream*
> *Dash salt*
> *Dash pepper*
> *Basic Omelet (page* 198)

Over low heat, sauté the potatoes in butter, but do not brown them. Add the clams long enough to heat them, pour in the cream and add the seasonings. Spoon the mixture into the center of the omelet just as soon as it is placed in the pan, or use it as a sauce over a plain omelet after it is on the serving dish. Serves 2.

▪ *OMELET CLAMART*

> 1 *teaspoon butter*
> ⅔ *cup cooked tiny green peas*
> ¼ *teaspoon lemon juice*
> *Basic Omelet (page* 198)
> *Printanier Butter (page* 288)

Heat the butter, and toss the peas in it without allowing them to cook; sprinkle with lemon juice while tossing. Spread this over the surface of the omelet just before folding and serve it after garnishing the top with a large pat of green Printanier Butter. Serves 2.

▪ *CORN OMELET*

> ½ *cup creamed corn (canned or fresh)*
> 1 *teaspoon butter*
> *Basic Omelet (page* 198)

Heat the corn in the butter, and spread it evenly over the surface of the omelet as soon as it is placed in the pan. Fold the omelet and transfer it to a plate; brush with butter before serving. Serves 2.

▪ *COTTAGE CHEESE OMELET*

> ½ *cup large-curd cottage cheese*
> 2 *teaspoons sour cream*
> *Pinch shallots or chives, if desired*
> *Dash pepper, if desired*
> *Basic Omelet (page* 198)

In a double boiler, heat the cottage cheese until it gives up its excess liquid; strain well. Mix it with the sour cream and shallots or chives, and a dash of pepper if a sharper flavor is wanted. Spread this over the surface of the omelet just before folding. Serves 2.

▪ *COTTAGE CHEESE OMELET PAYSANNE* (*Cottage Cheese Omelet, Peasant Style*) is served flat; the warmed cottage cheese is mixed with the eggs before cooking.

▪ *CRAB OMELET*

> 1 *tablespoon heavy cream*
> *Dash nutmeg*
> ¾ *cup flaked crab meat*
> *Basic Omelet (page* 198)

Warm the cream while blending the nutmeg with it. Pour the cream over the crab meat, and mix the crab meat mixture with the eggs as they are beaten. Cook the omelet, fold it and brush it with butter before serving. Serves 2.

▪ *OMELET CRÉCY*

> ½ *cup puréed cooked carrots*
> 2 *teaspoons cream*
> ¼ *teaspoon powdered allspice*
> *Basic Omelet (page* 198)

Blend the carrot purée, cream and allspice in a double boiler; spoon the mixture over the surface of the omelet just before folding. Transfer the omelet to a plate and brush with butter. Serves 2.

▪ *CREOLE OMELET*

This is one of the most abused omelets in the nation, listed on the menu of every wayside restaurant where the kitchen boasts a can of tomatoes and an onion. It is almost always served up as a pallid, watery ghost of its real self.

> 1 *teaspoon butter*
> 1 *tablespoon julienne-cut green pepper*
> 2 *tablespoons chopped mushrooms*
> 1 *teaspoon Worcestershire sauce*
> ¼ *teaspoon Tabasco sauce*
> ¼ *cup tomato juice or thinned tomato paste*
> *Dash salt*
> *Basic Omelet (page 198)*

Melt the butter, sauté the green pepper until it begins to become tender and add the mushrooms. Mix the sauces with the tomato juice and pour them over the pepper and mushrooms; simmer 5 minutes, adjusting the salt to taste. Spoon the mushrooms and green pepper into the omelet just before folding, and pour the remaining sauce on after the omelet is on its serving plate. Onions are sometimes used instead of mushrooms. Serves 2.

▪ DENVER OMELET

> 1 *teaspoon butter*
> 2 *tablespoons diced green pepper*
> 2 *tablespoons cooked, diced ham or bacon*
> *Dash salt*
> *Dash pepper*
> *Basic Omelet (page 198)*

Melt the butter over medium heat, sauté the green pepper until just underdone and add the ham or bacon long enough to warm them. Season lightly with salt and pepper. Put this mixture on the liquid surface of the omelet as soon as it is in the pan; turn the omelet over and serve it flat. Serves 2.

Between the Mississippi River and the Atlantic, this is called a *Western Omelet.*

▪ DIEPPE OMELET

> ¾ *cup finely chopped steamed mussels*
> 2 *teaspoons butter*
> 1 *tablespoon heavy cream*
> *Basic Omelet (page 198)*

Heat the mussels in the butter, but do not cook them. Pour in the cream and simmer not more than 2 minutes. Spoon the mussels into the center of the omelet just before folding. Brush with butter before serving. Serves 2.

■ *OMELET DU BARRY*

> ½ *cup parboiled tiny cauliflower flowerets*
> 1 *teaspoon butter*
> *Basic Omelet* (*page* 198)

Heat the cauliflower in the butter, but do not cook it. Spread it over the entire surface of the omelet as soon as it is in the pan; turn the omelet and serve it flat instead of folded. Serves 2.

■ *OMELET FERMIÈRE* (*Farmer's Omelet*)

> 1 *teaspoon butter*
> 2 *tablespoons very lean cooked ham, diced fine*
> 2 *tablespoons cooked carrots and celery, diced fine*
> 1 *tablespoon parsley, chopped fine*
> *Basic Omelet* (*page* 198)

Melt the butter and toss the ham and vegetables in it; sprinkle with half the parsley. Spread the mixture over the surface of the omelet just before folding it; after it is on the serving plate, brush it with butter and garnish it with the remaining parsley. Serves 2.

■ *OMELET AUX FINES HERBES*

> 1 *teaspoon chopped parsley*
> 1 *teaspoon chopped chervil*
> 1 *teaspoon chopped tarragon*
> 1 *teaspoon chopped chives*
> *Basic Omelet* (*page* 198)

Mix the herbs well together and sprinkle them over the surface of the omelet as soon as it is in the pan. Fold and serve. Many like to sprinkle additional herbs on the buttered surface of the omelet. Serves 2.

■ *OMELET FLAMANDE*

> ½ *cup coarsely chopped endive*
> 1 *teaspoon butter*
> 1 *teaspoon milk*
> *Dash nutmeg*
> ½ *cup Béchamel Sauce* (*page* 280)
> *Basic Omelet* (*page* 198)

Braise the endive with the butter in a skillet that can be tightly covered; leave it over a medium flame no longer than 2 minutes. In a double boiler, stir the milk and nutmeg into the Béchamel Sauce and add the endive. Spoon the endive and part of the sauce into the center of the omelet just before folding; fold the omelet, transfer it to a plate and pour the remaining sauce over it. Serves 2.

■ *HAM OMELET*

> ½ *cup finely diced, very lean ham*
> ½ *teaspoon butter*
> *Basic Omelet* (*page* 198)

Toss the ham in the butter over low heat in a skillet. Spread it evenly over the surface of the omelet as soon as it is poured into the pan. Fold and serve the omelet after brushing its surface with butter from the pan in which the ham was heated. Serves 2.

Ham omelets appear under a variety of names; usually the name is taken from the type of ham used in preparing them: *Omelet Bayonne,* from the salty ham of the Pyrenees; *Omelet Gascogne,* when the spicy hard ham of Gascony is used; and *Omelet Hongroise,* when Polish or Hungarian hams are used and the omelet is sprinkled lightly with paprika. A ham omelet that also contains mushrooms may be called an *Omelet Duxelles.*

■ *KIDNEY OMELET*

> 1 *parboiled kidney*
> 1 *teaspoon butter*
> 1 *tablespoon Madeira*
> *Basic Omelet* (*page* 198)

Choose the kind and size of kidney you prefer and parboil it to your individual taste; some like kidneys pink, others want them well cooked. Heat the butter, dice the kidney and warm it thoroughly in the butter. After it is warm, pour in the Madeira and bring up the heat for 2 to 3 minutes to marry the butter and wine. The usual method of serving this omelet is to fold and transfer it to its plate, then to cut through the omelet at right angles to the fold, spread the halves apart and spoon the diced kidney into the triangle this forms. The wined butter is poured over the kidney and omelet halves. Serves 2.

▪ *LUCHOW'S BOILED BEEF HASH OMELET*

New York's famous German restaurant seems to have put its brand indelibly on this one.

> 2 *tablespoons butter*
> ½ *cup chopped onions*
> 1 *cup diced boiled beef*
> *Dash salt*
> *Dash pepper*
> 2 *slices crisp, well-drained bacon*
> *Basic Omelet (page* 198*), using* 5 *eggs*

Heat the butter over medium heat, add the onions and sauté them until they begin to become transparent. Add the diced beef; cook 2 minutes more while mixing the beef and onions and sprinkling on salt and pepper. Crumble in the bacon and stir while it warms. Pour the omelet into its pan and as quickly as the bottom crust forms, distribute the hash over its surface. Allow it to cook until the top is firm; fold it, slide it onto a warm platter, brush with butter and serve. Serves 2.

▪ *OMELET MÉNAGÈRE* (*Thrifty Wife's Omelet*) is the ancestor of Luchow's Omelet; the original uses the same ingredients minus bacon. It is garnished with chopped parsley.

▪ *OMELET LYONNAISE*

> ¾ *cup chopped onions*
> 3 *tablespoons butter*
> *Basic Omelet (page* 198*)*
> 1 *tablespoon lemon juice or* 1 *teaspoon vinegar*

Sauté the onions in 1 tablespoon butter until they are completely transparent. Spread them over the surface of the omelet just before it is folded. When it is transferred to a warm plate, melt the remaining butter in a saucepan until it bubbles and begins to brown; dash in the lemon juice (which gives you drawn butter) or vinegar (for Beurre Noir, page 117), swirl it a moment and pour it over the omelet. Serves 2.

▪ *ARCHDUKE OMELET* calls for the cooking onions to be generously sprinkled with paprika and placed on the surface of the batter as soon as it is put in the pan. The finished folded omelet is dusted with a design in paprika, such as a "W" or a "V," on its buttered top.

▪ *OMELET MASCOTTE* (*Favorite Omelet*)

> ½ cup Cream Sauce (page 281)
> 1 tablespoon milk
> Dash nutmeg
> ¼ cup parboiled, chopped artichoke hearts
> ¼ cup chopped boiled potatoes
> Basic Omelet (page 198)

Thin the sauce in a double boiler with the milk; add the nutmeg, chopped artichoke and potatoes. Simmer a minute, but do not boil. Spoon the bits of artichoke and potato into the center of the omelet with a little sauce, just before folding. Fold the omelet, slide it onto a service plate and pour over it the remaining sauce. Serves 2.

▪ *OMELET MONSELET* omits the potatoes, but uses a sliver of truffle as a garnish. Both Omelet Mascotte and Omelet Monselet are as often as not called an *Artichoke Omelet*.

▪ *OMELET MISTRAL* (*North Wind Omelet*)

> 1 tablespoon shredded tomato pulp
> Basic Omelet (page 198)
> ⅓ cup sautéed and finely diced eggplant
> 3 tablespoons Sauce Choron (page 283) or Tomato
>   Sauce (page 278)

Stir the tomato pulp into the omelet batter; pour it into the pan and add the eggplant immediately. Turn the omelet over, slide it onto a service plate and pour the sauce on top. The omelet is served folded as often as it is turned and served flat, and the choice of sauces is also the option of the cook. Serves 2.

Without tomato, or sometimes with it, this dish is also called *Eggplant Omelet* or *Omelet Aubergine.*

▪ *MUSHROOM OMELET*

Again we come to a universally popular omelet known by a variety of names. Frequently it is identified by the type of cryptogram used in its preparation: cèpes, morels and so on. The mushrooms can be sautéed, parboiled or simmered in wine or in cream. There is no firm standard; this is another case of cook's option.

> *¾ cup chopped cooked mushrooms*
> *2 tablespoons heavy cream*
> *Dash coarsely ground pepper*
> *Basic Omelet (page 198)*

If the mushrooms have been parboiled, they may be added to the cream as it simmers in a double boiler; if they have been sautéed, they may also be added to the cream, or the cream can be omitted. The mushrooms should, however, be warm and lightly peppered when they are added to the omelet batter, just after the eggs go into the pan. When the top of the omelet sets, fold it and serve. Serves 2.

▪ *OMELET ANDRÉ-THEURIET* is a Mushroom Omelet garnished on the platter, with creamed asparagus tips.

▪ *OMELET DUXELLES* is traditionally made from the classic mushroom hash of French cuisine; frequently a dice of ham is added.

▪ *OMELET FEYDEAU* is a Mushroom Omelet with three tiny poached eggs put on its top after folding; it is then brushed with Sauce Espagnole (page 275) and glazed under the broiler before serving.

▪ *OMELET FORESTIÈRE* (*Forester's Omelet*) uses only field, or wild, mushrooms; a few bacon crumbles are added, and the mushrooms may be sautéed in bacon drippings.

▪ *OMELET PARISIENNE* calls for minced onions to be added to the mushrooms and is garnished with a pair of small link sausages atop its folded surface.

▪ *NANTUA OMELET*

Traditionally this omelet is filled with chopped boiled crayfish, but the French crayfish is not like the one found in the United States; it is closer in size to a big prawn. Start with uncooked prawns or shrimp, then, which will give you the broth needed to make the omelet's traditional Nantua Sauce.

> *4 raw prawns, crayfish or large shrimp*
> *Large pinch salt*
> *½ cup Béchamel Sauce (page 280)*
> *1 tablespoon light cream*
> *Dash cayenne*
> *Basic Omelet (page 198)*

Boil the shellfish in 2 cups cold water to which is added a large pinch of salt. When they are done, remove them; shell and devein them, reserving the water in which they were cooked. Boil this water down until it is reduced two-thirds, strain it and return it to the saucepan. Cut the shellfish into thirds: reserve the tender tail sections, chop the center sections and make a purée of the coarser large sections; use the blender and a dash of milk, or pound them in a mortar. With the reduced cooking water at a low simmer, add the Béchamel Sauce and cream, then the purée, stirring to blend well. Taste for seasoning; additional salt may be needed. Add the cayenne. Simmer the chopped sections of the shellfish in the sauce a moment to warm.

Spoon the meat from the sauce and a little of the sauce into the center of the omelet just before folding. After folding and transferring it to its service plate, garnish it with the tail sections and spoon the sauce over it. Serves 2.

▪ *SHRIMP OMELET* is both another name for the Nantua Omelet and an omelet made with creamed shrimp; usually a little Madeira is used to thin the Cream Sauce (page 281) for a more challenging flavor.

▪ *OMELET PARMENTIER*

> *½ cup finely diced boiled potatoes*
> *1 tablespoon butter*
> *Dash salt*
> *1 teaspoon chopped parsley*
> *Basic Omelet (page 198)*

Gently sauté the potatoes in the butter; sprinkle them with salt and roll them in the chopped parsley. Add the potatoes to the cooking omelet just before folding it; transfer it to a plate and brush it with butter. Serves 2.

■ OMELET PAUVRE FEMME (*Poor Woman's Omelet*)

> ½ *cup diced firm bread*
> 1 *tablespoon butter*
> *Basic Omelet* (*page* 198)

Sauté the diced bread in the butter, turning it to be sure it is crisp and evenly browned. Spread it on the very liquid surface of the omelet as soon as it has been placed in the pan. Fold, brush with butter and serve. Serves 2.

■ OMELET POLONAISE

> ½ *cup mutton hash made with onions and potatoes*
> *Basic Omelet* (*page* 198)
> 3 *tablespoons Tomato Sauce* (*page* 278)

Warm the hash in a lightly oiled skillet, and spread it evenly over the surface of the omelet just before folding. Spoon the Tomato Sauce over the omelet just before serving. Serves 2.

Mutton hash is available canned, but it can be easily made by sautéeing canned corned mutton or precooked fresh mutton with diced potatoes and onions.

■ OMELET PORTUGAISE

> ¾ *cup flaked cooked codfish*
> ½ *teaspoon olive oil*
> *Basic Omelet* (*page* 198)
> 3 *tablespoons Tomato Sauce* (*page* 278)

Warm the codfish flakes in the olive oil, but do not cook them. Remove the flakes from the pan and replace them with the eggs. Immediately spread the codfish over the very liquid surface of the omelet. When the omelet is cooked, fold it, slip it onto its warm plate and spoon on the Tomato Sauce. Serves 2.

Tuna, haddock, mackerel and other fish are often used in this basic omelet. It is also identified by many other names, most frequently the

name of one of the religious orders whose members observed many
fast days when only eggs and fish could be eaten.

▪ *ROMAN OMELET*

> 1 *teaspoon olive oil or butter*
> 2 *tablespoons cooked, chopped spinach*
> *Dash salt*
> *Dash pepper*
> *Basic Omelet (page 198)*

Melt the butter and heat the spinach in it, adding the seasonings.
Put the warm spinach on the firming surface of the omelet just be-
fore it is folded. Often the omelet is sprinkled with drawn butter,
Buerre Noir (page 117), or Sauce Vinaigrette (page 287). Serves 2.
  Florentine Omelet is another name for the same dish.

▪ *SPINACH OMELET* usually is prepared with creamed spinach
and garnished with a portion of the cream or with Cream Sauce.

▪ *OMELET SANTÉ (Health Omelet)*

> *Basic Omelet (page 198)*
> 1 *tablespoon chopped mushrooms, parboiled or*
>   *sautéed*
> 1½ *tablespoons chopped chives*
> 1½ *tablespoons chopped parsley*
> 1½ *tablespoons Tomato Sauce (page 278)*
> 3 *or 4 sprigs watercress*

While the surface of the omelet is very liquid, sprinkle it evenly with
the mixed mushrooms, chives and parsley. Fold it when it is ready,
and slide it onto a warm plate. Brush the omelet with the Tomato
Sauce, glaze it a moment under the broiler and garnish with sprigs
of watercress. Serves 2.

▪ *SORREL OMELET*

> ⅓ *cup tender, young sorrel leaves*
> 2 *tablespoons light cream*
> *Basic Omelet (page 198)*

Blanch the sorrel by plunging it into boiling water. Drain it at once,
and simmer it in the cream a minute or two. Spoon it into the center

of the omelet just before folding; serve it after brushing the top with butter. Serves 2.

■ *ZUCCHINI OMELET*

> ½ *cup diced sautéed zucchini*
> *Dash garlic salt*
> *Basic Omelet (page* 198*)*
> 3 *tablespoons Tomato Sauce (page* 278*)*

Sprinkle the zucchini with the garlic salt while it is still warm; spread it over the surface of the very liquid omelet. When the top is firm, fold the omelet and slide it onto a warmed plate. Pour on the Tomato Sauce. Serves 2.

■ SPECIAL OMELETS

All omelets are special to a degree, but like Orwell's animals, some are more special than others. Diversity or rarity of fillings, special sauces or some other factor lifts them from the classification of "simple." Included in this group is a famous "secret" omelet that really isn't a secret, after all.

■ *OMELET AHMED PASHA*

Created for a single ostrich egg, this omelet was originated by the eunuch cook of Ahmed Pasha, Bey of Algiers. It was served to, and its recipe given to, Alexandre Dumas when the writer–gourmet visited the Bey in the 1840s. If you have a fresh ostrich egg, by all means use it, but do not try to crack the shell; instead, drill a hole at each end and blow out the egg's contents. Lacking an ostrich egg, use five hen's eggs. But begin with the savory filling.

> ½ *cup olive oil*
> 3 *tablespoons chopped green pepper*
> 3 *tablespoons chopped onion*
> 4 *tablespoons diced eggplant*
> 4 *tablespoons diced drained tomato*
> 4 *drained anchovy fillets, chopped fine*
> *Basic Omelet (page* 198*), using* 5 *eggs*
> *Dash salt*
> *Dash cayenne*

Heat the oil over medium heat; sauté the green pepper, onion and eggplant, adding them in that order, and finally add the tomato. Remove the mixture from the heat before adding the anchovy fillets and seasonings. Stir well, and spread the filling across the center of the omelet just before it is ready to be folded; use any excess filling as a garnish over the top of the omelet after it is dished up. Serves 4.

▪ OMELET ALBINA

> *Truffle grating or Truffle Essence*
> *Basic Omelet (page 198)*
> *2 teaspoons heavy cream*
> *⅔ cup ground or minced cooked chicken meat*
> *Dash salt*
> *Dash pepper*

Add the truffle grating to the eggs as they are beaten. Warm the cream and blend in the chicken meat and seasonings. Put them on the surface of the cooking omelet just before folding. Brush the top with butter after it is in its plate. Serves 2.

Omelet Princesse and *Omelet à la Reine* are other names often given to an omelet filled with chicken meat and truffle-flavored.

▪ OMELET BRILLAT-SAVARIN

> *¼ cup carp roe*
> *2 tablespoons butter*
> *½ cup well-drained, flaked tuna*
> *Dash salt*
> *Dash cayenne*
> *Basic Omelet (page 198)*
> *¼ cup tarragon vinegar*

Poach the roe in melted butter over very low heat, adding the tuna just long enough to warm it; mix it well, dusting with salt and pepper. Drain all the butter possible back into the pan. Spread the tuna–roe mixture over the surface of the omelet as soon as it is in the pan. Fold it and slide it onto a plate. Bring the heat up under the butter in the pan, dash in the vinegar and pour it over the omelet. Serves 2.

▪ OMELET DIANE

> *⅔ cup cooked meat of game birds: pheasant, quail,*
>   *woodcock, etc.*

> *2 tablespoons Sauce Chasseur* (*page 276*)
> *Basic Omelet* (*page 198*)
> *1 tablespoon Sauce Espagnole* (*page 275*)

Warm the meat, either minced or ground, in the Sauce Chasseur; it should form a very loose purée. Spoon it onto the center of the omelet just before folding. Transfer the omelet to a plate, brush it lightly with Sauce Espagnole and glaze it under the broiler before serving. Serves 2.

▪ *OMELET ST. HUBERT* is the name applied to an omelet filled with the minced meat of game: venison, etc.; it is not glazed, but served with Sauce Poivrade (page 278).

▪ *OMELET JARDINIÈRE* (*Gardener's Omelet*)

> *½ cup diced vegetables, boiled in meat stock: carrots,*
> *potatoes, celery, green peas*
> *Dash salt*
> *Basic Omelet* (*page 198*)
> *¼ cup tiny cauliflower flowerets*
> *½ cup Cream Sauce* (*page 281*)

Have the diced vegetables warm, salt them lightly and spread them over the surface of an omelet as soon as it is in the pan. Finish cooking the omelet, fold it and transfer it to a platter. Warm the cauliflower bits in Cream Sauce; pour it over the top of the omelet before serving. Serves 2.

▪ *OMELET JURASSIENNE*

> *½ cup diced uncooked bacon*
> *½ cup minced uncooked onions*
> *Pinch powdered sorrel*
> *Dash salt*
> *Dash pepper*
> *Basic Omelet* (*page 198*)

Sauté the bacon and onions together; both should be nicely browned. Season them while cooking with the sorrel, salt and pepper. Reserve the drippings. Spread the bacon and onions over the liquid surface of an omelet that has just been placed in the pan, finish its cooking and fold. Before serving, brush its surface with the pan drippings. Serves 2.

▪ *OMELET LORRAINE*

> ¼ *cup coarsely diced soft-cooked bacon*
> ½ *cup grated Gruyère cheese*
> *Basic Omelet* (*page* 198)

Mix the just-cooked bacon with the cheese; spread it over the soft surface of the omelet as soon as it is in the pan. Fold the omelet, or turn it and serve it flat; one style of presentation is as common as the other. Serves 2.

▪ *OMELET MAINTENON*

> ½ *cup finely chopped cooked breast of chicken*
> ¼ *cup finely chopped sautéed mushrooms*
> *Grated truffle or Truffle Essence*
> *Dash nutmeg*
> 3 *tablespoons heavy cream*
> *Basic Omelet* (*page* 198)
> 3 *tablespoons Béchamel Sauce* (*page* 280)

Combine the chicken, mushrooms, truffle and nutmeg in the cream while it is heating. Spoon them into the center of the omelet just before it is folded. When it is on the plate, pour over it the warmed Béchamel Sauce. Serves 2.

▪ *OMELET MÈRE POULARD* (*Mother Poulard's Omelet*)

This may well be the most famous omelet in Christendom. It is certainly the one most often reprinted, in varying forms, in magazines and books containing omelet recipes; usually the recipe is offered as the revelation of the "long-lost secret" of the famous omelet served at the Inn of the Abbey of Mont St. Michel to the hundreds of thousands of pilgrims and tourists who have visited the Abbey on its dramatic rise of rock. Since the original Mère Poulard who operated the inn died in 1918, and since the omelet is not mixed individually, but ladled into small pans from a huge pot of ready-mixed batter, no one can really swear that there is any validity to these "revelations." However, a number of noted chefs, including Escoffier and deGouy, are in agreement that the "secret" omelet may be duplicated very closely; the sum of their deductions is represented in this recipe.

>5 *eggs*
>10 *tablespoons heavy cream*
>*Dash salt*
>*Dash pepper*
>2 *tablespoons butter*

Beat each egg into the batter individually; begin with 1 egg and 1 tablespoon cream, and beat well; add another egg and another tablespoon of cream as the beating continues; and so on until all the eggs and half the cream are used. Add the seasonings, and while still beating begin to add flakes of butter until the 2 tablespoons have been incorporated in the batter. Set aside to stand 15 minutes. Butter the pan and bring it to high heat; the butter should be just below smoking temperature. Pour in the eggs. Allow the bottom skin to form, then quickly stir into the very soft omelet the remaining cream. Fold it at once and serve. No filling or sauce is offered; the omelet should be very soft at its center. Serves 4.

▪ *OMELET NORMANDE*

In preparing the filling for this omelet, canned or frozen seafoods may be used as successfully as fresh ones. If canned ingredients are used, they should be placed in the sauce just long enough to heat them thoroughly. If frozen ingredients are used, parboil them without thawing, drain and transfer to the sauce. Cook fresh ingredients in water to cover and drain them before putting in the sauce. The oysters, however, are traditionally served raw.

>1 *tablespoon chopped mussels*
>1 *tablespoon chopped shrimp*
>1 *tablespoon chopped mushrooms*
>2 *tablespoons Sauce Velouté* (*page* 279)
>2 *tablespoons light cream*
>*Dash salt*
>*Dash pepper*
>*Pinch cayenne*
>*Basic Omelet* (*page* 198)
>2 *raw oysters*

Prepare the mussels, shrimp and mushrooms. Simmer them in the Sauce Velouté to which the cream, salt, pepper and cayenne have been added. Do not allow to boil. Prepare the Basic Omelet; before folding it, spoon the solids from the sauce and a little of the liquid into its center, then fold and slide onto a warm plate. Pour over it the remaining sauce, and lay the two oysters on top. Serves 2.

■ *OKRA OMELET*

> ¼ *cup minced onion*
> ½ *cup tender small okra, sliced across the pod*
> 1½ *tablespoons butter*
> *Dash salt*
> *Dash cayenne*
> 1 *teaspoon minced well-drained pimiento*
> *Basic Omelet (page* 198*)*
> 3 *tablespoons Tomato Sauce (page* 278*)*

Sauté the onion and okra together in the butter; drain them well, over the pan, so that the butter drips back into the utensil. Season the vegetables while cooking with the salt and cayenne. Remove the vegetables from the pan and mix in the pimiento. Spread the mixture over the surface of the omelet as soon as it is in its pan; fold the omelet and slip it onto a plate. Blend the Tomato Sauce with the butter left in the pan and pour it over the omelet before serving. Serves 2.

■ *OYSTER OMELET (I)*

Since some like the oysters in an omelet sautéed and others want them creamed, two recipes are given.

> ½ *dozen small or* 3 *large oysters*
> 1 *tablespoon flour or very fine breadcrumbs*
> 2 *tablespoons cooking oil or fat*
> *Dash salt*
> *Dash cayenne*
> *Basic Omelet (page* 198*)*

Roll the oysters in the flour or breadcrumbs; sauté them in very hot oil; after they are in the pan season them with salt and cayenne. Just before folding the omelet, cover half its surface with the oysters. Fold and serve the omelet; lemon wedges, drawn butter, or Beurre Noir (page 117) should be offered warm in a separate bowl. Serves 2.

■ *OYSTER OMELET (II)*

> 3 *tablespoons heavy cream*
> *Dash salt*

Dash pepper
3 or 4 drops Tabasco sauce
½ dozen small or 3 large oysters
Basic Omelet (page 198)

Warm the cream until it is simmering; add the salt, pepper and Tabasco, and drop in the oysters. Poach them 3 to 4 minutes, but do not boil. While the surface of the omelet is still very liquid, lay the oysters on it. Fold and serve the omelet, brushing the top with butter after it is on its warmed plate. Serves 2.

▪ *OMELET PAYSANNE (Peasant Omelet)*

1 tablespoon oil or fat
2 tablespoons grated boiled potato
2 tablespoons diced cooked ham or bacon
3 or 4 finely chopped sorrel leaves
Basic Omelet (page 198)
Dash salt
Dash pepper

Bring the oil to high heat, and sauté the grated potato until it is very crisp. Add the ham or bacon long enough to warm it. Drain well, and sprinkle with the sorrel, salt and pepper. Sprinkle the mixture evenly over the surface of the omelet as soon as it has been placed in the pan; turn the omelet and serve it flat. It should be allowed to cook until firm. Serves 2.

▪ *PROVENÇALE OMELET*

3 small, ripe tomatoes
1 tablespoon olive oil
Dash salt
Dash pepper
1 tablespoon finely chopped parsley
Basic Omelet (page 198)

Peel, drain, deseed and dice the tomatoes. Bring the oil to a high heat and sauté the tomatoes until soft, seasoning them with salt and pepper. Roll the tomatoes in the chopped parsley, and spread them evenly on the very liquid surface of the omelet, as soon as it is in the pan. Turn the omelet, and serve it flat. Serves 2.

■ *SAVOYARD OMELET*

> 1½ *tablespoons butter*
> ½ *cup coarsely chopped leeks*
> ¼ *cup diced boiled potatoes*
> *Dash salt*
> *Dash pepper*
> *Basic Omelet* (*page* 198)

Melt the butter; sauté the leeks until they are translucent. Add the potato dice and seasonings. When the potatoes are lightly browned, spoon them into the center of the omelet just before it is folded. Brush the top with butter before serving. Serves 2.

Another version of the Savoyard Omelet uses cheese cubes instead of potatoes; the cubes are partly melted in the pan with the leeks. Take your choice.

■ *SHAD ROE OMELET*

> ½ *cup shad roe*
> 1 *tablespoon butter*
> 1½ *tablespoons flaked, boiled or baked fish: tuna,*
>   *haddock, etc.*
> *Basic Omelet* (*page* 198)
> 3 *tablespoons Sauce Mornay* (*page* 281)

Sauté the roe in the butter, adding the fish flakes during the final minutes of cooking so that they will be warm. Spread this mixture on the liquid surface of the omelet as soon as it is in the pan. Fold the omelet, slide it onto a platter and cover with the warm Sauce Mornay. Serves 2.

■ *OMELET TALLYRAND*

> 2 *tablespoons chopped onions*
> 2 *tablespoons butter*
> *Dash curry powder*
> *Basic Omelet* (*page* 198)
> 2 *parboiled calves' sweetbreads*
> 2 *tablespoons Sauce Velouté* (*page* 279)
> 1 *teaspoon heavy cream*

Sauté the onions in half the butter, and spread them with curry powder. Distribute them evenly over the liquid surface of the omelet as soon as it is in the pan. Turn the omelet; serve it flat. Sauté the sweetbreads with the remaining 1 tablespoon butter added to the butter in the pan in which the onions were cooked, so that a trace of curry powder will cling to them. Lay the sweetbreads on the omelet, thin the Sauce Velouté with the cream and pour the warm sauce over the omelet before serving. Serves 2.

■ *OMELET VERDURIÈRE (Greengrocer's Omelet)*

> 1 *tablespoon chopped parsley*
> ½ *tablespoon chopped young chervil*
> ¼ *tablespoon chopped tender sorrel*
> ½ *tablespoon chopped chives*
> 1 *tablespoon shredded heart of lettuce*
> *Basic Omelet (page* 198)
> *Beurre Noir (page* 117)

Toss the herbs and lettuce together and sprinkle them generously over the surface of the liquid omelet as soon as it is in the pan. Fold the omelet, pour the Beurre Noir over the top and serve at once. Serves 2.

Some offer this omelet turned and served flat, but when it is cooked this way the herbs often come into contact with the cooking pan and char, which mars the flavor of the dish.

■ *OMELET VIVEUR (Roué's Omelet)*

> 2 *tablespoons finely diced raw artichoke heart*
> 2 *tablespoons finely diced raw celeriac*
> 2 *tablespoons butter*
> ½ *cup raw beef cut in small dice*
> 1 *teaspoon flour*
> *Dash salt*
> *Dash pepper*
> *Basic Omelet (page* 198)

Sauté the artichoke and celeriac in the butter over low heat until they begin to become tender. Raise the heat and add the beef. Mix together the flour, salt and pepper and sprinkle them over the artichoke, celeriac and beef, stirring so that they will become crusted and brown. Prepare the Basic Omelet; spread the artichoke, celeriac and beef mixture on its surface when the omelet is first put into its pan. Turn the omelet instead of folding; when brown, slide it onto a warm plate and brush the top with butter. Serves 2.

▪ SURPRISING OMELETS

As with other surprising egg dishes, the element of novelty might be in the ingredients themselves, the manner in which they are combined or the presentation of the finished dish. We will meet in this group the double-decker omelet that resembles a sandwich, as well as the *mousseline*, which is kin to a soufflé.

▪ *AVOCADO OMELET*

Only one trick to master for this one: choosing an avocado ripe enough to have lost the milky bitterness characteristic of underripe avocados, yet firm enough to keep its shape well. The easiest to judge are the thin-skinned Fuerte type.

> 1 *medium avocado*
> *Dash onion salt*
> *Dash cayenne*
> *Basic Omelet (page 198)*

Peel the avocado starting at the stem and cut ½ cup of dice from its fleshy neck; make 2 or 3 semicircular slices by cutting around the fruit to the seed and freeing the sections with a spoon.

Sprinkle the onion salt and cayenne on the avocado pieces. Put the diced bits into the center of the omelet just before it is folded, and when it is on its plate arrange the semicircular slices as a garnish on top. Serves 2.

▪ *BLUE FLOWER OMELET*

> 2 *tablespoons chopped chives*
> *Basic Omelet (page 198)*
> 10 *or* 12 *chive blossoms*

Sprinkle the chopped chives on the surface of the liquid omelet as soon as it is in the pan; a moment before folding, dot half the chive blossoms over the surface. After the folded omelet is on its plate, brush it with butter and arrange the remaining blossoms as a garnish. Serves 2.

■ *OMELET BOUCHÈRE* (*Butcher's Omelet*)

Big beef thighbones can usually be gotten from your butcher by asking him to save them for you; have him saw them in 6-inch lengths. Poach the bones in lightly salted water to cover for a half-hour or longer. If you can persuade the butcher to leave some meat on the bones, you also will have broth. A boning knife is the best tool to use in getting the marrow out intact.

> *½ cup diced poached marrow*
> *3 or 4 slices poached marrow*
> *1 tablespoon butter*
> *Dash salt*
> *2 or 3 coarsely broken peppercorns*
> *Basic Omelet (page 198)*
> *3 tablespoons Sauce Espagnole (page 275)*

Sauté the diced and sliced marrow in the butter; after removing it from the pan, sprinkle it with the salt and peppercorns. Spread the diced marrow evenly over the surface of the omelet as soon as it is in the pan, and fold it when it is ready. When it is on its plate, lay the sliced marrow on top and pour the warmed sauce over it. Serves 2.

■ *BREADCRUMB OMELET*

Keep in mind that ordinary commercial baker's bread is not designed to be used in cooking. You need a firm-textured bread, not the squish-loaf with its fluffed-up softness.

> *2 cups coarse breadcrumbs*
> *½ cup warm milk*
> *3 tablespoons chopped chives*
> *Dash salt*
> *Dash pepper*
> *Dash nutmeg*
> *Basic Omelet (page 198)*

Soak the breadcrumbs in the milk; add the chives and seasonings. Beat them into the omelet as it is being mixed. Serve the omelet flat rather than folded. Serves 2.

▪ *OMELET CAFÉ DES SPORTS*

A house specialty from the Café des Sports of Paris. The omelet should be a large one.

> 1 *tablespoon butter*
> ¾ *cup parboiled, diced beef or veal kidneys*
> 1 *whole parboiled kidney*
> 1½ *cups red wine*
> 2 *tablespoons heavy cream*
> *Dash cayenne*
> 1 *egg white*
> *Basic Omelet (page* 198)
> 2 *tablespoons Tomato Sauce (page* 278) *or catsup*

Over low heat melt the butter; sauté both the diced and the whole kidney. Remove the whole kidney and reserve it. Over the kidney dice slowly pour the wine, stir it well and simmer 3 to 4 minutes. Add the cream and the cayenne; simmer but do not boil. Beat the egg white until it forms a stiff peak. Beat the eggs for the omelet, substituting Tomato Sauce or catsup for the cream in the Basic Omelet recipe. Just before pouring the omelet into its own pan, stir the beaten egg white into the batter in small spoonfuls; do not beat or stir it vigorously. When the omelet is ready to be folded, remove the diced kidney and spoon it with a little of the sauce into the center; fold the omelet and transfer it to its warmed plate. Slice the whole kidney very thin, lay over the top of the omelet and pour the wine sauce over it. Serves 2.

▪ *CHINESE OMELET*

Though designed for *wok* cookery, this can be very successfully prepared in a skillet or omelet pan. The trick is to begin stirring the minute the eggs hit the pan, and to stop stirring once the bottom skin starts to form.

> 3 *tablespoons peanut oil*
> ½ *cup cold boiled rice*
> ¼ *cup chopped cooked meat: ham, veal, chicken, etc.*
> 2 *tablespoons chopped onion tops or shallots*
> 1 *tablespoon green peas*
> 2 *tablespoons chopped bean sprouts*
> *Dash salt*

Dash pepper

3 eggs

Heat the oil over high heat, and quickly add all the ingredients but the eggs; stir to mix well. Pour the beaten eggs over the mixture in the pan, stir once or twice, then let it alone until the top surface firms and the omelet is ready to fold. Serves 2.

This is a common dish in China, and there are several versions, including one from Szechwan that calls for the inclusion of tiny red-hot peppers.

▪ OMELET DIPLOMATE

There is a small family of these double-decker omelets; the Omelet Diplomate just happens to be alphabetically first. All of them have an element of surprise in their service; many also use unusual ingredients. Incidentally, if you're in love with pots and pans, the preparation of the omelets in this family is easier if you have two pans; a good excuse for you to get a "His" and "Hers" set.

¼ cup Béchamel Sauce (page 280)
1 tablespoon brandy
¾ cup chopped lobster meat
2 Basic Omelets (page 198)
½ cup Sauce Mornay (page 281)
Breadcrumbs

Combine the Béchamel Sauce and brandy in a double boiler and simmer the chopped lobster meat in it; do not allow it to boil.

Cook two small flat omelets. Place one on a warm serving dish and cover it with the lobster–Béchamel mixture; top it with the second, and cover with warmed Sauce Mornay. Sprinkle with breadcrumbs and glaze under the broiler until the crumbs are browned. Serves 4.

▪ OMELET AUX FRUITS DE MER (*Seafood Omelet*) is the only omelet generally served in a casserole, though there is no reason why others of the double-decker type should not be adapted to the casserole. One omelet is placed on the bottom of the casserole, covered with a generous mixture of mixed seafoods: minced clam, shrimp, mussels, lobster, flaked fish, all in Cream Sauce (page 281); the top omelet is spread with Shrimp Butter (page 288), and the casserole warmed a moment in the oven before being brought to the table.

▪ GREEK OMELET incorporates minced onion in one of its halves, chopped pimiento in the other; the filling between the two layers is mutton hash, and the whole is covered with Tomato Sauce (page 278).

■ *OMELET LOUIS FOREST* calls for the bottom omelet to be spread with a thick purée of truffled *foie gras;* veal gravy into which a few splashes of Beurre Noir (page 117) have been stirred is spooned over the top.

■ *OMELET MONTBRY* has minced onions rolled in horseradish stirred in the batter of both the top and bottom layers; between the two is a purée of onion-seasoned celeriac. The structure is covered with Sauce Mornay (page 281) and glazed.

■ *OMELET NANCÉIENNE* puts chopped sautéed onions rolled in finely chopped parsley in the cooking omelets, both top and bottom; its filling is a layer of thin slices of black (blood) sausage. Veal gravy is poured over the top omelet.

■ *OMELET SAINT-FLOUR* combines onion with one of its layers as it is cooked, crumbled bacon with the other. The filling is tender cabbage leaves braised with bacon drippings; it is covered with Tomato Sauce (page 278).

These are the traditional double-deckers, but there is no really valid reason why any filling might not be used between two small omelets if this type of service strikes your fancy.

■ *FAROE OMELET*

Only those few people living on the stony Faroe Islands, which lie between Iceland and the Scandinavian Peninsula, can experience this omelet in its traditional form, for it is made with the eggs of wild seabirds and its filling is a seaweed gathered from the shores of the islands themselves. The substitute ingredients are reasonable approximations for the native items.

> 1 *teaspoon olive oil*
> ½ *cup cooked, chopped kale*
> 3 *coarsely chopped anchovy fillets*
> ½ *teaspoon chopped capers*
> *Basic Omelet (page 198)*

Warm the olive oil and toss the kale, anchovy fillets and capers in it. Spoon the mixture into the center of the omelet just before it is folded.

If additional flavor is desired, the omelet can be brushed with Anchovy Butter (page 288). Serves 2.

▪ *OMELET MAXIM*

Since Maxim's restaurant was the traditional headquarters of tourists
from the United States in pre-World War I days, this specialty of the
house may have been responsible for the Americans' slang term for
Frenchmen.

> *2 frogs' legs*
> *1 tablespoon butter*
> *Basic Omelet (page 198)*
> *4 small cooked shrimp*
> *3 tablespoons Sauce Mornay (page 281)*

Sauté the frogs' legs in the butter. Prepare the folded omelet and
transfer it to its plate; garnish the top with the shrimp, spoon on the
sauce and lay a frog's leg on either side of the omelet. Serves 2.

▪ *OMELET MOUSSELINE*

Any omelet may be cooked *mousseline,* or souffléd. The term describes a manner of preparation, a cooking process. Some omelets are
traditionally served *mousseline;* their recipes are given following the
description of the process that produces this type of omelet. From 3
to 6 eggs may be used for each omelet.

> *3 eggs, separated*
> *2 tablespoons light cream* per egg
> *Dash salt*
> *Dash pepper*

Beat the egg yolks with the cream and seasonings until they are
frothy. Beat the egg whites until they form soft peaks. Fold one-third
of the beaten whites into the yolks, then fold this mixture into the
remaining whites. Pour it into a very hot pan, turn when the bottom crust is formed and cook until the second side is brown. This
omelet is almost always served flat, as its puffiness makes it difficult
to fold. Like the soufflé it resembles, it must be served at once. Serves 2.

Generally, chopped parsley is the ingredient associated with the
plain Omelet Mousseline; it is often called a *Souffléd Parsley Omelet.*

■ *OMELET BIGOURDINE* has 2 tablespoons of finely shredded *foie gras* and some truffle gratings beaten into the yolk. This is also called *Omelet Rossini*.

■ *OMELET NIÇOISE* substitutes tomato juice for the cream beaten into the yolks and is garnished with a pair of anchovy fillets.

■ *SQUASH BLOSSOM OMELET* has a half-dozen blanched squash blossoms chopped coarsely and added to the whites; a few perfect blossoms are used to garnish the omelet's top before serving.

■ *TRUFFLED OMELET* has a generous sprinkling of truffle gratings beaten into the egg yolks.

Other variations or fillings that lend themselves to use in the fluffy Omelet Mousseline are those given for the Blue Flower Omelet (page 223); Omelet Santé (page 213); and Omelet aux Fines Herbes (page 206). There are a number of others which will certainly occur to you. Sauces are best avoided with omelets of this type; sprinkle them with Beurre Noir (page 117) or Sauce Vinaigrette (page 287) if you wish extra flavor.

■ *ONION RING OMELET*

> 1 *egg white*
> 1½ *teaspoons flour*
> *Dash salt*
> *Dash pepper*
> 2 *thick slices from a large sweet onion*
> *Oil or fat for deep frying*
> *Basic Omelet (page 198)*

Beat the egg white, flour and seasonings into a light batter; separate the onion slices into rings, dip them in the batter and fry them in deep fat until crisp. Space the smaller onion rings on the liquid surface of the omelet as soon as it is in the pan. Fold when it is ready, slide it onto a service plate, brush with butter and garnish with the large onion rings. Serves 2.

■ *OMELET PANACHÉE (Two-Toned Omelet)*

> *Basic Omelet (page 198), using 5 eggs*
> 2 *teaspoons tomato paste thinned with ½ teaspoon water*
> 2 *tablespoons grated Gruyère cheese*

Divide the batter to make 1 small omelet and 1 large one. Into the batter for the small omelet, beat the thinned tomato paste; cook it and set it aside. Into the batter for the large omelet beat half the grated cheese. When the large omelet is ready to be folded, place the small omelet on its surface and fold so that it is completely covered by the large omelet. Slide it onto a plate, sprinkle the remaining grated cheese on top and glaze it under the broiler until the cheese begins to melt. Serves 2 generously; can be stretched to serve 4 if offered as first course.

▪ RED FLANNEL OMELET

New England's famous Red Flannel Hash lends its name and ingredients to this recipe.

> ½ cup grated boiled beets
> ½ cup finely chopped boiled beef
> 1 tablespoon butter
> Dash salt
> Dash pepper
> Basic Omelet (page 198)

Sauté the beets and beef in the butter; do not overcook or brown. Mix them well and season them as they cook. Spread the mixture over the surface of the omelet just before folding. Brush the top with butter and serve. Serves 2.

▪ OMELET ROUENNAISE

> 2 or 3 duck livers
> 1 tablespoon butter
> Flour for dredging
> Dash salt
> 1 tablespoon grated orange peel
> Dash nutmeg
> Basic Omelet (page 198)
> ½ cup applesauce
> 1 teaspoon cinnamon

Sauté the duck livers in the butter until the outsides are browned; dusting with flour and salt helps brown them without allowing them to overcook. Chop the livers coarsely and return them to the pan with the grated orange peel added; dust with the nutmeg and with additional salt if needed. Spread the liver–orange peel mixture over the liquid surface of the omelet as soon as it is in the pan. Fold the omelet and remove it to a plate; mix the applesauce with the cinnamon and lay it in a ring around the omelet. Brush the omelet with butter, glaze it and sprinkle it with a touch more cinnamon. Serves 2.

▪ *TAN CHIAO* (*Half-Moon Omelets*)

This is the ancestor and traditional service of the egg roll, designed for home kitchens.

> *5 eggs*
> *½ cup ground cooked pork*
> *2 tablespoons chopped bean sprouts*
> *1 teaspoon sugar*
> *1 tablespoon sherry (rice wine is traditional, but sherry makes an acceptable substitute)*
> *1 teaspoon soy sauce*
> *2 tablespoons peanut oil*
> *2 cups cooked green peas*
> *½ teaspoon salt*

Beat the eggs, and set them aside to rest. Mix the pork, bean sprouts, sugar, sherry and soy sauce. Into a lightly greased skillet over low heat drop 1 tablespoon beaten egg; cook until it begins to set. Put 1 teaspoon of the meat mixture in its center and fold the egg over it to form a half-moon; turn for a moment to allow the pork filling to heat. Continue until all the eggs and meat are used. In a heavy saucepan that can be tightly covered heat the peanut oil; add the peas (if frozen peas are used, do not precook them, as they are blanched in the freezing and need no other cooking) and the salt. Arrange the omelets over the peas, cover the pan, reduce the heat to the very lowest and steam 5 minutes. In serving, a spoonful of peas is taken up with each of the little omelets. Serves 4.

▪ DESSERT OMELETS

▪ *APPLE OMELET*

This was created about 1750 for Frederick II of Prussia by his famous chef, Urban-Dubois.

> 2 *whole eggs plus 2 egg yolks*
> 2 *tablespoons flour*
> 1 *cup milk*
> 1 *tablespoon sugar*
> *Dash salt*
> *Dash nutmeg*
> 2 *tablespoons butter*
> 6 *tart apples, peeled, cored and sliced*
> 2 *tablespoons brown sugar*
> 1 *teaspoon cinnamon*

Beat the whole eggs with the egg yolks, adding the flour, milk, sugar, salt and nutmeg while beating. When the mixture is smooth and creamy, set it aside to rest for 10 minutes. Heat the butter, and add the sliced apples; as soon as the apples become transparent add the egg mixture. Lift its edges with a spatula and tilt the pan to allow all the liquid to reach the hot metal. When the top begins to set, turn it and cook 2 more minutes; slide it onto a warm plate and sprinkle with brown sugar mixed with cinnamon. Glaze under the broiler a minute to soften the sugar. Serves 2.

■ JELLY OMELET

Few dishes are unhappier than the usual offering of a jelly omelet; it generally takes the form of a plain omelet with a halfhearted dab of jelly in its folds or smeared over its surface. The result is a cacophony instead of a symphony. A genuine jelly omelet can be a fine dish, as witness this one.

> 3 *eggs*
> 1½ *tablespoons light cream*
> *Dash salt*
> *Dash nutmeg*
> 1½ *tablespoons butter*
> 2 *tablespoons jelly: grape, currant, etc.*
> *Sugar*

Beat the eggs, cream and seasonings until they are frothy, then begin to add the butter and 1 tablespoon of the jelly to the eggs in alternate small quantities while continuing to beat. When all the butter and the 1 tablespoon jelly are added, set the mixture to rest for 10 to 15 minutes. Thin the remaining jelly to the consistency of warm honey by pouring a few drops of bar syrup (equal parts sugar and water) into it while stirring.

Pour the eggs into the pan at high heat; lift the edges to allow any liquid to reach the pan. When the top firms, pour the thinned jelly over half the omelet, and fold. Transfer to a warm platter, and pour the remaining jelly over the top. Serves 2.

■ *SWEET POTATO OMELET*

> *½ cup parboiled diced sweet potatoes*
> *1 tablespoon butter*
> *Large pinch powdered allspice*
> *Basic Omelet (page 198)*

Sauté the sweet potato dice in the butter, sprinkling it with the allspice. Drain it and distribute it over the surface of the omelet as soon as it is placed in the pan. Fold the omelet and serve, or turn it to cook on both sides and serve flat; butter the surface before serving. Serves 2.

If you wish to make this a sweeter omelet, sprinkle the potatoes with brown sugar as they cook; butter the finished omelet's surface heavily, spread with brown sugar and glaze under the broiler.

■ SOUFFLÉS

Having exhausted the subject of omelets, it's time to look at the omelet's kissing cousin, the soufflé. Both dishes share another kinship in that both have been victims of propaganda regarding the difficulty of their preparation. Recently, though, the emphasis has switched from stressing the difficulties to emphasizing how simple both dishes really are.

Most of those who turn pale and begin shivering at the very idea of attempting a "tricky, complicated" dish like the soufflé are those who simply haven't had the courage to try. The soufflé is not reserved as the exclusive province of the *cordon bleu;* no deep mystery surrounds its preparation and cooking. And being familiar with the technique of the soufflé opens a wide door, for there are hundreds of variations both for general service with cheeses, meats and vegetables, and for desserts with fruit syrups, purées and liqueurs. But still some tremble, fearing that they will try and fail.

There are really only three reasons why a soufflé will fail, and few cookbooks or articles on the subject take the trouble to explain these three reasons. Once you know what not to do under any circumstances, the rest of the road is smooth.

Most commonly, the reason a soufflé fails is an impatient cook, the kind who "just must crack the oven door open a tiny bit to see how it's doing." This causes a fatal draft of cold air to be drawn into the oven as its hot air escapes through the cracked-open door; the cold blast wafts across the rising crown of the soufflé, and it collapses dejectedly. The second most common cause of failure is the use of an unsuitable dish; there is no substitute for the straight-sided soufflé dish, unless it's another just like it. As a soufflé cooks, the eggs rise along the sides of the dish at the same time that heat reaches the center of the soufflé batter, causing the center also to rise. Unless the heating is uniform, and unless the surface tension created by the rising edges also is uniform, the center will not crown. The third cause of failure is lack of understanding by the cook that adjustments must be made in quantities of ingredients to compensate for the varying water contents of the vegetables or fruits used; the delicate batter is overloaded with "wet" ingredients.

This last isn't as complicated as it seems at first glance. Foods tend to fall into certain groups; there is little variation of moisture content among the red meats—though there is a large difference between red meats and fish. There is a fairly wide variation in the water percentages of vegetables: squash and cucumbers, for instance, are much "wetter" than mushrooms and turnips. This difference is important because as vegetables, meats, cheeses, fish or fruits cook in a soufflé, they release their moisture as steam. The amounts aren't large, but the dish isn't large, either. It takes only a tiny bit too much water to cause the delicate structure of air bubbles to collapse and bring unpleasant sogginess to the soufflé's center.

So much for the physics involved. Once the causes of soufflé failure are understood, they can be overcome, and no one need fear the soufflé for a moment. The soufflé is both impressive and tasty, and if the properly shaped cooking utensil is used, the quantity of ingredients adjusted for moisture and the oven door left closed, your soufflé will be perfection nine times out of ten. Even master chefs allow themselves this percentage of failure.

Soufflés must be served at once, carried at a run from oven to table, for they lose their puffy texture very quickly. Many cookbooks suggest that the height of a soufflé's crown can be increased by tying a strip of brown paper or foil around the soufflé dish, extending an inch or two above the rim of the utensil. All this does is expose a greater area of the cooked soufflé to cold air and bring about its collapse faster than would be the case if the extension of the utensil's height was not attempted. A thicker layer of grease around the rim of the dish is much better; the soufflé will rise a bit higher, but with a pro-tective film which the paper or foil will not allow to form.

There are many types of soufflé, but only one recipe is needed for all of them. The adjustment is made only in the quantity of filling or character ingredients used, and this adjustment is on the basis of whether an ingredient is classed as "wet" or "dry." Only the name of its flavoring ingredient is used to describe a soufflé; it is a "corn soufflé," a "cheese soufflé," or a "ham soufflé," depending on what the filling happens to be. For that reason, only the basic soufflé recipe will be given; following it will be a list of suggested filling ingre-dients, their classification and any special treatment an individual ingredient might require. Most of them work best when puréed; here is where your blender comes into its own or, if you have no blender, see the section on Purées (page 289) for hints.

There is another branch of the soufflé family, the dessert soufflé; it will be dealt with in the next chapter, which is devoted to the egg as dessert.

■ *BASIC SOUFFLÉ*

> 3 *tablespoons butter*
> 3 *tablespoons flour*
> 1 *cup milk or cream*
> *Dash pepper*
> *Pinch nutmeg*
> 3 *egg yolks*
> *Filling or character ingredient*
> 5 *egg whites*
> ½ *teaspoon salt*

Melt the butter in a saucepan, and stir in the flour; stir over low heat until the mixture begins to bubble, but do not allow it to brown. About 2 minutes' cooking time will be required. Remove from the heat. Warm the milk, stir it into the flour–butter mixture and blend it vigorously until smooth. Add the seasonings at this point.

Beat the egg yolks until they are frothy. Return the milk to very low heat and begin to add the egg yolks a spoonful at a time, beating all the while. When all the yolks are added, remove them from the heat, but continue beating until the mixture is the texture of a light custard and very creamy. The filling or flavoring ingredient, minced or puréed, is added to the egg yolk mixture at this point, and is blended well with it.

Beat the egg whites until they form stiff peaks, adding a pinch of salt while beating. Stir one-third of the whites into the yolk mixture, then cut the yolk mixture into the remaining beaten whites by dropping a tablespoon at a time on top of the whites and cutting it into them with a knife or narrow spatula. The use of a spoon here only releases the air bubbles you have beaten into the egg whites.

Pour into a well-buttered 1-quart soufflé dish; place it in a preheated 400-degree oven for 3 minutes, then reduce the heat to 350 degrees and cook 25 minutes *without opening the oven door.* Serve at once! Serves 4.

▪ *SOUFFLÉS WITH CHEESE*

To the egg yolks, add ¾ cup of any of the following cheeses, grated medium-fine to fine, as described in the basic recipe:

Brick	*Longhorn*
Cheddar	*Parmesan*
Gouda	*Roquefort (½ cup, crumbled fine)*
Gruyère	*Swiss*

The addition of ¼ teaspoon of finely grated Sapsago cheese to any and all cheese omelets is recommended; the Sapsago acts as a flavor amplifier. No successful way has ever been found to use the mild cream-type cheeses such as Camembert and Brie in a soufflé.

▪ *SOUFFLÉS WITH MEAT*

To the egg yolks, add ¾ cup of meat, minced very fine or ground, as described in the basic recipe:

> *Bacon: cooked crisp, drained well, crumbled fine*
> *Chicken: ground or puréed, moistened with 1 teaspoon chicken stock*
> *Ham: lean only, cooked crisp, drained well, ground fine*
> *Kidneys: veal, beef or lamb, sautéed, minced fine, with ½ teaspoon Sauce Espagnole*
> *Pheasant and game birds: minced fine, tossed in butter*

Pork: only smoked cuts, ground fine
Sausage: cooked crisp, drained well, crumbled fine
Sweetbreads: sautéed, minced fine or puréed, with ½
teaspoon Sauce Espagnole
Turkey: treat white meat as chicken, dark meat as
game
Veal: treat as chicken

Beef does not live well in a soufflé; if it is used, treat it by moistening the ground beef with ½ teaspoon Sauce Espagnole.

▪ *SOUFFLÉS WITH SEAFOOD*

To the egg yolks, add ½ cup of fish, preferably cooked by broiling or baking on a rack to remove the excess oils that are in many fish (such as fresh salmon). Shellfish should be steamed, puréed or ground; flake the flesh of fish. Canned tuna or salmon should be flaked, then blotted to remove all excess oil. Oysters should be baked or poached and drained well, then puréed. The use of smoked fish and such preserved fish as anchovies is not recommended; their flavor tends to be too overpowering.

▪ *SOUFFLÉS WITH VEGETABLES*

To the egg yolks, add ½ cup of the following "wet" vegetables, puréed:

Asparagus	*Green peppers*
Corn, cream-style canned	*Peas*
Cucumbers	*Spinach (and all greens)*
Green (or string) beans	*Squash*

To the egg yolks, add ¾ cup of the following "dry" vegetables, puréed:

Artichoke hearts	*Corn, whole-kernel canned or*
Beans, dried (kidney, lentils,	*fresh*
navy, pinto)	*Mushrooms*
Celeriac	*Potatoes*
	Turnips

Combinations of meat and cheese, meat and vegetables or cheese and vegetables can be used to extend the soufflé's range of flavors still further. When using vegetables, season them to taste with salt and pepper independently of any seasoning put in the soufflé itself; a little nutmeg is a great help to marry flavors without adding a strong flavor of its own.

9 ■■

The Sweet Egg

TELL SOMEONE you're going to serve eggs for dessert, and you'll get a look which ranges from polite disbelief to a revelation of your listener's conviction that you've gone slightly mad. Explain that you mean angel food cake or an egg custard, and the listener's faith in your sanity is restored. But when you look at the structure of our usual desserts—leaving aside the lazy packaged substitutes with their chemical taste—it's hard to think of desserts in which eggs *don't* play a part.

An angel food cake just misses being what is variously called an "aircake," a Pâté Royale or a Génoise, those cakelike confections which depend on eggs for texture, leavening and body. A *crème* or custard is built on the egg's homogenizing, emulsifying and stabilizing abilities. The richest, smoothest ice creams are those with eggs in their batter. Meringues, custards, *crèmes*, aircakes—you'll meet them all in this chapter, along with a few that may be strangers to your kitchen and table. Most egg desserts are light and delicate, but a few are as substantial as any dessert has a right to be. Some are stunningly simple, some are staggeringly elaborate, but is your reputation as a cook more important than the time spent in preparing an elaborate dish?

There are no categories to the recipes in this section, though when families are encountered they will be dealt with as a group. There also is no uniformity in the number a recipe will serve, though it will be indicated in the recipe.

■ *ALMOND FROTH* (*Bataclan*)

> 10 *eggs, separated*
> 3 *cups blanched almonds*
> 2 *cups confectioners' sugar*
> ⅛ *teaspoon salt*
> 2 *tablespoons brandy or cognac*
> 2 *tablespoons very fine white breadcrumbs*
> 1½ *cups heavy cream*
> 1 *teaspoon dark rum*

Beat the egg yolks until they are creamy. Pound the almonds or pass them through a blender until they are very fine. Into the egg yolks beat all but 3 tablespoons of the sugar, adding it a little at a time; then add the almonds, salt, brandy and breadcrumbs while continuing to beat. Beat the egg whites until they form soft peaks; whip ¾ cup of the cream stiff and fold it into the yolks, then fold the yolk mixture into the whites. Bake the cake in an ungreased tube pan (angel food pan) 45 minutes in a preheated 450-degree oven. Leave it in the oven 5 to 10 minutes after cooking with the door partly open to let it cool gradually, then invert the pan over a wire rack. It should settle from the pan onto the rack within an hour; if it does not, remove it by gently running a narrow spatula between the cake and the pan.

Whip the remaining cream, adding the remaining sugar and the rum while whipping; it must be very thick. Split the cake into two layers, and spread the bottom layer with filling; use the leftover filling to fill the hole left by the pan's tube, and to frost the top lightly. Sprinkle the top with slivered toasted almonds. Serves 8 to 10.

■ *ALMOND SCHAUM TORTE* (*Foamy Almond Torte*)

> 6 *egg whites*
> 2 *cups sugar*
> ½ *teaspoon vanilla extract*
> 1 *teaspoon almond extract*

1 *teaspoon vinegar*
Sifted flour

Beat the egg whites, adding sugar a spoonful at a time as you beat. When the whites form stiff peaks, add the vanilla extract, almond extract and vinegar a few drops at a time, beating them in. Very lightly sprinkle the bottom and sides of a deep baking dish with sifted flour. Turn the batter into the pan, bake in a preheated 250-degree oven for 10 minutes, then raise the heat to 325 degrees for 5 to 6 minutes more. The top should be brown. Serves 6 to 8.

This mock-torte can be frosted, or cut into layers spread with whipped cream, or served by itself after a heavy meal or offered as a very delicate accompaniment to ice cream.

■ ANGEL PARFAIT

No eggs in a parfait, you say? There are in this one.

3 *egg whites*
½ *teaspoon salt*
¾ *cup sugar*
2 *teaspoons unflavored gelatin*
2 *cups heavy cream*
1½ *teaspoons cognac or liqueur*

Beat the egg whites with the salt until they form soft peaks. Melt the sugar in ½ cup cold water until it threads (about 250 degrees on a candy thermometer). Soften the gelatin in 2 teaspoons cool water, and combine it with the sugar syrup. Whip the cream with the cognac. Beat the syrup–gelatin mixture into the egg whites and continue to beat until they form stiff peaks. Fold the whipped cream into the egg whites. Fill parfait glasses; chill well before serving. Serves 6.

■ CHRISTMAS CAKE (Eggnog Cake)

Though either of the names arbitrarily given to this confection describes it accurately, its true name is lost. A native of Czechoslovakia, it is made with Slivovitz in its homeland, and is served on other festive occasions besides Christmas.

1 *ounce (*1½ *teaspoons) plain gelatin*
6 *eggs, separated*

> ½ *cup bourbon whiskey*
> ¼ *cup dark rum*
> ½ *cup granulated sugar*
> 1 *pint heavy cream*
> ¼ *teaspoon nutmeg*
> *Maraschino cherry or nut halves*

Soften the gelatin in 2 teaspoons water; dissolve it by adding ½ cup boiling water, then cool. Beat the egg yolks until creamy, slowly add the bourbon and rum; continue to beat until they are well mixed. Beat the egg whites until they form soft peaks, adding the sugar a little at a time. Whip the cream with the nutmeg, then combine them gently with the egg whites. Beat the gelatin into the yolks, and fold the yolks into the whites. Turn the batter out into a shallow square or rectangular baking tin lined with waxed paper—or use a Teflon-lined pan. Refrigerate 24 hours. Invert the pan over a lightly floured breadboard or platter, and when the cake has dropped to it, remove the paper. Cut it into small squares, and decorate each with half a maraschino cherry or nut. Makes about 18 small squares.

▪ CRÈME ANGLAISE or CRÈME FRANÇAISE

Here starts another family, the *crèmes*, which depend on eggs for their light, smooth consistency. There are many of them, and only the best-known names are given. The basic recipe is the Crème Anglaise, as it is known in France, or Crème Française, as the same recipe is called in England. All the other recipes are merely slight variations on the basic one.

> 3 *cups milk*
> ¾ *cup granulated sugar*
> 12 *egg yolks*
> ½ *teaspoon vanilla extract*

Bring the milk to the scalding point and dissolve the sugar in it with a little stirring; remove from heat. Beat the egg yolks briskly into the warm milk, and add the vanilla at the last moment of beating. Return to very lowest heat, or use a double boiler, and cook 20 minutes, stirring constantly. Do not allow it to boil. Turn it into molds or cups, or one large bowl or mold. When it is cool, chill it in the refrigerator, but this custard should not be overrefrigerated. Serve it alone or with a fruit purée or syrup, or use one of the variations given here. Serves 8 to 10.

■ *CRÈME ANDALOUSE*

Substitute lemon juice for the vanilla extract in the Crème Anglaise (page 242) and stir 1 tablespoon finely grated lemon rind into the custard before it is set to cool.

This recipe gives you the clue for other variations: a Crème Amande, with almond milk substituted for plain milk and grated almonds stirred in before cooling; a Crème Moka, with a coffee-based liqueur used instead of vanilla extract; or a *crème* with any of the fruit or berry liqueurs substituted. The *crèmes* may be garnished with a fruit syrup or purée, or served in tartshells—your cupboard can provide countless variations.

■ *CRÈME BRULÉE*

While the Crème Anglaise (page 242) is cooling in its pan, line shallow individual buttered molds with sugar and place them into a hot oven until the sugar caramelizes, or caramelize the sugar in a saucepan and line the buttered molds. When they are cool, fill the molds with the *crème*. Unmold on a service plate when chilled; cover with a light caramel syrup.

■ *CRÈME CHOCOLAT* (*Pot au Crème*)

As the milk for the Crème Anglaise (page 242) heats, add to it ½ pound melted bittersweet chocolate; blend well. Follow the recipe in other details, but remember that the traditional method of serving is in small individual soufflé dishes.

■ *CRÈME FRANGIPANE*

Prepare the Crème Anglaise (page 242), adding at the time it is set to cool ½ cup macaroon crumbs; stir them in. (This is one of the rare dishes bearing the name of the papal count who earned his honor and name by giving bread to the poor.)

▪ *DULCE DE NARANJAS* (*Orange Sweet*)

About the only way to get orange flavor into a dessert—and have you ever thought how rarely it is encountered?—is to use the fruit itself, which is what this Spanish custard does.

> 1½ *cups granulated sugar*
> 5 *eggs*
> 3 *egg yolks*
> 1½ *cups strained orange juice*
> *Finely grated rind from 2 oranges*
> 1 *cup heavy cream*

Caramelize ¾ cup sugar in a heavy skillet over high heat, stirring occasionally. When the sugar liquefies, pour it into a heated casserole or soufflé dish; tilt the dish until its bottom is completely coated. Set it aside to cool. Beat the eggs and egg yolks together, adding the remaining sugar, until the mixture is thick and creamy. Beat in the orange juice, orange rind and cream; add them slowly while beating. Pour the custard into the prepared casserole and bake it 1 hour in a *bain-marie* in a preheated 400-degree oven; the water must reach two-thirds up the sides of the cooking utensil. This custard will still be very soft when it is removed from the oven, but do not worry; it finishes cooking while it cools, and overcooking invites toughness. Cool it an hour, then chill 2 hours in the refrigerator before serving. Serves 4 to 6.

▪ *GALATOBURECHO* (*Custard-Filled Pastry*)

A Greek cook would scorn to offer this custard unless it were baked in a crust of *filo*, the Aegean pastry made up of countless tissue-thin layers of fine dough, but learning to make *filo* can in itself be a lifetime career. In large cities where there are Greek bakeries and specialty food shops, you may be able to buy the *filo* ready to be used, but lacking it, roll your favorite rich pastry dough very thin for the delicate topping of the pan in which you cook your Galatoburecho.

> 10 *eggs*
> 9 *cups milk*
> 4 *cups sugar*
> 1 *teaspoon salt*
> 1¼ *cups butter*

> *¾ cup farina*
> *1 teaspoon vanilla*
> *Pastry Dough (page 291)*
> *2 tablespoons lemon juice*
> *Grated peel of 1 lemon*
> *1 teaspoon cinnamon*

Beat the eggs until they are frothy. Scald the milk, reduce the heat to very low and stir ¾ cup sugar and the salt, butter and farina into the milk. Cook 5 to 10 minutes, stirring briskly, until the mixture thickens. Remove from the heat and beat in the eggs and vanilla. Line a baking pan with very thin Pastry Dough, and pour in the custard; cover the top, making several slashes or vents in it. Cook 30 minutes in a preheated 350-degree oven; reduce the heat to 300 degrees and cook 20 minutes longer.

While the custard cooks, dissolve the remainder of the sugar in 2 cups water; add the lemon juice, lemon peel and cinnamon, and bring to a quick boil, then reduce the heat and simmer 10 minutes. Cool, then pour it over the top crust of the custard-filled pastry the moment it is out of the oven. When it is cooled, cut it into squares. Makes about 20 small squares.

▪ *GOLD NUGGETS*

> *6 egg yolks*
> *1½ cups sugar*
> *3 or 4 whole cloves*

Beat the egg yolks until they are creamy, divide them among small well-buttered molds and bake 10 to 12 minutes in a preheated 375-degree oven. Dissolve the sugar in 1 cup water, add the cloves and bring to a boil. Simmer 5 minutes. Turn the baked molds out carefully into the syrup, bring the heat up to medium and cook 3 minutes; baste the "nuggets" if there is not enough syrup to cover them. Lift each nugget to an individual serving dish and refrigerate 30 to 45 minutes. Just before serving, pour a little of the remaining syrup over each one. Serves 6.

▪ *LEMON MERINGUE JUBILEE*

If you have a secret yearning for the flamboyant service of a dessert served *flambéed*, your craving will be satisfied when you light this dramatic dish.

>6 *eggs, separated*
>4 *lemons*
>1 *cup sugar*
>2 *tablespoons almond flour or cornstarch*
>2 *cups cherries*
>1 *cup brandy or cognac*

Beat the egg yolks and egg whites separately. Cut the lemons into thick slices, discarding the end pieces. Cook the lemons in a syrup made by dissolving the sugar in 1 cup water; bring it to a quick boil and reduce the heat before adding the lemons. Simmer 10 minutes, pressing on the lemons as they cook with a large spoon, to extract their juices. Strain the syrup, discarding the lemon slices. Cool the syrup and add it to the egg yolks, beating well; beat the cornstarch into the yolks. Fold the yolks into the whites, and blend well; turn the meringue out into a service bowl. Chill 1 hour, take from refrigerator 20 to 30 minutes before serving. Soak the cherries in brandy at least 1 hour. Just before the meringue goes to the table, warm the brandy and cherries and pour them over the top of the bowl holding the meringue. Light the brandy, serving the dish *flambéed*. Serves 6 to 8.

▪ *MONT BLANC*

The favorite for filling this towering set-piece of a dessert is a chestnut *crème* (see the basic *crème* recipe on page 242). But use any flavor that meets your taste to fill the meringue mountain.

>8 *egg whites*
>2 *cups sugar*
>Crème *filling: chestnut, chocolate, fruit, etc.*
>2 *cups heavy cream*

Beat the egg whites until they form stiff peaks, adding the sugar a little at a time. Grease a cookie sheet and dust it lightly with flour; on it mark an 8-inch circle. With a spatula, make a layer of the beaten whites 2 inches thick, filling the circle. Transfer the remaining whites to a pastry tube, and using its biggest opening (size 12 or bigger) pipe a layer of the meringue around the rim of the circle of whites; add successive layers, spacing each a little closer to the center, to form a cone with its top open. Bake 45 minutes in a preheated 225-degree oven; the meringue must set firmly, but should not be browned. Remove it from the oven and cool. Fill the cone with the flavored Crème Anglaise (page 242); whip the cream stiff and form it into a peak on top of the cone. Chill a half-hour before serving, but do not overrefrigerate it. Serves 8 to 10.

Lacking a pastry tube, you can achieve the same effect by baking your meringues in tiny balls, about 1 inch in diameter, and arranging them in the form of a mountain. Technically, this is a Croquembouche, but it will taste the same as a Mont Blanc.

■ *MOUSSE AU CHOCOLAT*

> *7 eggs, separated*
> *Dash salt*
> *6 ounces semisweet chocolate (not milk chocolate)*
> *1 tablespoon bitter chocolate*
> *2 tablespoons strong black coffee (cool)*
> *1 tablespoon dark rum*

Beat the egg yolks until they are creamy. Beat the egg whites until they form sharp peaks, adding the salt. Melt the semisweet and bitter chocolate together in a double boiler or over lowest heat; blend with it the coffee and rum. After cooling the chocolate, beat it into the egg yolks; fold this mixture into the whites and blend well. Fill parfait glasses, sherbet glasses, individual molds or one large mold; depending on the size of the molds used, refrigerate 4 to 6 hours. For a dress-up touch, top each serving or the large mold with a cap of whipped cream and a few fine shavings of sweet chocolate. Serves 8.

Eggs do not usually go into a mousse, but this egg mousse will not melt down while awaiting service, nor will it take on an unhappy ice-streaked texture. Fruit purée may be substituted for chocolate, but if this is done, also substitute 1 tablespoon bar syrup for the coffee.

■ *MOUSSE AU MIEL* (*Mousse with Honey*)

In this honey mousse, any fruit syrup may be substituted, but the honey gives by far the most delicate flavor.

> *6 egg yolks*
> *1½ cups honey*
> *4 egg whites*
> *1 pint heavy cream*

Beat the egg yolks until they are frothy in a double boiler or over very lowest heat; add the honey to them. Simmer 5 minutes, stirring constantly. Cool thoroughly. Beat the egg whites until they form stiff peaks; whip the cream until it is firm. Fold one-third of the beaten egg whites into the yolks, then fold this mixture into the cream, then into the remaining egg whites. Fill parfait glasses or molds or 1 large mold; chill 4 to 6 hours, depending on the size of the mold. Serves 8.

▪ *MOUSSELINE*

Here's the ancestor—perhaps ancestress would be a better word—of another family of light, delicate egg custards. While the basic recipe is often served as an individual dish, it can be sprinkled with chopped almonds or walnuts, garnished with whipped cream, dotted with maraschino cherries or drenched with a syrup or purée of fruit or berries, or it can be served with whole or half apricots or with peaches or pears poached with a liqueur or brandy.

> ¼ *pound butter*
> ¼ *pound confectioners' sugar*
> 10 *egg yolks*
> 7 *egg whites*

Cream the butter and sugar together; beat 2 egg yolks and begin blending the butter–sugar mixture with them in a double boiler or over lowest heat; add the other egg yolks one by one as you beat and blend. When all the yolks are added, allow the mixture to simmer and thicken; it is ready when a clean spoon plunged into it comes out lightly coated. Set aside to cool. Beat the egg whites until they form stiff peaks, and fold the cooled yolk mixture into the whites. Pour it into a mold—a ring mold is generally used—and cook in a *bain-marie* 25 to 30 minutes in a preheated 325-degree oven. Allow the mold to cook 15 to 20 minutes before turning it out. Serves 8 to 10.

▪ *OEUFS À LA NEIGE* (*Snow Eggs*)

> 8 *egg whites*
> ½ *cup sugar*
> 5 *cups milk*

¼ *teaspoon vanilla extract*
4 *egg yolks*

Beat the egg whites until they form stiff peaks, adding 4 tablespoons of the sugar as you beat. Heat the milk in a double boiler or over low heat. Stir in the remaining sugar and the vanilla, stirring frequently; do not allow the milk to boil. Drop small spoonsful of the beaten whites into the simmering milk; they will puff up as they poach, so do not crowd the pan. Turn each meringue once as it cooks; remove them with a slotted spoon and place them on absorbent cloth or a paper towel to drain. Beat the egg yolks and stir them into the remaining milk. Stir and simmer the mixture until it thickens into a smooth, creamy custard; do not allow it to boil. Strain it into a large mold or individual serving dishes such as sherbet glasses. Chill 30 minutes, then place the "egg" meringues on top of the chilled custard. Return to the refrigerator for about 10 minutes more chilling before serving. Do not overrefrigerate. Serves 6 to 8.

▪ *PFANNKUCHEN* (*Pancakes*)

In Austria, where this dish was born, there are as many versions of Pfannkuchen as there are cooks and kitchens. Some have cinnamon, Kirsch, nutmeg or other ingredients added to the batter; the fillings embrace raspberry, apricot and other jams or puréed cooked fruits, and the topping varies as well. The dish may be offered in small individual servings or as one huge platter-filling cake, although the style given in this recipe is probably the most common.

4 *eggs*
1½ *cups milk*
¼ *cup whole wheat flour*
1 *teaspoon salt*
½ *cup applesauce*
1 *tablespoon powdered sugar*

Beat the eggs well, adding the milk slowly; continue to beat while adding the whole wheat flour and salt. Butter a large skillet very lightly—the biggest skillet you have—and allow it to warm over medium heat. Pour into the skillet enough batter to cover its bottom completely with a very thin coating, no more than ⅛ inch; just as the top of the batter firms, place the applesauce in a thick line down its center. Fold the cake over from two sides, lift it onto a warmed platter and sprinkle with powdered sugar. Serves 4.

▪ *RHENISH CUSTARD*

Although this light wine-flavored custard stands well alone, it also can be garnished with a peach or apricot half-marinated in wine or sprinkled with liqueur, or with cherries soaked in Kirsch or cognac. It can also be served over baked apples or pears, or used to fill tartlet shells.

> 4 *eggs, separated*
> 3 *tablespoons cornstarch*
> 2 *cups Rhine wine*
> 1 *cup sugar*

Beat the egg yolks and egg whites separately: the yolks until they are frothy, the whites to soft peaks. Beat the cornstarch, wine, sugar and 1 cup of water into the yolks and beat until creamy, in a double boiler or over very lowest heat. Beat until the mixture is very thick, cool it thoroughly and fold it into the egg whites. Chill moderately before serving. Serves 6.

▪ *SALZBURG DUMPLINGS*

Few egg desserts lend themselves to preparation at the table, but this one does. The dumplings may be made ready in advance and the final touch of warm milk added as your guests watch.

> 6 *eggs, separated*
> 2 *tablespoons sifted flour*
> 2 *tablespoons granulated sugar*
> ½ *cup warm milk*
> ½ *cup melted butter*
> ⅛ *teaspoon vanilla extract*

Beat the egg yolks until they are frothy, then add the flour, sugar and 2 tablespoons warm milk, finally adding ¼ cup of the melted butter; continue to beat until the mixture is smooth and creamy. Beat the egg whites until they form stiff peaks, and fold the yolk mixture gently but thoroughly into the whites. Heat the remaining ¼ cup butter, pour it into the completed mixture and blend lightly. Butter a large, deep skillet and warm it; pour the mixture into the skillet and cook it on top of the stove over medium heat as you would cook a pancake. When the bottom browns, turn the dough and cover the skillet; cook until delicately browned. Remove to waxed paper on a flat surface and cut into wide dumplings.

To serve, place the dumplings on service plates. Add vanilla to the remaining milk, warm it gently and trickle it into each dumpling with a spoon until the dumpling has absorbed all the milk it will hold. Dust lightly with sugar and serve. Serves 6 to 8.

■ DESSERT SOUFFLÉS

Like the soufflés served as entrées or appetizers, the dessert soufflé can be varied to infinity. Like the others, too, slight adjustments are needed to get the best results when the flavoring is changed from a fairly wet, thick purée of fruits to a syrup or liqueur. These two variations are given; following them are some of the many dessert soufflés that have acquired an identity beyond the one provided by their principal flavoring ingredient.

■ *LIQUID-FLAVORED DESSERT SOUFFLÉ*

> 1 *cup milk*
> 1½ *teaspoons granulated sugar*
> 1 *tablespoon flour, liquefied in* 1 *spoonful of milk*
> 1 *tablespoon butter*
> 3 *egg yolks*
> 5 *egg whites*
> 2 *to* 2½ *ounces flavoring syrup or* 1½ *to* 2 *ounces flavoring liqueur, depending on dominance of flavor desired*
> *Confectioners' sugar*

Heat the milk, dissolve the sugar in it over low heat and stir in the liquefied flour. Simmer 2 minutes, stirring constantly. Remove from the heat and stir in the butter. Set aside to cool.

Beat the egg yolks until they are blended; beat the egg whites until they form soft peaks. Beat the cooled milk mixture into the yolks, and add the fruit syrup or liqueur, then beat until creamy. Fold one-third of the beaten whites into the yolk mixture, then fold the mixture into the remaining whites, cutting it in by dropping a spoonful at a time on top of the whites and drawing it down with a knifeblade or spatula.

Butter a 1-quart soufflé dish generously, and coat the inside with confectioners' sugar. (The easy way: put a spoonful into the dish, invert a pie tin on top, shake the soufflé dish like a cocktail shaker and turn it upside down, leaving the excess sugar on the pie tin and the soufflé dish neatly and evenly coated.) Pour the soufflé mixture into the dish, and cook in a preheated 325-degree oven for 25 minutes without opening the oven door. Serve immediately! Serves 4.

It's impossible to give precise measurements of syrups and liqueurs. The flavor of a fruit syrup will vary between brands, and except for such proprietary liqueurs as Benedictine, Grand Marnier and a few others, the generic liqueurs such as Crème de Menthe, Kummel, Kirsch and so on will vary from one brand to the next.

■ *FRUIT-PURÉE-FLAVORED DESSERT SOUFFLÉ*

> ½ *cup milk*
> 1 *tablespoon granulated sugar*
> 1 *tablespoon flour, liquefied in 1 tablespoon cool milk*
> 1 *tablespoon butter*
> 3 *egg yolks*
> 6 *egg whites*
> ½ *cup puréed fruit or berries, unsweetened*
> *Confectioners' sugar*

Heat the milk, dissolve the sugar in it, stir in the liquefied flour and simmer on low heat for 2 minutes, stirring constantly. Remove from the heat, stir in the butter and set aside to cool.

Beat the egg yolks, combine them with the cooled milk mixture and beat until creamy. Beat 3 egg whites until they are frothy and begin to beat into them the puréed fruit or berries, adding the purée a little at a time until the eggs form soft peaks. In a separate bowl, beat the 3 remaining egg whites until they form stiff peaks. Fold the two batches of beaten whites together very gently; cut in the egg-yolk mixture by dropping a spoonful at a time on the whites and cutting down with a knifeblade through the beaten whites.

Butter a 1-quart soufflé dish, coat the inside with confectioners' sugar and pour in the mixture. Bake in a preheated 325-degree oven 25 minutes without opening the oven door. Serves 4.

Like syrups and liqueurs, the flavors of fruits and berries vary considerably. They may be reinforced with a dash of a compatible liqueur if desired; if the fruit or berries are not completely ripe, a few drops of bar syrup may be needed in the purée. Generally, the aciduous fruits and berries make the most flavorful soufflés.

There are several members of the dessert soufflé family that have come to have identities of their own, beyond the name of the flavoring ingredient. Those following are only the better-known ones, and the list is by no means complete. It should give you ideas for combinations of your own creation, though.

■ *SOUFFLÉ AMBASSADRICE*

Prepare the fruit-flavored soufflé (page 252); substitute for the purée 2 tablespoons plain macaroons crumbled fine, the crumbs sprinkled generously with dark rum and well moistened with 1 tablespoon vanilla extract. To the yolks add 1 tablespoon finely chopped toasted almonds.

■ *SOUFFLÉ BRASIL*

Prepare the liquid-flavored soufflé (page 251); substitute very strong black coffee for 1 tablespoon of the milk, and use a coffee liqueur (Crème de Cacao, etc.). Add to the yolks 1 tablespoon finely chopped Brazil nuts.

■ *SOUFFLÉ CAMARGO*

Prepare the fruit-flavored soufflé (page 252); use for the purée tangerine pulp from which all skin and white membranes have been removed. Crush the pulp slightly and mix into it 1 tablespoon chopped filberts.

■ *SOUFFLÉ AU CHOCOLAT*

Prepare the fruit-flavored soufflé (page 252); instead of purée, use 1 egg white beaten very stiff, into which is folded gently ¼ cup bittersweet chocolate. (Do not try to use milk chocolate!) Before serving, drop a few chocolate shavings on top.

■ *CHRISTMAS SOUFFLÉ*

Prepare the fruit-flavored soufflé (page 252); instead of purée, use a fine mince of candied fruits: cherries, pineapple, citron, quince.

Moisten this generously with brandy and let it sit 2 hours; drain off the excess brandy. *Soufflé Rothschild* is another name given this dessert soufflé.

▪ JAVA SOUFFLÉ

Prepare the liquid-flavored soufflé (page 251); substitute double-strength black tea for ¼ cup of the milk; in place of syrup use double-strength black tea in which is dissolved 1 tablespoon sugar. To the yolks add 1 tablespoon finely chopped pistachio nuts.

▪ SOUFFLÉ AU MIEL (Soufflé with Honey)

Prepare the fruit-flavored soufflé (page 252); for the purée beat ½ cup honey with ¼ cup butter until the mixture is light, then beat in 1 teaspoon Kirsch. Before serving, drizzle a thread of warmed honey in a spiral on top.

▪ SOUFFLÉ MONTBRY

Prepare the fruit-flavored soufflé (page 252), using apple purée thinned with 1½ tablespoons Kirsch. With each serving of this soufflé it is customary to include 2 or 3 *marrons glacés* (available almost everywhere in cans), which have been drained and soaked 1 hour or 2 in Kirsch.

▪ SOUFFLÉ NOYAUX

Prepare the liquid-flavored soufflé (page 251), using Noyaux liqueur; add 1½ tablespoons very finely chopped toasted almonds to the egg yolks.

▪ SOUFFLÉ ORIENTALE

Prepare the fruit-flavored soufflé (page 252); for the purée use ¾ cup ladyfingers, crushed to fine crumbs and soaked in Grenadine; drain off the excess liquid before adding it to the soufflé mixture. This soufflé may also be made with ¼ cup Grenadine in which ½ cup of plain sugar mints have been dissolved; if using the dissolved mints, follow the liquid-flavored soufflé recipe (page 251).

Strictly speaking, the next two recipes are not true soufflés, though they bear the name and there is a strong family resemblance. Overlook the bar sinister in their ancestry; both will be appreciated.

▪ *REFRIGERATOR SOUFFLÉ*

> 4 *eggs, separated*
> 1 *cup granulated sugar*
> ½ *teaspoon salt*
> 1 *tablespoon unflavored gelatin*
> ½ *cup flavoring (syrup or a liqueur)*
> 1 *cup heavy cream*

Beat the egg yolks until they are frothy, adding while beating ½ cup of sugar and the salt. Cook in a double boiler, or over lowest heat, stirring constantly, 3 to 4 minutes. During the last minute of cooking, add the gelatin, which has been softened in ½ cup cold water. Remove from the heat, and stir in the syrup or liqueur desired, blending well. Cool thoroughly. Beat the egg whites until they form sharp peaks, adding the remaining sugar a little at a time. Whip the cream until it will hold a peak; fold the cream, then the egg-yolk mixture, into the whites. Pour into a 1-quart soufflé dish, and refrigerate 2 hours before serving. Serves 4.

As with dessert soufflés, almost any syrup or liqueur can be used in this recipe; often it will be necessary to adjust the quantity called for to meet your taste.

▪ *RUSSIAN APPLE SOUFFLÉ*

> 6 *egg whites*
> *Dash salt*
> 1½ *cups apple purée*
> 1 *teaspoon cinnamon*
> ½ *teaspoon vanilla extract*
> 2 *tablespoons cider (if not available, use 1 tablespoon*
> *bar syrup)*

Beat the egg whites and salt until they form stiff peaks. Blend the cinnamon and vanilla extract with the apple purée and moisten the purée with the cider. Fold into the purée one-third of the egg whites;

fold this mixture into the remaining whites. Pour the soufflé into a buttered 1-quart soufflé dish, and bake 20 minutes in a preheated 375-degree oven. Serves 4.

▪ SOUFFLÉED PUDDINGS

The popularity of this dessert family is attributed to Carême, who is credited with originating the most popular service of the dish, a fluffy pudding in a ring mold and a filling of rich creamy custard. This does not mean that you must follow the great master chef's example; the dessert may be offered with the pudding in a turret mold and the custard circling it in small individual molds, or vice versa. As usual with these families, the basic recipe is given, followed by its best-known variations.

▪ *BASIC SOUFFLÉED PUDDING*

▪ *Pudding*

> *¼ pound butter*
> *4 tablespoons sifted flour*
> *4 tablespoons confectioners' sugar*
> *1½ cups milk*
> *5 eggs, separated*
> *1 tablespoon vanilla extract*

Cream the butter with the flour and sugar; heat the milk to scalding and reduce the heat to low; as it simmers stir in the butter–sugar mixture. Stir constantly until smooth; when it has been stirred and simmered 10 minutes, set it aside to cool. Beat the egg yolks until they are frothy, adding the vanilla extract; beat this into the cool milk mixture and continue beating until it becomes creamy. Beat the egg whites until they are stiff; fold the yolk mixture into the whites. Fill a ring mold, and poach it in a *bain-marie* 35 to 40 minutes in a preheated 300-degree oven. Unmold the pudding on a large round plate and fill with the custard.

▪ *Custard*

> *1 pint milk*
> *7 tablespoons sugar*
> *1 teaspoon vanilla extract*
> *2 eggs plus 4 egg yolks*

Boil the milk, skim off the froth and set it aside to cool. When it is cool, dissolve the sugar in the milk, and add the vanilla. Beat the eggs and the extra egg yolks lightly, adding the milk while beating. Beat until the custard is thick and very creamy in texture. Strain it into the center of a ring mold; chill until firm. Serves 8.

This is the basic souffléed pudding, known also as a "Saxon Pudding." It is usually referred to by the names of its variations.

▪ *CITRON PUDDING* (*Lemon Pudding*)

In the Basic Souffléed Pudding (page 256), substitute lemon juice for the vanilla extract in both the pudding and the custard; add 1 tablespoon grated lemon rind to the custard.

▪ *DENISE PUDDING*

In the Basic Souffléed Pudding (page 256), use Almond Milk instead of cow's milk, and substitute Kirsch for the vanilla extract. (Almond Milk, if not available commercially, may be made by pounding 4 ounces of peeled almonds to a paste, adding a few drops of water while pounding; when the paste is formed, add water to bring the total to 1 pint. Strain the liquid through a cloth, twisting it to extract all the moisture.)

▪ *PUDDING INDIENNE* (*Indian Pudding*)

In the Basic Souffléed Pudding (page 256), omit the vanilla extract; substitute in both the pudding and the custard 1 tablespoon warm tea in which 1 teaspoon powdered ginger has been dissolved. Add to the custard 2 tablespoons candied ginger, diced small.

▪ *LANGUEDOCIENNE PUDDING*

In the Basic Souffléed Pudding (page 256), reduce the amount of milk in the pudding by one-third, and reduce the quantity of sugar to 5 tablespoons; substitute ¾ cup sweetened puréed apricots.

■ *LIMOUSIN PUDDING*

In the Basic Souffléed Pudding (page 256), reduce the quantity of milk in the pudding by one-third and the quantity of sugar by one-half; substitute a purée made from ¾ cup chopped chestnuts simmered with 4 tablespoons sugar in 1 cup water. (Put them through a blender, if you have one; otherwise, mash them through a sieve.)

■ *LIQUEUR PUDDING*

In the Basic Souffléed Pudding (page 256), substitute your choice of liqueur for the vanilla extract in both the pudding and the custard.

■ *REGAL PUDDING*

In the Basic Souffléed Pudding (page 256), 1 tablespoon crushed plain macaroons is added to the pudding and 1 tablespoon finely chopped pistachio nuts to the custard.

■ *RÉGENCE PUDDING*

No substitutions are reqquired in the basic recipe (page 256); the dish is coated with caramelized sugar, or the mold—ring or turret—is heavily buttered and covered inside with caramelized sugar before use.

■ *ROYALE PUDDING*

No substitutes are needed in the basic recipe (page 256), but the dish is served on a sponge cake equal in diameter to the ring mold, the cake being split and filled with a layer of currant jelly.

■ *VÉSUVIENNE PUDDING*

In the Basic Souffléed Pudding (page 256), the quantity of sugar is reduced one-third in the pudding and 1½ tablespoons tomato jam added; ½ cup raisins is added to the custard.

▪ *SURPRISE OMELET OR BAKED ALASKA*

These are not the only two names by which this old warhorse of a set-piece dessert is known. It is also called a Norvégienne, or a bombe, or a Bombe Vésuvienne. In addition, it has a host of variations, each bearing its own name. But in the United States, it is best known as Baked Alaska.

There are two versions of how the dessert came into being. One gives credit to a Chinese mission to France, whose chef is supposed to have given the dish to a Parisian hotel's chef in 1862. The better claim seems to be that of Benjamin Thompson, Count Rumford, a Massachusetts-born physicist whose specialty was heating and heat conductivity, which is the entire basis of the dish. Thompson, or Rumford (he was given the title for services to the principality of Bavaria), is supposed to have originated the novelty about 1792. There is not much doubt that he based the creation on the already known dessert called the Norvégienne, which was a mound of seasoned whipped cream on a base of light cake, covered with an egg-white meringue, which was browned in the oven.

Thompson's contribution was not inspired by his interest in gastronomy. He had originated the first convection-heated oven, and needed a dramatic way to demonstrate its virtues. He recognized that the meringue formed such a good insulating barrier that it could be browned quickly enough to avoid melting ice cream or sherbet if they were used in place of whipped cream.

Whatever its source, the Baked Alaska gained its great popularity in the United States during the Gilded Age following the Civil War; it was unquestionably brought back from Europe during those years. For the next two decades or more, no large dinner was complete without it. Then it fell into near-oblivion, and is just regaining popularity.

Called by any name, the dessert is about the same, so again a basic recipe will be given, followed by some of the best-known variations.

▪ *BASIC SURPRISE OMELET*

The base of the dish is an aircake usually called a "Génoise," which traditionally is baked in an oval pan; the ice cream is frozen in a mold the same shape and size as the baking pan.

12 *eggs*
3 *cups confectioners' sugar*
1½ *cups sifted flour*
½ *pound melted butter*
1 *teaspoon vanilla extract*
3 *tablespoons cognac or brandy*
10 *egg whites*
1½ *tablespoons granulated sugar*
1 *to* 1½ *quarts ice cream or sherbet*

Beat the 12 whole eggs in a saucepan over very low heat or in a double boiler; add the confectioners' sugar while beating, and beat until the eggs follow a spoon lifted from the mixture, then settle slowly to level again. Mix the flour, butter, vanilla and cognac, and beat them into the eggs slowly and smoothly. When the batter is smooth, pour it into its pan; there should be no more than 2 inches of batter in the pan. Bake in a preheated 350-degree oven for 1½ hours. Invert the pan over a wire rack; the cake will settle onto the rack as it cools.

When the base is completely cold, beat the 10 egg whites with the granulated sugar until they form stiff peaks. Have the ice cream or sherbet to be used frozen very hard in its mold. Dip the mold in hot water, and unmold the ice cream on the cake base. Cover quickly with the beaten egg whites, place in a preheated 375-degree oven and remove to serve as soon as the meringue is brown, about 6 to 10 minutes. Serves 8.

There is no set formula for the type of ice cream used in the Baked Alaska; however, there are traditional variations of the dessert. The best-known ones follow to stimulate your creative instincts.

▪ *CHERRY SURPRISE*

Mix softened cherry or raspberry sherbet with 2 tablespoons Kirsch, and add ½ cup halved maraschino cherries. Mold, and refreeze until hard. Use as the ice cream in the basic recipe on page 259.

▪ *CHRISTMAS SURPRISE*

Soften pistachio and cherry or strawberry ice cream and fill the mold with them in alternate layers. When the meringue is applied, sprinkle it with stripes of granulated sugar dyed red and green with food coloring.

■ *SURPRISE ELIZABETH*

Soften vanilla ice cream and mix into it a generous amount of crystallized violets. Space a few of the violets on the meringue before it goes to the oven; do not allow the meringue to brown.

■ *SURPRISE MILADY*

Poach drained peach halves in their syrup to which has been added 1 tablespoon cognac per cup of syrup, and line the mold with them; fill with softened raspberry ice and freeze very firm. (If fresh peaches are used, poach them in bar syrup: 1 tablespoon sugar to each tablespoon water, simmered a moment on low heat.) Cover with meringue.

■ *SURPRISE MILORD*

Soften vanilla ice cream, line the mold with it, then add a layer of sliced canned (or fresh poached) pears; alternate the layers of ice cream and pears until the mold is full. Proceed as in the basic recipe on page 259.

■ *NEAPOLITAN SURPRISE OR BOMBE VÉSUVIENNE*

Fill the mold with alternate layers of strawberry ice cream, sliced and drained *marrons glacés*, vanilla ice cream, and more *marrons*, until the mold is filled. Proceed as in the basic recipe (page 259), but do not allow the meringue to brown. When the meringue is taken from the oven, sprinkle it with Cherries Jubilee (Bing cherries soaked in warm brandy) and light the brandy; serve *flambéed*.

■ *NORVÉGIENNE*

This recipe is added just to keep the record straight, as the ancestor of the Baked Alaska.

Add to 1½ pints whipped cream as it is whipped 2 tablespoons of the liquor from maraschino cherries, ½ cup of shredded maraschino cherries and 1 tablespoon slivered toasted almonds. Pour it into a mold and chill it well, but do not allow it to freeze; proceed with the Basic Surprise recipe (page 259).

■ TORTES

Nobody ever thinks of Vienna's famous tortes as egg desserts, but how else can they be classified? The thin cake dividing the filling is an aircake based on eggs as a leaven; the filling or frosting is an egg custard. The two best-known recipes are given; there are many others.

■ *DUBOSH TORTE*

> 10 *egg yolks*
> 1 *cup sugar*
> 1 *cup sifted flour*
> 6 *egg whites*
> 5 *ounces bittersweet chocolate*
> 3 *tablespoons strong black coffee*
> 1 *tablespoon dark rum*
> 1/4 *pound butter*

Beat 6 egg yolks, adding 1/2 cup sugar, until very thick and creamy. Begin sifting the flour into the yolks, beating and blending thoroughly. Beat the egg whites until they form soft peaks; beat one-third of the whites into the yolks, then fold the mixture into the remaining whites. Spread in a very thin layer in a large, shallow square or rectangular cake pan, or divide among several pans; bake 8 to 10 minutes in a preheated 350-degree oven. Cool on a rack.

Beat the 4 remaining egg yolks, adding the remaining 1/2 cup of sugar. Melt the chocolate over very low heat, or in a double boiler, and stir in the coffee and rum; blend well. Remove from heat and work in the butter 1 tablespoonful at a time, working until the butter is used up and the mixture is very smooth.

On waxed paper, spread a rectangle of the chocolate about 4 by 8 inches. Cut a rectangle of cake the same size and lay it on the chocolate; add layers of chocolate and cake until the torte is about 4 inches high; cover the top and sides with chocolate. Chill to harden the chocolate, but serve at room temperature. Makes 1 torte, 4 by 8 inches.

▪ *SACHER TORTE*

> ½ cup butter
> 2 tablespoons milk
> ¾ cup sugar
> 1½ cups sifted flour
> 6 eggs, separated
> 1½ teaspoons vanilla extract
> 1½ cups semisweet chocolate
> 1½ cups confectioners' sugar
> 2 tablespoons dark rum
> ¾ cup apricot jam

Work the butter with a teaspoon or two of milk until it is foamy, then blend in the sugar and flour, using only enough of the milk to create a soft, smooth paste. Beat the egg yolks until they froth, adding the vanilla, and blend in the sugar–butter–flour paste. Beat the egg whites until they form stiff peaks, and fold the yolk mixture into the whites, mixing well. Pour into a very lightly greased loaf-sized baking tin, and bake 30 minutes in a preheated 275-degree oven. Remove, and cool in the pan.

Blend the chocolate, confectioners' sugar, 2 tablespoons hot water and the rum into a smooth paste. Split the cake lengthwise, spread the bottom layer with a thick coating of apricot jam, return the top layer and cover the top with a thin coating of the jam. Spread the chocolate frosting on the sides and top; chill in the refrigerator to allow the icing to set, but serve at room temperature. Serves 8 to 10.

▪ *TUILES* (Tiles)

These are a traditional feature of French pâtisserie; their curved shape resembles the roofing tiles which give them their name.

> 3 egg whites
> ¼ cup confectioners' sugar
> ⅓ cup sifted flour
> ¼ teaspoon salt
> 1 teaspoon vanilla extract
> 1 teaspoon cognac or brandy
> 3 tablespoons melted butter
> ⅔ cup chopped almonds

Beat the egg whites until they form soft peaks, then add the sugar, flour and salt a little at a time while beating the whites until they peak stiffly. Whip the vanilla and cognac into the melted butter and add the chopped almonds. Fold this into the beaten egg whites. Drop by teaspoonfuls onto a greased cookie sheet, and bake 10 minutes in a preheated 350-degree oven. While still warm, shape each cookie into a curve around a rolling pin, then transfer to a rack for cooling. Makes about 20 Tuiles.

▪ *ZABAGLIONE*

Most strongly identified with Italy and Marsala wine, this is truly an international dessert. In France, as Sabayon, it is made with cognac or a liqueur; in Spain, as Yemada, it will be tossed up with sherry or *anis del mono;* in England it becomes Posset and is made with Madeira or Port; in the United States it is a flip, and may be made with bourbon or a white rum. Still, it all began as Zabaglione. The original, or Italian version, is given.

> 8 *egg yolks*
> ½ *cup sugar*
> ¼ *cup Marsala*

In a double boiler or over very lowest heat, beat the egg yolks, adding the sugar a little at a time. When the yolks begin to turn frothy, add the wine. Beat until the mixture has doubled in bulk, but never boil, and do not overcook.

Depending on the meal it follows or the season of the year, Zabaglione is served warm or chilled. It may also be stiffened by folding in ½ pint lightly whipped cream; in this case it should be refrigerated 30 minutes and served like a custard or ice cream. Serves 4.

The Sipping Egg

MAN'S FIRST ENCOUNTER with the egg as food must have occurred in prehistory, before he began to use fire; his first use of an egg must have been the straightforward matter of cracking its shell and gulping. From that unrecorded day to this overly communicative age, man has continued to add eggs to his drinks.

Some ancient instinct is still at work; there is buried in his subconscious the belief that the egg is a powerful soother of restless stomachs, a reviver of the drooping spirit. While it is true that an egg taken raw with a dash of sharp seasoning will often settle a stomach roiled after overindulgence by coating its inner lining with bland albumen, the egg as a reviver functions more as a psychological than a physiological lift.

This does not change the fact that an egg makes a beverage foamy and light, as in fizzes, and acts as a broker in the marriage of milk and brandy or whiskey as in eggnogs. There are scores of drinks to which an egg is added as an accessory, but relatively few in which its presence is essential. These few, both alcoholic and nonalcoholic, as well as the revivers and restorers, are in this short chapter.

▪ *DIETETIC EGG*

Break one or two eggs into a wineglass, squeeze a quarter of a lemon on top and dust with paprika. Gulp. Makes 1 portion.

▪ *EGG LEMONADE*

Carbonated beverages have all but banished the Egg Lemonade, but for many years it was a popular beverage, especially Down East in the New England states.

Beat a whole egg lightly while pouring into it a glass of pre-sweetened lemonade, pour it over cracked ice in a tall glass. Makes 1 portion.

▪ *EGG SODA*

There is a story that a famous chain of drugstores survived the depression following the 1929 stock market crash by instructing its fountain attendants to ask, when a customer ordered an ice cream soda, "Do you want one egg, or two, in the soda?" One egg meant an extra five cents per soda, two eggs an extra dime. Led by the carefully phrased question, most customers agreed to the inclusion of at least one egg, and on the extra nickels the chain maintained a precarious margin of profit.

Put a scoop of ice cream, any flavor, in a tall glass. Soften 1 tablespoon of ice cream and 1 tablespoon of milk, beat with 1 or 2 eggs and pour over the ice cream in the glass. Makes 1 portion.

▪ EGGNOGS

No two people agree on what a good eggnog must contain—besides eggs. There are dozens of favorite personal recipes for this descendant of the flip; it would be possible to fill a small book with nothing but eggnog formulas. The four offered here give a fair sampling of the field; one is for the temperance group, three for those who prefer their eggs with a sprightly portion of nog.

■ *NONALCOHOLIC EGGNOG*

> 1 *egg, separated*
> 2 *tablespoons heavy cream*
> ½ *teaspoon sugar*
> *Dash nutmeg*

Beat the egg yolk with the cream, adding the sugar while beating; beat until frothy. Beat the egg white until it forms soft peaks. Fold the yolk into the white, pour it into a glass and dust the top with nutmeg. Makes 1 portion.

■ *EGGNOG (I)*

> 1 *egg*
> 1 *teaspoon sugar*
> ½ *cup milk*
> ½ *ounce cognac or brandy*
> ¼ *ounce light rum*
> 2 *ounces dry sherry*
> *Nutmeg*

Beat the egg, sugar and milk in a large bar glass. Stir in the cognac, rum and sherry. Add 2 or 3 lumps of ice (not cracked or chipped ice, please) and stir well; better still, cover the glass and shake 3 or 4 times. Strain into a thin goblet, and dust the top with nutmeg. To prepare larger quantities, simply multiply the ingredients by the number to be served. Makes 1 portion.

■ *EGGNOG (II)*

> 10 *eggs, separated*
> ¾ *cup sugar*
> 1 *pint bourbon whiskey*
> ½ *pint dark rum*
> 1 *quart heavy cream*
> *Nutmeg*

Beat the egg whites until they form very soft peaks. Beat the egg yolks until they are just mixed, then begin adding the sugar while continuing to beat; add the sugar slowly until it is absorbed, then, while beating slowly, pour into the yolks all the bourbon and rum.

Whip the cream very lightly and stir it into the beaten yolks, then fold the yolk mixture into the whites. Top each serving from the bowl with a sprinkle of nutmeg on top of the glass. Serves 12 to 15.

▪ *EGGNOG (III)*

> 1 *cup sugar*
> 4 *eggs*
> 1 *pint bourbon whiskey*
> 1 *pint brandy*
> 1 *pint heavy cream*
> 1 *quart milk*
> *Nutmeg*

Make bar syrup, by dissolving the sugar in 1 cup warm water; cool. Beat the eggs, adding the bourbon, brandy, cream and milk in that order, pouring in the bar syrup last. Beat until well blended. Dust the top of each glass with nutmeg. Serves 12 to 15.

▪ FIZZES

For winter the eggnog, for summer the fizz; between them the range of seasons need not worry anyone. In warm climates, each region has its locally famous fizz, but three are universal, and many of the local concoctions are only one of these three called by another name.

Preparing a good fizz was once a difficult job, calling for more muscle than most bartenders liked to admit having; today, the blender has made it possible for a fizz to be enjoyed without any more muscle strain than is involved in flicking a blender switch. There is only one trick: the ice must go in and be whirled briefly before any other ingredient is added. Use ¼ cup cracked ice for each drink, put the ice in the blender and turn the switch off and on as fast as your finger will work. Pour in everything else, give the switch another quick flip—as fast as you can say "Gin Fizz" is long enough—then pour the frothy mix into a glass, fill with cold club soda and enjoy.

▪ *GOLDEN FIZZ*

> 1 *egg*
> 1½ *jiggers gin*

2 teaspoons lemon juice
1 jigger thick cream
1 teaspoon sugar
½ jigger Kirsch or Orange Water
Club soda

Break the egg into a shaker (if the blender is not being used), add the next 5 ingredients and half-fill the shaker with cracked ice. Shake very briskly for 2 minutes and strain into a tall, thin glass or large goblet. Fill the glass with club soda, then stir once. Makes 1 portion.

▪ RAMOS FIZZ OR NEW ORLEANS FIZZ

1 jigger gin
2 jiggers light cream
½ jigger lemon juice
½ jigger orange juice
½ jigger lime juice
1 egg white
Club soda

Half-fill a shaker with cracked ice. Pour in the gin, the cream and the juices; add the egg white last. Shake very hard several minutes and strain into a tall glass or goblet; fill the glass with club soda, then stir once. Makes 1 portion.

▪ SILVER FIZZ

1½ jiggers gin
1 jigger lemon juice
2 jiggers thick cream
2 egg whites
Club soda

Half-fill a shaker with cracked ice. Put in the gin, lemon juice and cream, then the egg whites. Shake hard, strain into a tall glass, fill with club soda and stir once. Makes 1 portion.

There are a number of well-known fizzes, all following the same basic formula: Creole Fizz, using sloe gin; Tropical Fizz, using pineapple juice instead of lemon; Amer Picon Fizz, which substitutes this apéritif wine for gin; and probably another 50 or 60 local versions around the Caribbean and the China Sea.

▪ *FLIP*

Break 1 egg into a wineglass; add 1 jigger dry sherry, ½ jigger brandy, 2 jiggers cream and ½ teaspoon sugar. Stir well. Makes 1 portion.

▪ *MULLED WINE WITH EGGS*

Use a poker to mull the wine, if you have a fireplace and are devoted to tradition, but the kitchen range does it equally well.

> 1 *bottle dry red wine*
> 6 *eggs, separated*
> *Nutmeg or cinnamon*

Pour the wine into a saucepan, half-fill the wine bottle with water and pour it into the wine. Beat the egg whites until they form soft peaks; beat the yolks until they are frothy. Heat the wine over high heat, and as it begins to simmer just before boiling fold the egg yolks into the whites, add them to the wine and remove from the heat. Stir well and serve in large mugs from a heavy pitcher, dusting the top of each serving with nutmeg or cinnamon; or, put a stick of cinnamon into each mug before pouring in the hot wine. This must not be reheated. Serves 6 to 8.

▪ *TOM AND JERRY*

> 1 *egg, separated*
> 1½ *jiggers brandy*
> 1½ *jiggers dark rum*
> 1 *teaspoon sugar*
> *Nutmeg*

Beat the egg yolk and egg white separately. Fold the yolk into the white and put them in a thick mug; add the brandy and rum and fill the mug with very hot water. Stir in the sugar, stir a moment longer and dust the top with nutmeg. Makes 1 portion.

▪ RESTORERS

These are the traditional morning-after soothers, the best known of another fairly large family that has relatives in every land.

■ *THE DOCTOR*

Break an egg into a wineglass, stir into it 2 tablespoons light cream and 1 teaspoon sugar. Stir well while filling the glass with cognac. Makes 1 portion.

■ *PRAIRIE CHICKEN*

Break an egg into a wineglass; add a dash of salt and pepper and cover the egg with gin or vodka. Gulp. Makes 1 portion.

■ *PRAIRIE OYSTER*

Separate an egg and put the unbroken yolk into a wineglass; add a pinch of salt, ½ teaspoon vinegar, a drop or two of Tabasco sauce and 1 teaspoon each of lemon juice, Worcestershire sauce and catsup. Swirl the glass several times to mix, dust the top with cayenne and swallow at a gulp. Makes 1 portion.

■ *THE SURGEON-MAJOR*

Break an egg into a wineglass, add a jigger of cognac and stir lightly while quickly filling the glass with champagne. Makes 1 portion.

11

Sauces and Auxiliaries

IN COOKERY as in architecture, a good building depends on a good foundation and attention to the final details. In egg cookery, the foundation of many dishes designed for individual service is not just the egg, but the base of toast or crusty pastry on which the dish is served. And the final detail is the sauce.

▪ SAUCES

It is an oversimplification, but a practical oversimplification, to say that there are only three warm sauces. Yet it is true. There are the white sauces, based on broth and cream; the brown sauces, based on condensed meat stock and browned flour; and the wine sauces, which overlap into both whites and browns. From these three sauces can be produced almost all of the sauces in common use; there are exceptions, but they are rare.

Most of the legends that inhibit the use of sauces in everyday cooking come from the fear that saucing is "difficult," that all sauces call for rare ingredients, great kitchen wisdom and long hours of work. Once this was very true, when stoves were uncertain, and the only way to condense a broth or bouillon was to simmer it for hours. The legend persists because most of the authoritative writers on cooking lived, practiced and wrote of their craft at a time when instinct was the thermometer, apprentice hands replaced the blender and time had not been shortened by the commercial steam kettle or the freeze-drying drum. Succeeding writers, either too lazy to experiment for themselves or too busy writing to cook, have simply copied what was written fifty or a hundred years ago and perpetuated the misconception.

Almost all the great warm sauces reflect the days of the French *haute cuisine,* which dragged to its death about 1910. Vestiges of it are left today, but only as a reflection of the past. Worldwide, only a very few of the very greatest restaurants follow the old tradition of cooking in which a sauce starts as bones and meat in a huge pot of cold water and takes hours to appear on the finished dish. And why should they, any more than a motorist should try to refine his own gasoline, when commercial processes offer the same product?

Please do not read into the words "commercial processes" a recommendation for manufactured "instant sauces." There is a difference between reducing meat broth to its essence and canning or freeze-drying a finished sauce without losing the subtle flavors of herbs and spices which give the sauce its character. These flavors will not survive either the high temperatures of pressure-canning or the extreme cold of the freeze-drying drums used in processing dry-packed "instant" foods. Both canned and packeted "instant sauces" suffer the flavor loss common to mass-produced foods. They are unidentifiably bland, vague compromises which add to a dish more liquid than flavor. The few moments you think to gain by using an "instant sauce" are lost trying to restore flavors removed by the processing. Forget your fear that saucing is difficult and plunge into the simple job of preparing your own supply of Espagnole and Veloutè, the two basic sauces from which most other brown and white sauces can be made in a matter of minutes.

When the sauces themselves are analyzed, fear of them vanishes. When it's understood that the simplest white sauce, Velouté, can be turned in three to five minutes into Béchamel, Mornay, Chivry, Aurore, Suprême, Soubise or a half-dozen others, the mystery is gone. When the cook knows how to produce the basic Sauce Espagnole in two minutes, and how in three minutes more to transform it into Poivrade, Périgueux, or Bordelaise; or to turn the Bordelaise into Chasseur or Hongroise or any of the sauces stemming from Espagnole the terror ends.

If a stock of Sauce Velouté, a quart or more, is kept in the refrigerator; if the modern substitute for Sauce Espagnole is kept on the pantry shelf, preparing any one of fifty sauces is as easy as making instant coffee, and the result far more rewarding. Saucing is now a matter of minutes, not of hours. Even the egg sauces can be prepared in seconds, if you have a blender. Without a blender, they may take as long as ten or fifteen minutes to prepare. And for sauces, there is really no substitute. Cooks may continue the argument whether it is the sauce which makes the dish or the dish which makes the sauce; the two are interdependent and cannot be divorced.

Sauces cannot disguise deficiencies in cooking; they are designed to point up flavor or to introduce a note of contrast, not to conceal shortcomings. They must be used rather sparingly, or the food drowns. However, years of scorning sauces or fearing them has made for unimaginative cooking. We tend to replace sauces with raw salt and pepper piled on in incredible quantities. About all that can be said for this habit is: If enough salt and pepper are put on any food, it will taste just like salt and pepper.

▪ BROWN SAUCES

The basis of the family of brown sauces is the Sauce Espagnole, or Demi-Glaze. This is cooking's most often-used sauce. Unfortunately, for those who insist on following tradition, it is the most elaborate and most time-consuming to prepare. Fortunately, there is a shortcut. Most of the time used in making Sauce Espagnole from its beginning stages is devoted to reducing liquids, straining and skimming them. This is a stage we can skip, if we will only use the meat essences available on the market as the basis on which to build the Sauce Espagnole. The essential product is the packaged meat paste—the result carried to extremes of any saucing process—sold under various trade names; B-V and Bovril are two of them. When thinned to the proper consistency with warm water in which a bouillon cube has been dissolved, and smoothed with a *beurre manié*, the result is a Sauce Espagnole that need not hang its head in any but the most exalted company. The instant process below is followed by the more involved ritual for traditionalists.

Now, no claim is made that the Instant Espagnole will have the subtleties of flavor to be found in the traditional recipe. But it will be tasty, have a good texture, and be available without six hours of work. In essentials of taste and use, it will be the equivalent; it can be used to prepare the brown sauces that follow, which are based on Sauce Espagnole; it can also be used as a glaze when called for.

■ *SAUCE ESPAGNOLE OR DEMI-GLAZE* (*Instant*)

> ½ *teaspoon flour*
> ½ *teaspoon butter*
> 1 *chicken bouillon cube* (*or equivalent in granules*)
> 1 *tablespoon meat concentrate* (*Bovril, B-V, etc.*)

Make a *beurre manié* by mixing the flour and butter together into a smooth, firm paste; roll it into a little ball and set aside. Dissolve the bouillon cube in 1 tablespoon hot water in a very small saucepan over lowest heat; stir in the meat concentrate. While stirring, add tiny flakes of the *beurre manié* until the sauce is the consistency of rich cream. If it appears grainy, add a flake of pure butter and stir.

Since quantities are even, they need only be increased in proportion to the quantity of sauce you will require. The quantity of the *manié* will not need to be increased in this ratio; a tablespoon is the most you should ever need for any quantity of sauce up to a quart.

■ *SAUCE ESPAGNOLE OR DEMI-GLAZE* (*Traditional*)

> 2½ *quarts strained beef stock, from meat including a*
> *marrow bone*
> ¼ *cup butter*
> ¼ *cup flour*
> 1 *thick slice bacon*
> ½ *carrot*
> ½ *onion*
> 1 *sprig thyme*
> 1 *bayleaf*
> ¼ *cup white wine*
> 1 *cup tomato purée*

Reduce 2 quarts of the beef stock by one-half, boiling and skimming as needed. Heat the butter, sprinkle the flour on it and stir as it browns. Add the reduced meat stock, and stir until smooth. Simmer 10 to 15 minutes, stirring occasionally. In a separate skillet, cook the bacon until light brown, mince the carrot and onion fine and simmer them in the bacon fat until very soft and browned. Add the thyme and bayleaf to them during the last minutes of cooking. Pour off the excess fat from the skillet; the mixture should be moist, but without free liquid fat in the pan. Over very low heat, pour the wine over the mixture in the skillet and blend thoroughly, mashing the carrot and onion pieces. After this has cooked 10 minutes, add it to the meat stock and simmer for 1 hour, skimming if necessary, and stirring occasionally. At the end of the hour, add the remaining half-quart of meat stock, stir well and simmer for 1½ hours, stirring occasionally. Strain into a bowl, stirring as the liquid cools. Refrigerate until all the fat rises to the surface; skim off this fat and discard it. When free of fat, return the liquid to the saucepan, heat until it simmers, add the tomato purée and simmer ½ hour. Strain into a jar for refrigerated storage. The finished sauce should be between a thick creamed soup and a thin purée in consistency. Makes 1 quart.

■ SAUCE BORDELAISE

> 1 tablespoon chopped shallots
> Pinch thyme
> Pinch powdered bayleaf
> 1 cup dry red wine
> 1 cup Sauce Espagnole (page 275)
> 2 tablespoons butter
> Small dash salt

Add the shallots, thyme and bayleaf to the wine; simmer fast over medium-high heat about 5 minutes, until it is reduced two-thirds in volume. Strain the wine into heated Sauce Espagnole and simmer over medium heat about 10 minutes until the liquid is reduced one-third. Remove from heat, stir in the butter and stir until smooth. Adjust by adding salt to taste. Makes ½ pint sauce.

■ SAUCE CHASSEUR

> 1 tablespoon chopped mushrooms
> 1 teaspoon butter
> 1 cup Sauce Bordelaise (page 276)

Lightly sauté the finely chopped mushrooms in half the butter (if canned mushrooms are used, merely warm them), and stir them into the simmering Sauce Bordelaise. Simmer over very low heat 5 minutes, remove from heat, stir in the remaining butter and stir until smooth. Makes 1 cup.

▪ *CHATEAUBRIAND SAUCE*

> 1 *teaspoon chopped shallots*
> ½ *cup white wine*
> ¾ *cup Sauce Espagnole (page 275)*
> 6 *tablespoons butter*
> ⅛ *teaspoon cayenne*
> 1 *teaspoon lemon juice*

Over medium heat, simmer the shallots in the wine until its volume is reduced one-half, about 3 to 4 minutes. Strain the wine into the simmering Sauce Espagnole. Add the butter a little at a time, stirring well, then stir in the cayenne. Remove from the heat, add the lemon juice and stir until smooth. Makes ½ pint sauce.

▪ *SAUCE HONGROISE (Hungarian Sauce)*

> ¼ *cup chicken broth (from cube or granules)*
> ¾ *cup Sauce Bordelaise (page 276)*
> ¼ *teaspoon paprika*

Simmer the broth and Sauce Bordelaise together 5 minutes; stir in the paprika. Makes ½ pint sauce.

▪ *MADEIRA SAUCE (Sauce Madère)*

> 1 *cup Sauce Espagnole (page 275)*
> 3 *tablespoons Madeira*
> ¼ *teaspoon butter*

Simmer the Sauce Espagnole and Madeira together 5 minutes, remove from heat and stir in the butter; stir until smooth. Makes ½ pint sauce.

▪ *SAUCE PÉRIGUEUX*

> 6 *drops Truffle Essence or 1 tablespoon grated truffle*
> 1 *tablespoon Madeira*
> 1 *cup Sauce Espagnole (page 275)*

Blend the Truffle Essence with the Madeira, stir it into the simmering Sauce Espagnole and simmer 3 to 5 minutes. (If gratings of truffle are used the sauce should be simmered 10 minutes, then strained.) Makes ½ pint sauce.

▪ SAUCE POIVRADE

> 1 *teaspoon chopped shallots*
> *Pinch powdered bayleaf*
> *Pinch thyme*
> 1 *cup Sauce Espagnole* (*page 275*)
> ½ *cup red wine vinegar*
> ½ *teaspoon peppercorns*

Add the shallots, bayleaf and thyme to the simmering Sauce Espagnole; simmer 5 minutes. Add the vinegar, raise the heat to medium and simmer 5 more minutes. Crack the peppercorns and add them during the last minute of cooking. Strain through a cloth; if the sauce is too thick, stir in a small amount of butter. Makes ⅔ pint sauce.

▪ SAUCE ROBERT

> 1 *cup Sauce Espagnole* (*page 275*)
> ¼ *teaspoon onion salt*
> ¼ *teaspoon dry mustard*

Into the simmering Sauce Espagnole, stir the onion salt and mustard; stir until they are dissolved. Makes ½ pint sauce.

Escoffier originated a process for bottling this sauce; it is sold commercially.

▪ TOMATO SAUCE

> ¼ *cup tomato purée*
> ¾ *cup Sauce Espagnole* (*page 275*)
> 1 *tablespoon butter*

Stir the purée into the simmering Sauce Espagnole. Simmer 3 to 5 minutes, remove from the heat and stir in the butter; stir until smooth. Makes ½ pint sauce.

▪ WHITE SAUCES

There is really no shortcut needed in making the basic white sauce, Sauce Velouté. It is the easiest of all sauces to produce from the traditional recipe; the only time-cutting step in the process would be getting the required quart of veal stock from a can or cubes, but so far no successful way has been found to produce a concentrated veal cube without losing the meat's characteristic and delicate flavor. Diluted veal broth is not the same, nor is chicken broth modified with beef. There is the promise that a new process of granulation may do the trick, but at this time there is no product on the market that you could use.

So simmer a few veal bones with some meat on them for two hours in lightly salted water, adding a little water when the level drops and skimming when necessary. The simmering requires no time or attention, and the broth can be used for other dishes besides making Sauce Velouté. With a stock of Sauce Velouté in your refrigerator, you also are equipped to produce a dozen white sauces that use it for a base.

▪ SAUCE VELOUTÉ

> 1 *quart strained veal stock*
> ½ *cup butter*
> ½ *cup flour*
> *Dash salt*
> *Dash pepper*
> *Dash nutmeg*

Simmer the veal stock. Heat the butter in a skillet and sprinkle the flour on it, stirring until smooth; keep the heat low under the skillet and do not let the flour brown in the 5 minutes required to blend the butter and flour well. Pour the stock over the butter–flour mixture and simmer 10 to 20 minutes over lowest heat, adding the seasonings early. Strain into a jar for covered refrigerated storage. Makes 1 quart sauce.

▪ SAUCE ALLEMANDE

> ⅔ *cup concentrated chicken broth*
> 2 *cups Sauce Velouté (page 279)*
> 3 *egg yolks*
> 1 *teaspoon lemon juice*

Make the concentrated chicken broth by dissolving a bouillon cube in one-third less water than label directions specify for broth, or similarly dissolve any of the granulated or powdered products.

Simmer the Sauce Velouté in a double boiler and slowly beat in the egg yolks; beat until smooth and creamy. Stir the warm stock into the sauce and simmer with frequent stirring until the sauce becomes very thick and creamy. Remove from the heat and stir in the lemon juice until it is well blended and the sauce is smooth. Makes 1 pint sauce.

▪ *SAUCE AURORE*

> 2 *tablespoons Tomato Sauce* (*page 278*)
> ¾ *cup Sauce Velouté* (*page 279*)
> 4 *tablespoons butter*

In a double boiler, stir the Tomato Sauce into the simmering Sauce Velouté; stir in the butter a spoonful at a time to achieve a smoothly blended texture and flavor. Makes ½ pint sauce.

▪ *BÉCHAMEL SAUCE*

> 2 *cups Sauce Velouté* (*page 279*)
> ½ *cup consommé* (*canned or cube*)
> 1½ *cups heavy cream*
> *Dash nutmeg*

Over low heat reduce the Sauce Velouté one-half, stirring frequently to prevent its burning or sticking to the sides of the pan. Add the consommé, cream and nutmeg, and reduce one-third, stirring constantly. Makes ½ pint sauce.

▪ *SAUCE CHIVRY*

> ½ *cup white wine*
> ½ *tablespoon chopped shallots, chervil and tarragon
>   in equal parts*
> 1 *cup Sauce Velouté* (*page 279*)
> 2 *tablespoons flour*
> 2 *tablespoons butter*

Over medium heat, simmer the wine with the shallots, chervil and tarragon, mashing the herbs as they soften until a smooth, thick paste is created. Add this to the simmering Sauce Velouté; reduce the sauce one-third while stirring regularly. Blend the flour with ½ cup water, stir it into the sauce and blend well. Strain, and while it is still hot, stir in the butter to smooth its texture. Makes 1¼ pints sauce.

▪ *CREAM SAUCE*

> ¾ *cup heavy cream*
> 1 *cup Béchamel Sauce* (*page* 280)
> 3 *tablespoons butter*

Over lowest heat, add ½ cup of the cream to the Béchamel Sauce, and reduce one-third, stirring regularly. Remove from the heat, stir in the butter and the remaining cream and stir vigorously until smooth. Makes 1 pint sauce.

▪ *SAUCE MORNAY*

> ½ *cup light cream*
> 1 *cup Béchamel Sauce* (*page* 280)
> ½ *cup grated Gruyère cheese*
> 1 *tablespoon grated Parmesan cheese*
> 3 *tablespoons butter*

Over lowest heat, add the cream to the simmering Béchamel Sauce; stir frequently while reducing the sauce one-third. Add the Gruyère and Parmesan, and stir until thoroughly blended. Remove from the heat, stir in the butter and stir until smooth. If a few undissolved crumbs of Parmesan remain, strain the sauce through cheesecloth. Makes 1 pint sauce.

▪ *SAUCE SOUBISE*

> ½ *cup onions*
> 1 *teaspoon butter*
> 1 *cup Sauce Velouté* (*page* 279)
> *Dash salt*
> *Dash nutmeg*

Sauté the onions gently in the butter, mashing them into a smooth paste when they are soft; or put them through the blender. Bring the Sauce Velouté to a simmer over medium heat and reduce it one-third while stirring regularly; add the salt and nutmeg, then the onion purée. Stir until smooth. It may be necessary to add a small quantity of butter for a finer texture; do this after removing from the heat. Makes ½ pint sauce.

■ *SAUCE SUPRÊME*

> ¾ *cup chicken broth or stock*
> ¾ *cup Sauce Velouté* (*page* 279)
> 1 *tablespoon butter*
> 3 *tablespoons lemon juice*

Stir the stock into the Sauce Velouté; simmer over medium heat to reduce one-third, stirring frequently. Remove from the heat and stir in the butter until it is blended, then add the lemon juice. Stir vigorously to blend well and smooth the sauce. Makes ½ pint sauce.

■ WINE SAUCES

As easy to prepare as the white sauces—in fact, quicker—are the wine sauces, for unlike the creamy, thick whites, the wines are speedily reduced in volume until only the concentrated essence of their flavor is left.

■ *SAUCE BÉARNAISE*

> 1 *cup white wine*
> ½ *cup white wine vinegar*
> 1 *tablespoon chopped shallots*
> 2 *tablespoons chopped tarragon*
> 2 *tablespoons chopped chervil*
> *Pinch thyme*
> *Pinch powdered bayleaf*
> 2 *egg yolks*
> ¼ *pound butter*
> *Dash cayenne*
> 1 *teaspoon lemon juice*

Heat the wine and add the wine vinegar, shallots, tarragon, chervil, thyme and bayleaf; simmer over medium-low heat until the volume is reduced two-thirds. Remove from the heat. Beat the egg yolks lightly, adding a little water. Strain the wine into a double boiler and beat in the egg yolks, beating until the mixture is smooth and creamy. Melt the butter and add it slowly while still beating; add the cayenne. Remove from the heat, beat in the lemon juice and stir vigorously until smooth. If necessary for texture and smoothness, beat in a little additional butter. Makes ½ pint sauce.

■ *SAUCE CHORON*

> *1 cup Sauce Béarnaise (page 282)*
> *¼ cup Tomato Sauce (page 278)*

In a double boiler, over low heat stir the Sauce Béarnaise and Tomato Sauce together until they are well blended. Makes ¾ pint sauce.

■ *RED WINE SAUCE*

This sauce is commonly called by the name of the wine used in making it: Chambertin, Bordeaux, and so on. Only the very affluent can afford the drops of liquid gold which are Chambertin and some of the other great and scarce wines, but the sauce does well with any wine you would drink at the table.

> *1½ cups red wine*
> *1½ cups consommé (canned or cube)*
> *Pinch thyme*
> *½ bayleaf*
> *½ chopped clove garlic*
> *1½ cups Sauce Espagnole (page 275)*
> *3 tablespoons butter*

Over medium heat, add the wine to 1 cup of the simmering consommé; put in the thyme, bayleaf and garlic. Simmer to reduce one-half, stirring occasionally. Add the Sauce Espagnole and reduce one-third. Strain, return to the heat, add the remaining consommé and reduce one-third. Remove from the heat; stir in the butter a little at a time, stirring vigorously until the sauce is smooth. Makes 1 to 1¼ pints sauce.

■ *WHITE WINE SAUCE*

> *2 cups white wine*
> *1 cup consommé (canned or cube)*
> *1 tablespoon chopped chives*
> *1 tablespoon chopped tarragon*
> *1 teaspoon butter*
> *1 teaspoon flour*
> *Dash salt*

Over medium heat, add the wine to the consommé, put in the chives and tarragon and reduce one-half, stirring occasionally. Strain, and return to very low heat. Make a *manié* of the butter and flour and flake it into the sauce, stirring well, until it is smooth and creamy. Add a small pinch of salt if required. The sauce should simmer at least 5 minutes after the last of the *manié* has been added to insure thorough cooking of the flour; otherwise it will have a starchy taste. Makes ½ pint sauce.

■ EGG SAUCES

Making the world's two great egg sauces, Hollandaise and Mayonnaise, is greatly simplified if a blender is used. Here is the one place in egg cooking where extreme speed and complete emulsification are needed, and the blender's whirring blades give it. Either of the two can be made in seconds in this utensil. But even without it, there is no real strain to producing a good Hollandaise or a smooth Mayonnaise; if the Duc de Richelieu could make history's first Mayonnaise in a tent during a military campaign, you should be able to do it in your kitchen. No effort will be made to argue on either side of the never-to-be-settled argument: whether Richelieu intended his sauce to be named in recognition of his victory at Bayonne, or in honor of General Mahon.

Both conventional and blender versions of both sauces are given.

■ *HOLLANDAISE SAUCE (Conventional Method)*

> ¼ *cup white wine vinegar*
> 5 *egg yolks*
> ½ *pound butter*
> 1 *tablespoon lemon juice*
> *Dash salt*
> *Dash pepper*

Over medium heat simmer the vinegar with ¼ cup cold water until it is reduced two-thirds. Transfer it to a double boiler and beat the egg yolks in one by one, beating between the addition of each yolk to keep the mixture creamy and smooth. Then begin beating in the butter a little at a time, working vigorously. When the sauce is creamy, add the lemon juice, salt and pepper and give it a final beating to blend. (Hollandaise may be kept for a short time, a day or two, in refrigerated storage, and reheated in a double boiler; do not allow it to get either too cold while in the refrigerator or too warm while reheating, or it is apt to separate. Sauce made in a blender will separate less easily than sauce made by hand.) Makes approximately 1 pint sauce.

▪ *HOLLANDAISE SAUCE* (*Blender*)

> 4 *egg yolks*
> ½ *teaspoon salt*
> *Dash cayenne*
> ½ *pound butter* (*no substitute*)
> 2½ *tablespoons lemon juice*
> ½ *tablespoon white wine vinegar*

Place the egg yolks, salt and cayenne in the blender. Melt the butter, but do not allow it to brown. Add the lemon juice and vinegar to the eggs in the blender; cover, turn it to low speed for 5 seconds, then begin to pour in the butter (if your blender does not have the small opening in the cover, it is safe to take off the top; the splattering occurs in the first half-second when the blender starts up). Pour the butter in a steady stream; turn off blender the moment the sauce thickens—about 15 to 20 seconds. Makes approximately 1 pint sauce.

▪ *MAYONNAISE* (*Conventional Method*)

> 3 *egg yolks*
> 1 *tablespoon lemon juice*
> ¼ *teaspoon prepared Dijon-type mustard*
> *Dash salt*
> *Dash pepper*
> *Dash cayenne*
> 2½ *cups olive or peanut oil*

Beat the eggs with the lemon juice, adding the seasonings; beat until the egg yolks are creamy. Begin adding the oil, first a few drops at a time, then in a very thin, steady stream, while beating vigorously. When all the oil has been used, continue beating until the sauce is a little thicker than you want it to be. Add 1½ tablespoons boiling water while continuing to beat; this will keep the mayonnaise from separating. Makes 1½ pints sauce.

▪ *MAYONNAISE (Blender)*

> 1 *egg*
> ½ *teaspoon sugar*
> ¾ *tablespoon salt*
> ½ *teaspoon Dijon-type prepared mustard*
> 3 *tablespoons lemon juice (or* 1½ *tablespoons each of*
>   *lemon juice and wine vinegar)*
> 1 *cup olive or peanut oil*

Place the egg in the blender. Toss the sugar and salt in a fold of waxed paper to blend them; add them to the egg. Add the mustard, lemon juice and one-third of the oil. Cover the blender and turn it on low speed 5 to 7 seconds; remove the cover or cover insert, and turn to high speed as you pour the remaining oil in steadily in a thick stream. Blend 5 to 10 seconds after the oil is all used, depending on the consistency you prefer; the longer the blending, the thicker the sauce. Makes ¾ to 1 pint sauce.

▪ INSTANT OR TABLE SAUCES

Included in this category are the sauces that must be served as soon as they are blended, or those that can be made from simple ingredients just before the moment of serving, and which are often made at the table.

▪ *BEURRE NOIR (Black Butter)*

> 2 *tablespoons butter (no substitute)*
> 1 *tablespoon grain vinegar*

Heat the butter over a high flame until it is a rich brown; dash in the vinegar very quickly, and swirl the pan or stir to mix. When the spitting ends, the sauce is ready to be served. It will not keep. Makes 3 tablespoons Beurre Noir.

▪ *SAUCE PROVENÇALE*

> 1 *tablespoon olive oil (no substitute)*
> 3 *tablespoons vinegar*

Dash salt
Dash pepper
1 *teaspoon tomato purée*
1 *teaspoon chopped capers*
1 *tablespoon chopped parsley*

Mix the olive oil, vinegar, salt and pepper in a deep sauce bowl or wide-mouthed flask. Stir or shake well—shaking is better. Add the tomato purée, capers and parsley; stir or shake. If the sauce is to sit before being used, it should be shaken or stirred before use. Makes 4 tablespoons sauce.

▪ SAUCE VINAIGRETTE

1 *tablespoon olive oil* (*no substitute*)
3 *tablespoons vinegar*
Dash salt
Dash pepper

Mix the oil, vinegar and seasonings by brisk stirring in a deep bowl or by shaking in a wide-mouthed flask. If it is to sit before being used, stir or shake it again before using. Makes 4 tablespoons Sauce Vinaigrette.

▪ COMPOUND BUTTERS

All compound butters are essentially the same. No precise measurements of quantity can be given here because of the variation between butters, herbs, spices and other ingredients; you must be guided by your taste. In all the compounds the process is the same, kneading an ingredient into butter to form a smooth paste. Often the butters are spread on a dish before glazing; sometimes they are melted and offered as a sauce. To give you at least a rule-of-thumb guide, suggestions are made as to the ratio of butter to flavoring ingredient, but it should be used only as guide, not gospel.

Before using any butter—and margarine can be substituted in most cases—wash it free of excess salt by putting the amount you will use into twice its bulk of cold water and kneading it with your fingers; after a few moments, pour off the water and add fresh. Change the water three or four times. Before using the butter, pat and squeeze out the excess water.

▪ *ANCHOVY BUTTER*

Use ½ drained anchovy fillet or a pea-sized bit of anchovy paste to 1 tablespoon butter.

▪ *COLBERT BUTTER*

Use ¼ teaspoon Sauce Espagnole (page 275) and a pinch of minced tarragon to 1 tablespoon butter.

▪ *MAÎTRE D'HÔTEL BUTTER*

Use a generous pinch of chopped fresh parsley, 8 to 10 drops of lemon juice and a dash of freshly ground white pepper to 1 tablespoon butter.

▪ *PRINTANIER BUTTER*

Use any puréed green vegetable—asparagus, peas, spinach, beans—to equal parts of butter. This name is applied to any compound butter in which green vegetables are blended.

▪ *SHRIMP BUTTER*

Use equal parts of freshly cooked shrimp, pounded to a paste, and butter. This also is the ratio for any of the fish and shellfish group; when smoked or salted fish is used, only your taste can guide you.

There is only one thing limiting you in the creation of compound butters: your imagination. Here are a few suggestions to get you started. Mustard Butter, use a fine Dijon mustard; Robert Butter, use Sauce Robert; Tarragon Butter, made with finely crushed fresh tarragon leaves or tarragon vinegar; Parsley Butter, with pounded fresh parsley or dried parsley flakes; Garlic or Onion Butters, made from the fresh bulbs or the packaged powder; *Camarone* Butter, using the powdered dried shrimp imported from Mexico that will taste shrimpier than the fresh ones; Savory Butter, with crushed fresh savory.

These are only a few. Almost all herbs and herb vinegars; the classic brown sauces; bottled commercial sauces such as Worcestershire, A-1, Tabasco; all these can be used in creating compound butters. One caution, though: When using any strongly acid ingredient, such as a vinegar, butter will prove more satisfactory than its substitutes.

▪ PURÉES

Although technically purées are not sauces, they are a close kin, hovering in a sort of Never-Never Land between liquid and solid, between ingredient and accessory.

Preparing a good purée is no longer the tedious, messy task it was when the job was given to kitchen apprentices. You will find on the shelves of even the smallest grocery stores an abundant variety of purées: beef, veal, lamb, chicken, turkey, kidney, liver, most vegetables and many fruits. Because they are labeled "baby foods" many cooks overlook this source of ready-made purées. The small jars hold just about the right amount for preparing 2 servings, the large jars will garnish or accompany 4 portions. The purées sold as baby food are invariably seasoned very, very lightly and contain nothing which will conflict with the spices or herbs you may want to add to them. If they are too thick as they come from the jar, a few drops of milk or meat stock will bring them to the desired consistency.

An electric blender will, of course, purée almost anything in a matter of seconds. In the better-stocked housewares stores you will find foodmills especially designed for making purées. These are crank-operated utensils with interchangeable sieves graduated from coarse to very fine; they are easy to use and to clean. Almost equally good is the old-fashioned ricer used in making jams and preserves. It has one advantage in that it will accept unpeeled vegetables and fruits and pass only the pulp, retaining skin and pits or seeds; this reduces the number of operations required to produce the finished article. In a pinch, a potato masher will produce a passable purée, so will a sturdy kitchen strainer.

▪ AUXILIARIES

Today's spineless bread from the big mass-producing bakeries is useless as a base for a dish that must be served with sauce or gravy; the fluffed-up chemicalized sponge dissolves into an unpleasant paste when it is touched by moisture. There are a few firm breads sold under national brand names, most of them baked regionally; they survive saucing, but are almost all sold only in presliced form, which limits their usefulness when thicker pieces are required. The obvious answer is to bake your own.

Baking is not the onerous chore many believe it to be. The Brioche recipe that follows takes little time to prepare, can be baked in individual forms or loaf pans, and if desired can be prepared in double or triple batches; bread frozen while fresh from the oven can be thawed and still retain its fresh-baked flavor.

▪ *BRIOCHE*

> 1 *yeast cake or* 1 *package dry yeast*
> 8 *cups flour*
> ¼ *teaspoon salt*
> 1½ *teaspoons sugar*
> 1 *pound butter or margarine*
> 6 *eggs*
> 2 *tablespoons milk*

Combine the yeast with ½ cup lukewarm water and 2 cups of flour; set it in a warm place for ½ hour. To the remaining 6 cups flour add the salt and sugar; sift, then knead in one-fourth of the butter. Beat 4 eggs lightly into the milk. When the mixture begins to smooth, add another egg and continue beating, then add the final egg. Beat the remaining butter in, then combine the liquid with the flour and mix well. Turn out on a lightly floured breadboard or any flat surface, and work the yeast sponge into the flour. Place in a bowl, cover with a cloth and let it rise until double in bulk. Again place the dough on a lightly floured breadboard and beat with the palm of your hand until the dough is flat and compact. Place in loaf pans or individual brioche molds enough dough to fill them to one-fourth of their depth. Let the dough rise in a warm place until it has increased in bulk one-third. Bake 30 to 45 minutes in a preheated 350-degree oven if small individual molds are used; 45 minutes to 1 hour if large molds or loaf pans are used. The yield will be 3 standard-sized loaves or the equivalent in small individual molds.

■ *PASTRY DOUGH* (*for* Croustades *and Tartshells*)

When making *croustades* or filling pastry shells, you can of course use your own favorite piecrust recipe, or even one of the several commercial packaged mixes. The only drawback to this is that most of the recipes for piecrust and all of the packaged mixes result in a crust too fragile to be handled easily. Your need is for a crust that will be both tender and sturdy, one that can be baked either brown or pale and still survive reheating and some handling. The brown *croustades* or tartshells should be used when reheating is brief; the pale, slightly undercooked ones when their contents are to be baked several minutes. The pastry dough in the following recipe satisfies all these requirements, and is very simple to make. It can be used to bake a brown *croustade* or shell, or an undercooked one; both can be frozen for later use. When baking unfilled tartshells, fill the dough-lined molds with raw rice so they will hold their shape while cooking.

> 2 *egg yolks*
> 2 *cups flour*
> *Dash salt*
> 12 *tablespoons butter*

Stir the egg yolks lightly, sift the flour and salt into them a little at a time, then work in the butter by hand until smooth. Roll only once to the desired thickness; cut rounds for *croustades* or line tartshell molds. Bake 10 minutes in a preheated 425-degree oven for lightly brown *croustades* or shells, about 6 minutes for pale ones, 12 minutes for richly brown crusts. If freezing, place in sealed plastic bags only after they cool, and then put into the freezer at once. Makes 16 to 18 *croustades* 2 to 2½ inches in diameter.

■ *BREADCRUMB–CHEESE GLAZE*

Parmesan is easily grated by tossing a few small pieces in the blender. Use equal parts of grated Parmesan and dry breadcrumbs; store them in a tightly closed jar in the refrigerator. A cupful will last a long while.

▪ *FOIE GRAS*

One of the auxiliaries to egg cookery is *foie gras,* and the imported variety is both widely available and rather costly. It must be noted, too, that the great day of French *foie gras* has passed. Today's product is not the same as it was in the period when producers nailed the feet of their geese to sturdy planks so the fowl could not move and then force-fed them with grain. This practice is now officially forbidden, though it is said that in certain parts of Strasbourg there are dark cellars—much like the bootlegger's cellars in the days of American Prohibition—where the geese are still confined in this way. But the livers from these cellars cannot be more than a tiny fraction of all the *foie gras* produced. And good or only passable, the price is still high.

Now, the bulging liver of a force-fed goose has been the basis of *foie gras* for a long time, but it was not always thus. Chicken livers were once used to make the delicacy, and if you have a half-hour to spare and would like to experiment on a do-it-yourself basis, use this recipe.

> 12 *chicken livers*
> 3 *cups light cream*
> ½ *teaspoon nutmeg*
> 2 *whole cloves*
> 1 *teaspoon salt*
> 1 *pound pork fat*
> 1 *bayleaf*
> Pinch thyme
> 12 *tablespoons butter*
> ¼ *teaspoon freshly ground white pepper*
> Pinch marjoram

Choose chicken livers as large and fat as you can find, and run a skewer through each one 2 or 3 times. Warm the cream with the nutmeg, cloves and a tiny pinch of salt until it reaches the simmering point; remove it from the heat. Put the livers into the cream and allow them to stand until completely cold.

Render the pork fat over very low heat; it should not get too hot or take on any brown tinge from the meat. In the pan where the fat is being rendered put the bayleaf and thyme. Let the fat cool, and strain it through a cloth. To each level spoonful of the butter add a spoonful of this fat in a heavy skillet over very low heat.

Take the cold livers from the cream, dust them lightly with the teaspoon of salt mixed with the pepper and marjoram, and poach them in the fat until they are white. Test for doneness by piercing the livers with a skewer; they should not release a pink juice.

Put the livers in a 1- or 1½-pint terrine that can be covered, and strain the fat over them through a cloth; they should be completely covered. Cool thoroughly and store with the terrine covered in the refrigerator. When using the livers for cooking, or in making a *pâté*, include a small quantity of the fat with the portion of the liver being used. This recipe will yield between 1 and 1½ pints, depending on the size of the livers.

12 ....

Leftovers and Easter Eggs

▪ LEFTOVERS

Nobody likes a surplus of anything, except money. Leftovers can be a source of irritation and guilty consciences in any kitchen, and the egg has few rivals in helping the thrifty cook dispose of those annoying dribs and drabs of good food that remain after meals. Instead of putting them carefully into covered dishes and storing them in the refrigerator where they're forgotten until it's too late to salvage them, let the egg come to the rescue.

In the first chapter, passing reference was made to the egg as a budget-stretcher. The time has now come to explore that virtue in more detail.

Following is a cross-index of egg dishes according to the basic ingredient or ingredients used in them besides the egg itself. The index is intended primarily as a guide to help you in using leftovers, but it can also be helpful in other ways.

Consider. You have a stray cupful of carrots, not enough to offer of themselves, but too much to discard. The ingredients index provides four dishes in which carrots are combined with eggs. Or: the rich uncle coming for dinner tomorrow is exceedingly fond of onions, but is on a diet of light foods. The ingredients index clues you to a dozen egg–onion combinations. Or: a friend gives you a crate of spinach or artichokes or asparagus; consult the index for ways to combine the oversupply with eggs for adventure and variety.

When using the ingredients index, remember that it does not include those egg dishes identified by ingredient in the main index. And a separate ingredients index for omelets will be found later in this chapter.

CODFISH: Bénédictine; Portuguese; Creamed; Bamboche; Capucine.

CORN: Kentucky Scramble; Cobb.

CRAB: Trinidad; Creamed; Lorenzo.

CRAYFISH: Apicius.

CREAM CHEESE: Omelet Pie; Southern Fleece.

EGGPLANT: Suzanne; Agenaise; Omar Pasha; Provençale.

ENDIVE: à la Bruxelloise.

FISH: Milanese; Antiboise.

FOIE GRAS: Ambassadrice; Boieldieu; Bohémienne; Commodore; Rossini; Jockey Club; Tetrazzini; Béchamel; Verdier; Colbert; Troubador.

GHERKINS: Galtz; Bordalue.

GREEN BEANS: Chevreuse; Creamed.

GREEN PEAS: Armenonville; Choron; Clamart; Harvester's; Balmoral; Célestine; Creamed.

GREEN PEPPERS: Spanish; Aladdin; Andalouse; Omar Pasha; Reno; Creamed; à la King; Pipérade; Celia.

GROUND BEEF: Taco; San Francisco; Tartare.

HAM: Demi-Deuil; American; Virginian; Bayonne; Parma; Coquette; Benedict; Zingara; Duxelles; Lee; Suzanne; Panetière; Carmen; Mongole; Croquettes; Patties; Quiche Lorraine; Denver; Bohémienne; Alsacienne; Lully; Verdi; Rothomago; Josephine.

HOMINY: Sharecropper.

HOMINY GRITS: Arkansas.

HOP SHOOTS: Anversoise; Rubens.

KIDNEYS: Creamed; Croquettes; Patties; Carême; à l'Ancienne; Jockey Club; Meyerbeer; Courrone Normande.

KIPPERS: Kedgeree.

LENTILS: Esau.

LETTUCE: Sévigné; Clamart; Harvester's; Frissac; à la Maraîchère.

LOBSTER: Cardinal; Armoricaine; Creamed; Victoria; Carême.

MACARONI: Bagration; Palermitaine; Milanese; Lucanian; Lully.

MACKEREL: Languedoc; Kedgeree.

MARROW: Masséna.

MEATS: Creamed; Croquettes; Patties; Parisian Egg Ring; Soufflé-Capped.

MIXED VEGETABLES: Amalie; Carnavelet; Creamed; Louisiana; Printanier; Bamboche; Soufflé-Capped; Chartreuse.

MUSHROOMS: Waldorf; Brillat-Savarin; Brimont; Demi-Deuil; Troubador; Marivaux; Montrose; Windsor; à la Midinette; Montrouge; Boston; Berlioz; Duxelles; à la Forestière; Lee; Châtillon; Panetière; Bordelaise; à la King; Croquettes; Princess Mary; à la Parisienne; en Cocotte; Chimay; Danish; Montfermeil; alla Cacciatora; Florida; French Egg Pie; Sardinian.

MUSSELS: Carmelite; Normande.

ONIONS: Lyonnaise; Spring; Archduke; Swiss; Spanish; Agenaise; California; Creole; Florida; Matelote; Espagnole;

Rodriguez.

OYSTERS: Hangtown Fry; Normande.

PARSLEY: Villeroi.

PIMIENTO: Jacqueline; Creamed; Galli-Marie; Celia; Andalusian; en Belle Vue.

POTATOES, BAKED: en Berceau; Georgette; Parmentier.

POTATOES, BOILED: Harvester's; Balmoral; Ménagère.

POTATOES, MASHED: Cécile; Duchesse; Berlioz; Jacqueline; à la Reine; Monselet.

POTATOES, RAW: Boulanger; Kansas; Matelote; Marianne.

PUMPKIN: Bayonnaise.

RED PEPPER: Creamed; Las Vegas.

RICE: à l'Ancienne; Alabama; à l'Africaine; Caracas; Mirelle; Kedgeree.

SALMON: Scotch; Phillipsburg; Danish.

SALT PORK: Sharecropper; Alabama; Boulevardier; New England Chowder; Maine Chowder.

SAUERKRAUT: Alsacienne.

SAUSAGE: Cuban; Bellevilloise; à la Charcutière; Bercy; Auvergne; Rothomago; French Egg Pie; Chartreuse; Scotch.

SEMOLINA: à l'Africaine.

SHRIMP: Apicius; Carignan; Creamed; Danish Sandwich; Normande; Royale; Lafitte; Carême; Nantua.

SOUR CREAM: Dijon.

SPINACH: Carnavelet; Roman; Florentine; Martin; San Francisco; à la Maraîchère; Colbert.

SPLIT PEAS: Mongole.

SWEETBREADS: Creamed; Croquettes; Patties; Delmonico; Favart; Augier; Lucullus.

TOMATOES: Portuguese; Spanish; Andalouse; à la Charcutière; Bordelaise; Provençale; Tyrolese Egg Pie; Pipérade; Comte Potocki; Créole; Huevos en Rabo; Auber; Marianne.

TONGUE: Croquettes; Patties; Carême; Clarence; Edward VII; à la Parisienne; Bizet; Châtelaine.

TROUT: Rothschild.

TRUFFLES: Brillat-Savarin; Ambassadrice; Boieldieu; Carême; à la Chevalière; à la Comtesse; Rossini; Victoria; à l'Ancienne; Mortemart; Orloff; Princess Mary; Rachel; Rothschild; Truffled; Béchamel; Colinette.

TURKEY: Croquettes; Patties; Yvonne.

TURNIPS: Ménagère.

WATERCRESS: Cressonière.

WILD GAME: Diane; Yvonne.

ZUCCHINI: Arlésienne; Sicilian.

Omelets are often created at the drop-in of a guest who unexpectedly decides to stay to dinner, but equally as important are the omelets created for a special occasion. Impromptu or planned, omelets absorb leftovers; the ingredients index that follows should help you to find and try new omelets. It should also save you moments of striding the floor with corrugated brow while trying to recall the formal name of that delicious omelet that contains one ingredient of which you're sure, but one or two others which escape you. Frantic thumbing of indexes doesn't always help—unless the index begins where your memory leaves off, with the name of the ingredient that gives the omelet its character but doesn't appear in its name.

Remember when using the omelet ingredients index that it does not duplicate the main index, which lists those omelets known principally by the name of their chief ingredient. The following supplement lists only those whose menu names give no clue as to their contents.

ANCHOVY FILLETS: Ahmed Pasha; Faroe.

ARTICHOKE: Mascotte; Monselet; Vivieur.

ASPARAGUS: Argenteuil; Princesse.

BACON: Pascal; à la Forestière; Jurassienne; Lorraine; Paysanne; Denver.

BEEF: Vivieur.

BREAD: Pauvre Femme.

BRUSSELS SPROUTS: à la Bruxelloise.

CARROTS: Crécy; Fermière.

CAULIFLOWER: Du Barry; Jardinière.

CELERY: Fermière.

CHEESE: Quiche Lorraine; Two-Toned.

CHESTNUTS: Châtelaine.

CHICKEN: Albina; Maintenon.

CHICKEN LIVERS: au Chasseur.

CODFISH: Portuguese.

CRAYFISH: Nantua.

DUCK LIVERS: Rouennaise.

EGGPLANT: Mistral; Ahmed Pasha.

ENDIVE: à la Flamande.

FROG'S LEGS: Maxim.

GAME FOWL: Diane.

GAME MEATS: St. Hubert.

GREEN PEAS: Clamart.

HAM: Fermière; Denver; Paysanne.

HERBS: Verdiere.

HOP SHOOTS: Anversoise.

KALE: Faroe.

KIDNEY: Café des Sports.

LEEKS: Savoyard.

LETTUCE: Choisy.

LOBSTER: Diplomate.

MARROW: Bouchère.

MIXED VEGETABLES: Fermière; Jardinière.

MUSHROOMS: André-Theuriet; Duxelles; Feydeau; à la Forestière; à la Parisienne; Santé.

MUSSELS: Dieppe.

MUTTON: Polonaise.

ONION: Lyonnaise; Archduke; à la Parisienne; Ahmed Pasha; Jurasienne.

POTATO: Mascotte; Parmentier; Paysanne; Savoyard.

PRAWNS: Nantua.

SAUERKRAUT: Alsacienne.

SEAFOOD: Fruits de Mer.

SHRIMP: Nantua.

SPINACH: Roman.

SWEETBREADS: Tallyrand.

TOMATO: Ahmed Pasha; Provençale.

TONGUE: Agnès Sorel.

TUNA: Brillat-Savarin.

Between these supplementary indexes and the main index, there should be no lagging of interest in your approach to eggs.

▪ EASTER EGGS

Decorating Easter eggs is a job usually inherited by the cook, but annually the home service magazines devote space to instructions for copying the current egg decorating fads, so this presents no problem. The greater challenge to the cook's ingenuity is the economical and tasty disposal of a surplus of hard-cooked eggs beginning the Monday after Easter.

Like many similar problems, this one is best solved the Saturday before. Keep in mind, first, that it's tradition, not law, that calls for all Easter eggs to be hard-cooked. The tradition makes sense when small fry begin tossing eggs in an excess of high spirits, or when a too-well-hidden egg is stepped on by accident. If your small fry can be depended on, by virtue of age or discipline, not to throw eggs, then by all means cook some of your Easter eggs *mollet*. They are almost as durable as those that are hard-cooked, and can be decorated in the same manner. Mark them for identification, and serve them in after-Easter menus in some of the dishes that use eggs *mollet* or poached eggs interchangeably. This one bit of advance planning adds over seventy choices to your after-Easter meals.

There are also occasions when you might want to depart from the tradition of the hard-cooked Easter egg and follow the Russian and Mexican custom of the surprising filled eggshell. This involves blowing the egg while still raw and putting perfume or cologne or confetti into the shell, which is then sealed and decorated. These filled shells are designed to be cracked gaily on the heads of guests at your Easter party. Only your own conscience can guide you in deciding whether you want to try this. It is not recommended for parties involving the very young unless you, too, are young at heart. At adult entertainments, it does serve as an effective icebreaker and party-starter. It leads to a relaxed gathering, but it also leads to eggshells turning up all over the house in unlikely places for days afterward.

Should you decide to take the plunge, there are two methods used to remove the insides of an egg while leaving its shell intact. One is to pierce each end of the egg with a large needle, rotating the needle like a drill between your forefinger and thumb while applying firm but gentle pressure. The needle hole is enlarged with the tip of an exceedingly sharp knife until you have an opening ¼ inch or so in diameter. The second, faster, way is to use a small fine-grit sanding drum in an electric drill. Touch the whirling drum to each end of the egg until the abrasive creates the size opening desired. Wipe away sanding dust with damp cloth before emptying the egg.

Whichever method you choose, open the egg's big end first. At the large end there is usually an air pocket and a separation between shell and inner membrane, though even if the membrane is punctured, surface tension will generally keep the egg's insides from flowing until both ends have been opened. Then, a slow puff into either opening will send the contents cascading into a bowl or cup which you are holding ready.

After rinsing the shell and allowing it to dry, use white sealing wax to close one opening. Through the remaining hole insert a small quantity of perfume or cologne diluted with alcohol, or fill the shell with confetti, and seal it with the wax. The heated tip of an old knife is the best tool to use in smoothing the warm wax to shape. The shell is then decorated as simply or elaborately as you wish, remembering that its destiny is to be smashed.

Since the decorating door has been pushed ajar, let's open it a bit wider. After all, it is the cook's job to see that there are plenty of decorated eggs on hand for Easter Sunday. And you've preplanned your activities so well that you now have plenty of time to decorate a few eggs.

Not endless time, of course. The day is gone when Easter egg decoration involved boiling hay or walnut hulls to get brown dye, steeping sassafras for yellow, soaking eggs in beet juice to color them red or in bluing to give them a blue hue—or perhaps in alternate baths of beet juice and bluing to produce purple. There are easier ways to produce decorated eggs for Easter. They will not match the artistry of the Polish and Ukrainian craftsmen who apply thin layers of colored wax to eggshells and produce Easter eggs that properly belong in galleries or museums, but you can decorate eggs easily and quickly.

Borrow an old-fashioned technique from these old-world artists, though. Melt variously colored candle stubs in a pan of hot water. The wax rises to the top of the water and a gentle stirring will cause it to swirl in a rainbow-like layer. Dip an egg through the wax film, twirling as you dip. Or use separate colors of wax in individual pans and dip half an egg at a time. A thin coating of the colored wax on the shell glows with a jewel-like translucence.

Borrow a technique from the lithographer: scribble a design on an eggshell using a wax crayon, then dip the egg in cool dye. The wax-covered areas will not accept the dye, and thus you can produce designs of many hues against a contrasting or complementary background.

Borrow a technique from the etcher: using a finely tipped brush, trace a delicate design, a name or a message, on an undyed eggshell, using white shellac or ordinary white carpenter's glue. Let the design dry thoroughly. Like an etcher's resist, the shellac and glue will resist the dye-stain; when the egg has been dipped in the dye, your design will stand out white against a colored background.

Borrow a technique from the silhouette artist: paste pregummed legal seals, chart dots or stars to the eggshell as they come from the package, or trim them to your own fancy shapes. Brush dye onto the shell; the uncovered areas will accept it, the slick surface of the pasted-on decorations will not. When they are wiped clean they gleam and glisten brightly.

Borrow a technique from the china-maker: dip an egg in warm water and wrap it in a piece of varicolored "Madras tissue," then bring the tissue into firm contact with the shell by wrapping a cloth around the egg and twisting it to tighten. This type of tissue bleeds its colors when wet, just as the china-maker's tissue transfers do, and the colors of the tissue will remain on the egg when the cloth is unwrapped.

Borrow a technique from the stenciler: snip designs from paper placemats or doilies and hold them against the eggshell with tiny pieces of masking tape while you spray color from an aerosol can, being careful to choose a nontoxic paint. When it is dry, lift off the paper to reveal the design. Dye the shell before stenciling it if you want multiple colors.

Use nylon-tipped or felt-tipped marking pens in many colors to scrawl bold designs on eggshells, before or after dyeing. Use "ball-point embroidery" pens for sketching. Attach sequins or glitters with model-maker's cement or epoxy. Use Christmas-tree flocking material to produce velvety eggshells that feel like plush; dye the eggs first if you wish and put on a stencil cut from a paper doily, then remove the paper after applying the flock to achieve a two-toned effect in both color and texture.

None of these decorating techniques require great artistic ability or very much time. All of them lend themselves to production-line methods. And the materials are available almost anywhere, from five-and-dime stores, hobby shops and sewing shops, and by mail order. Nor are any of the materials expensive enough to put a large dent in your Easter budget. You'll still have plenty left with which to buy eggs.

It's time that we got back to our primary concern, which is the egg's insides left in the bowl or cup when the shell is emptied, or the hard-cooked egg that remains after the decorated shell has been peeled away. You have the makings of a massive serving of scrambled eggs for your Easter guests, or smaller servings for your family, using any of the seventy or so recipes for scrambled eggs given in the preceding pages. If you put only 4 or 6 eggs into each bowl, you have the premeasured makings of any of the hundred omelets for which recipes are given in Chapter 8. You have the basic ingredient for a number of special dishes such as Quiche Lorraine (page 100) or Délicacies Royale (page 191), or even for an Egg Sausage (page 185). And remember that you can freeze or preserve in your refrigerator any excess on hand after the shells have been emptied; procedures for both are given in Chapter 1.

But you're a traditionalist. You stick to the belief that an Easter egg must be a hard-cooked egg, no matter how many you have left over on Monday. Good enough, but think about shelling those hard-cooked eggs and offering them in aspic, if you are entertaining adults. The recipes given here for eggs in aspic only begin to give you ideas for combinations and decoration of eggs served in this style. Eggs molded in aspic provide an unstereotyped Easter party dish; they also offer an interesting variation for serving the family any after-Easter surplus of hard-cooked eggs.

There are many other recipes in earlier chapters that will relieve the monotony of the unadorned hard-cooked egg. Investigate the big family of stuffed eggs that begins with Eggs Farci (page 149) and that of creamed eggs (page 96). The range is broad and varied. It includes the egg chowders: New England (page 98) and New York (page 99); then goes on through Southern Shortcake (page 99), croquettes (pages 102-103) and patties (pages 103-104), into the casserole dishes. Your choice can be the simpler recipes such as Eggs Cécile (page 51) or Eggs Goldenrod (page 58), or it might extend to the more elaborate ones such as Egg Fillets (page 180), or even to Kedgeree (page 181).

An excess of hard-cooked eggs also offers a wonderful chance for you to lay down a batch of Smoked Eggs (page 183) or Pickled Eggs (page 184), and at a time when they will be available for the picnic season that follows Easter. If you can take the decorations off the eggshells, put down some Tea Eggs (page 182). And if you really believe in planning ahead, anticipate Easter by six months and greet it with a batch of Thousand-Year Eggs (page 182) which you began to prepare last October.

So the problem of what to do with leftover Easter eggs really need not rear its ugly head. A bit of preplanning will enable you to greet Easter Monday with assurance instead of dreading to face what might otherwise be a staggering surplus.

Index

305